Labyrinth 2

Plays by Don Nigro: 2001-2011

Jim McGhee

University Press of America,® Inc.
Lanham • Boulder • New York • Toronto • Plymouth, UK

Copyright © 2013 by University Press of America,® Inc.
4501 Forbes Boulevard, Suite 200, Lanham, Maryland 20706
UPA Aquisitions Department (301) 459-3366

10 Thornbury Road, Plymouth PL6 7PP, United Kingdom

Library of Congress Control Number: 2012945156
ISBN: 978-0-7618-5980-2 (paperback : alk. paper)—ISBN: 978-0-7618-5981-9 (electronic)

⊖™ The paper used in this publication meets the minimum requirements of American National Standard for Information Sciences Permanence of Paper for Printed Library Materials, ANSI/NISO Z39.48-1992.

Contents

Preface

My first account of Don Nigro's work—*Labyrinth: the Plays of Don Nigro*—dealt with plays published by January, 2002, as well as scripts that had not been published by that date. This second book describes monologues, short(er) plays, and full- length plays written since then, and Samuel French, Inc. now lists all of Nigro's work on its website: www.samuelfrench.com. I have followed the traditional alphabetical order for plays of varying length.

Since I first learned of Nigro's plays, I and my students at York College of Pennsylvania have produced over 20 of his scripts. Most recently, we presented *Chronicles* in December, 2009, *Paganini* in March, 2010, *Cinderella Waltz* in October, 2010, and *Lurker, Things That Go Bump in the Night, Bible*, and *The Sin-Eater* in November, 2011. Audience response has been enthusiastic and players who have graduated write that many of their fondest memories are connected with their experiences doing his plays.

We are all familiar with the stereotype of the struggling artist whose work, relatively unknown and unappreciated during his lifetime, becomes canonical for later generations. And although Nigro's plays are being produced in high schools, colleges, and universities, as well as in professional venues here, in Canada, and in Europe, I believe his work should be much better known. Information about plays written after January, 2012, may be found at goose.ycp.edu//~jmcghee/dnigro.

Acknowledgments

Publication of this book was facilitated in part by a grant from the Faculty Development Committee of the York College of Pennsylvania Academic Senate.

Chapter One

Full Length Plays

Animal Tales is a collection of eleven short plays that may be done as a full-length show, in small groups, or individually. Nigro writes that he very strongly discourages the use of animal costumes, actors getting down on all fours, and expressions of overt animal physicality. In *Three Turkeys Waiting for Corncobs,* two men and a woman portray three wild turkeys—Bob, George, and Penny—who are waiting in someone's back yard for corncobs to be thrown out. Penny asks the two males if they think there is more to life than corncobs and bugs. She says that she has always wanted to play the saxophone and that, someday, even though she doesn't have fingers or lips, she will be a world-famous saxophone player. She says she is going to search for a saxophone tree. George tells her that if she leaves them she will become flockless and have nobody to gobble with. She will walk alone forever and go mad. But she leaves and the males wonder if they should have been more supportive. Bob asks George what a saxophone is and George says that the corncobs are coming as he looks back to where Penny has gone; Bob looks towards the corncobs and the light fades out.

In *Dialogue with Lemmings,* two lemmings "in a bleak landscape" walk slowly at first and then with increasing speed. Their names are Lem and Em and they speak tersely as Em tries to find out what is bothering Lem, who feels an itching in his head. Em thinks that he, too, may be experiencing the same feeling. Lem says he has to go, but Em thinks there is a cliff "over there." Lem doesn't know why but he says he has to go. Em tells him that if they don't stop they are going to go over the cliff. He summarizes their situation: they don't know where they are going, nor why, but millions of them are going to fall off the cliff onto the sharp ocean rocks below. Lem says it's something in the head, and Em repeats the phrase as they walk now rapidly. "Here we go," Lem says, and the lights black out.

One character on a bare stage in *Platypus* is trying to discover who and what he is, trapped in a strange party costume he can't take off. He thinks his grandpa was a duck and his grandma a beaver, but he doesn't know and wonders what he is supposed to be. He says he doesn't fit in anywhere and that being odd is a terrible curse. He hates his claws and wishes he had fingers. He fears that one day he will be extinct, be nothing. He wishes he could find somebody like him and thinks he was cobbled together from leftover pieces of somebody else. He asks the audience if he can sit with them just for company but, realizing the futility of his request, apologizes as the lights go out.

Another lone actor, a mouse in *The Trap*, explains to the audience that he ought to know better but he finds the cheese in what he knows is a mouse trap compelling. He says that he has seen many others crushed horribly by the great metal prong snapping down, crushing their heads and spines, and he wonders what kind of hideously depraved creature could have created such a monstrous thing. But the cheese smells are so wonderful that he thinks, perhaps, if he is quick enough, he can get the cheese before the trap springs. He argues that nobody ever accomplished anything new if they presumed that the failures of the past would happen to them, too. He says he doesn't need the cheese, that he can live off the crumbs from the kitchen table or inside the stove. He says he can run rings around the cat and is a very careful mouse. He knows the trap is a trick devised to kill him, but he dreams about the cheese, wondering who is more evil, the person who invented the trap, or the one who invented cheese, because without cheese the trap wouldn't work. He thinks he might be able to just sniff the cheese, saying that desire is a trap, yet desire is all there is. He resolves to walk away, but then he reaches out his "little" arm. Blackout and the sound of a giant trap snapping shut.

A lone actor *In the Great Chipmunk Labyrinth* speaks to us "from inside his labyrinth of tunnels." He tells us that chipmunks, thought cheerful, are really torn by constant doubts and regrets. He wonders why the great Chipmunk God, who created snakes to kill inferior creatures like mice, allows the snakes to swallow the chipmunk babies. He loves the labyrinth of tunnels he and his forbears have created to confuse the snakes, tunnels given them, the chosen of God, by the Great Chipmunk to celebrate his mysterious handiwork. He says he can't stop thinking about the hawk that swooped down and took his mother, pregnant with brothers and sisters, to a nest in the trees to be torn apart. He urges himself not to think of the hawk and wonders if the tunnels he digs are perhaps the inside of the brain of the Chipmunk God, who is the hollow space inside the labyrinth inside his brain inside the labyrinth. He wants to think only of digging tunnels, his "lonely work in the dark." Lights fade out.

In *Groundhog at the Window* the actor tells us that something in his head makes him slow but thoughtful. He says he will eat anything but he tries to stay away from humans although he keeps returning to the basement window of a house near his den. One window-well in particular attracts him, not just because it is a good place to hunt toads after it rains but because he sees another groundhog looking back at him through the glass of the window. This groundhog imitates everything he does and he wonders what the other groundhog's life is like. Sometimes the human hears him scratching at the glass to let the other groundhog out and comes out to chase him away. He is troubled that the groundhog behind the glass imitates everything he does. He has a sense that something is following him across the grass, but all he can see is his shadow and he wonders if that shadow is the dark disguise of the groundhog in the window. He screams at the creature in the window well and it screams back at him. He says there is an itching in his head that makes him dizzy and thirsty. There is froth at his mouth and he thinks the dark thing that follows him across the grass has gotten into his head and is eating his soul.

In *Parrots* two actors move back and forth sideways as if on their perch in a cage created by shadows of bars. Pickles repeats everything Pecky says and Pecky tells us that the question is not why 'this jackass' keeps repeating everything he says but why he himself feels compelled to keep saying stupid things like, "Polly want a cracker?" since neither of the birds is named Polly and Pecky would rather have a cheeseburger with fries and a chocolate shake. Pecky thinks he is going mad, that there is another person inside him who keeps saying inane phrases that he must repeat. And he is trapped in a cage with a moron. Pecky asks Pickles to say, just once, something that Pecky hasn't said first. "I love you," Pickles says. Pecky replies that Pickles is a tape recorder with feathers and cannot say anything intelligent. "Ontogeny recapitulates phylogeny," Pickles responds and continues to utter random sentences from physics, police car radios, and aliens, and then starts singing songs. Pecky shouts at him to shut up, saying that he hates him and wishes he were ground up into cat food. Pecky expresses satisfaction with peace and quiet, but then asks Pickles, who is silent, if he is pouting. Pecky repeats some of the phrases he said at the beginning of the play, but gets no response. He asks if Pickles is dead and tells him that he loves him. But he gets no response to "Polly want a cracker?" and the lights fade out.

Two cats, Maggie and Tabby, on a rug in front of a fireplace in *String Theory*, talk about the meaning of life. Maggie says that life is dark and she sometimes thinks she is going crazy. Tabby suggests that if they run away all the stuff that seems to matter will just vanish. But Maggie wonders what it all means, although she doesn't want it to be over. She has no faith that there is anything on the other side of the fence. Tabby says there was another yard there yesterday and Maggie asks if she knows it is still there today and whether it is the same yard and what is over the fence of that yard. Tabby says she guesses it is all yards forever, like a big house where you can go through more and more rooms. Maggie says she is sick of her life and wants something else. When Tabby asks what, Maggie tells her that when she was chasing a string she wondered why she was doing it. Tabby says they are cats and cats chase things. Maggie says they chase mice and birds so they can eat them but why do they chase string? She says that when she saw the hand of the child that was moving the string, she stopped chasing the string because she didn't want to be manipulated. Tabby tells her that they are cats and she can play or not, that it's her choice. Maggie says life is meaningless and that what gives them pleasure is either illusory or an obscenity. She says that they are victims of a process they don't understand, controlled by other victims who don't understand. Tabby asks her if she enjoys chasing the string, and when she says she does, Tabby tells her to "chase the damned string."

One character in *Bat* hangs upside down in dim, gloomy light, telling us that the piece will be short because of the blood rushing to his head. He tells us of a war between the birds and the beasts and when the birds wanted the bat to join them he said he was a beast, but when the beasts wanted him to join them he said he could fly like the birds. When a treaty was made neither the birds nor the beasts wanted the bat. Hanging upside down in a cave he heard a rustling and realized that there were millions and millions of others just like him, but each one was alone. He doesn't know what it means. Even if he slept right side up the world would still seem upside down to him. "Not bird. Not beast. Not anything." He asks us what kind of animal we are and closes with "Suck you later. Maybe we can hang out together."

Ed, a baboon, in *The Baboon God*, speaks to us about the absurd, insulting, and blasphemous attempt to teach evolutionary thought in their baboon schools. He says it is obvious that they are made in the image of the blue ass and floppy red nose of the Great Baboon God and he urges immediate execution of those secular baboons "who would fill our children's heads with monstrous fairy tales about the humans being some form of cousin to us." He says such ignorance is insulting and appalling and urges those listening to "exterminate the vermin who spread these unholy lies," in the name of "the Most Holy Lord and Creator, the Great Blue-Assed Baboon God. Amen."

In *Waiting*, three cows—Bessie, Opal, and Eloise—are standing in line, wondering why they are there and what is going on. Opal says she has no idea what "they" do or why "they" do it, but Eloise is sure that everything will be fine, that "they" feed them and take good care of them. But, Bessie says, "they" have never loaded them in trucks and taken them to another place before. She says the place doesn't smell like a barn, that the hundreds of other cows, especially those at the head of the line, look worried. Eloise thinks that most unhappiness in cows is caused by worrying. She says the trick is to relax and be thankful for what they have. Bessie says they don't know if they're ever going home again, that they don't know where they're going or why they are here. Eloise tells her to be calm, put herself in the hands of Providence, and have faith that everything will be all right. Bessie says she smells fear and thinks something terrible is going on. Eloise says she believes that they were put on earth for a purpose, even though they may not know what that purpose is. They need to trust the powers that have always looked after them and everything will be all right. Opal says the line is moving again and as the light fades Bessie repeats, uneasily, Eloise's assurance, "The line is moving and everything is fine."

In *City of Dreadful Night,* four characters—Gus, in his thirties; his brother, Tony, in his thirties; Philly, in his twenties; and Anna, in her late twenties—enact the discovery of an unsuspected murder. The scene is New York City in the late 1940s and a unit set represents all locations simultaneously: a park bench DR, a coffee shop with curved counter and stools DL, a bedroom with bed and chair on a platform UC, and the street played across the downstage area. We hear the sound of pigeons in the dark and lights come up on Gus and Tony on the park bench as Anna, in the upstage shadows, sits before her mirror, and Philly leans on the counter of the coffee shop reading a newspaper. From the laconic conversation of Gus and Tony we learn that Gus wants Tony to spy on Anna. Gus thinks Anna is seeing someone and he wants Tony to find out who the man is. Tony suggests that perhaps Gus should forget about Anna but agrees to follow her. As Tony moves downstage, Anna asks him if he is following her. She thinks she recognizes him and suggests that he would like a piece of warm cherry pie. Tony says he might have liked one before the war but he isn't sure now. She says that perhaps he can have some pie when he gets done following her.

As Anna sits on the bench with Gus, Tony sits on a stool in the coffee shop and asks Philly if he recognizes the picture of Anna that Gus gave him. Philly warns Tony to watch out for her, that she is trouble. He says he has seen her with a man he thinks is a killer. Tony writes a phone number on a napkin and tells Philly to call him if the girl comes in again. Tony goes to Anna who is sitting on the bench feeding the pigeons. She says she saw him looking up at her window the previous night and thinks Gus is paying him to follow her. Tony denies being paid anything, and as Gus moves into Anna's room and sits in front of the mirror, she remembers seeing a photograph of Gus and Tony and a pretty girl taken at Coney Island before the war. Tony says that when he sees Anna moving from window to window in her red slip she reminds him of a girl he used to know. Anna asks Tony who got the girl in the photograph but he says he can't remember. Anna asks him to come up to her room, and when Tony says he's busy she says she'll leave her door unlocked if he wants to come up later.

She goes to her room where Gus has been waiting. He asks her where she has been and gets upset with her evasive answers. She asks him where he

goes at night and tells him that if what he does is none of her business then
what she does is none of his. Gus leaves and joins Tony on the bench, asking
him if he has found out if Anna is seeing somebody. Tony tells him that
sometimes Anna walks to see the monkeys in the zoo and sometimes goes to
Coney Island.

We hear the sound of seagulls and lapping water as Tony joins Anna
looking out at the water on Coney Island. Anna says there's somebody else
inside Tony, someone a lot more complicated. She thinks Tony wants her
and wonders what Gus would do if he caught them naked in bed together.
She says the gulls and the smell of the water remind her of Cape Cod and
doing everything with her sister until the war came and her father left and her
mother went insane and her sister went away.

She walks into the upstage shadows and Tony moves to the coffee shop.
Philly says the woman Tony was asking about came into the coffee shop with
some guy, a guy that looked like Tony, a few nights earlier. Tony gives
Philly a dime so that he can call him the next time the woman comes in. Tony
leaves the coffee shop and paces back and forth across from Anna's place,
talking disjointedly to himself, seeming to be almost remembering something. As he looks up at Anna's window, the light fades on him, ending the
first act.

Act Two begins as the lights come up on the bedroom with Anna just
opening the door for Tony. Philly is behind the counter in the coffee shop and
Gus sits on a stool drinking coffee. Tony tells Anna that he needs to talk to
her and she asks him to come in. She is trying to remember a nightmare
about her mother and sister, but Tony says that Gus will kill her if she is
cheating on him. She taunts Tony until he slaps her and she falls backward
across the bed. She asks Tony if he wants her and wonders if he hit the girl in
the picture at Coney Island. When Tony says that he is trying to save her,
Anna asks what Gus has on him. Tony says that his head got hurt in the war
and that Gus looks out for him by helping him remember things. Anna says
that Gus doesn't want him to remember and asks about the girl in the picture.
When Tony says he thinks she died, Anna asks if he killed her, if Gus helped
him get rid of the body. Tony says that she loved Gus and when Anna says
that Tony killed her, he grabs her around the throat and says loudly that he
didn't kill her. When he lets her go, he sits on the bed, and Anna asks him
who she looks like. He says she looks like Ida Lupino and like the girl in the
picture. In a long speech, Anna explains that the girl in the photograph was
her sister who ran off to live in the city, leaving Anna to take care of their
sick, drunk, half-crazy mother. The sister wrote letters every week but then
the letters stopped. The mother fell down the stairs and died and Anna came
to the city to look for her sister who had disappeared. From the photographs
her sister had sent, Anna was able to locate the coffee shop and, one day,

Gus. Then Tony started following her and now she wants to know which one of them killed her sister.

Lights come up on the coffee shop where Philly is telling Gus about Tony following Anna. Gus says he told Tony to follow her but is surprised when Philly tells him that Tony has been in Anna's room. Gus leaves the coffee shop and lights come up on Tony and Anna in her room. She wants to know who took the pictures of Gus, Tony, and her sister. Tony seems about to remember when Gus comes in, asking what's going on. Anna tells Gus that he knew her sister and shows him the Coney Island photo. Gus thinks she has taken it from his room but she insists her sister gave her a copy of the picture. Tony remembers that the name of the girl in the picture is Faith. Gus notices the mark on Anna's face where Tony hit her and says he will kill him if he touches her again. He accuses Anna of being with him just to find out what happened to her sister. Gus says he hasn't seen the girl since before the war and when Anna asks about the picture in his room Gus says it is a picture of his brother Tony. He is bothered that Anna pretended to like him even though she thought he might have killed her sister. When Anna tries to leave, Gus throws her on the bed, saying she is not going anywhere, that he needs to think. Tony asks Gus who took the pictures of the three of them and the lights fade on the bedroom and come up on the coffee shop where Philly is reading the paper.

Tony enters from the darkness and Philly serves him black coffee, asking if he wants a piece of cherry pie. When Anna enters, Philly gives her coffee with extra sugar and lots and lots of cream. Gus comes in and says he has a job to do. He asks Philly where his camera is but Philly says he doesn't have a camera any more, adding that he spent the war in prison because he did some stupid things because of mental problems. Tony remembers that Philly was the kid that used to follow them around before the war, and Gus wants to know what happened to the girl. Under pressure from Gus, Philly admits that he took the girl to Coney Island and thinks that she may have gone to see her sister. Philly says that Anna can't be the girl's sister because the girl told him her sister had dangerous mental problems and might have killed her mother and that was why she was going back home to Cape Cod to talk to her. Tony says he remembers getting a letter from the girl just before he went overseas, verifying what Philly says. Gus asks Anna what she has been doing since the war started. Anna admits that she had a nervous breakdown after her mother died and that she was put in a place where they gave her drugs and shock treatments. She tells the men of a bad dream she keeps having about walking on the beach with her sister and being angry with her for suggesting that she pushed their mother down the stairs. Anna says that in the dream she picks up a rock and hits her sister in the head and her sister falls face down in the water. Anna runs away but when she comes back her sister is not there. Anna says the dream keeps playing in her head over and over but that it's just a movie. She asks Philly for some pie. Gus wants to leave. Tony says he'll stay for a bit and tells Philly to give Anna some pie. Anna eats the pie, saying it's very good. Lights fade out.

The set for the 4-character (3m, 1w) *The Count of Monte Cristo in the Chateau D'If* is a two-level unit with a background of fog and crags. Two sets of curving stone steps lead up to a platform with Alexandre Dumas' desk and chair SR. Under the platform UC between the steps is a cave mouth. There is a door SR opening upstage and between it and the SR steps is a window. DR a table and chairs. A garden bench is downstage of the SL steps and further downstage, perpendicular to the edge of the stage, is a "stone" wall that characters must dig through. A small prop table is on the landing halfway up the SL stairs. Escape stairs lead off from halfway up both sets of stairs and from either side of the top of the platform. This unit set represents a dungeon cell in the Chateau d'If, a dark prison on an island in the Atlantic, the study of Dumas, an inn near the sea, the jagged island of Monte Cristo, and a garden. The action is fluid, without set changes or intermission.

A Chopin *Etude* and the conclusion of Rossini's *William Tell* Overture are heard as the house lights fade to darkness. A circle of light comes up on Edmund Dantes, sitting center stage on the floor of his cell. Dumas is barely visible at his desk, starting to ask ludicrous questions. Dantes responds with his own thoughts, concluding the scene by saying that his purpose is the conquest of time. As the lights go to black we hear the sound of a cell door creaking shut, then the sound of gulls and ocean and the voices of Mercedes and Dumas. Birdsong signals the light coming up on Mercedes on the bench in her garden. Auguste Maquet, a literary drudge, tells her that he loves her, and she says that she loves only Edmund Dantes. When Dumas says, "Oh, cries the rejected lover, running along like one demented and tearing his hair," Maquet looks up at him and asks if he thinks that's too much. Dumas repeats the line and Maquet follows directions, tearing his hair and running like one demented to the table DR. Dumas suggests to Maquet that perhaps something unfortunate should happen to Dantes. Maquet says that he cannot control Fate, but Dumas says that he, as author, can. He tells Maquet to denounce Dantes to the authorities as a traitor. Maquet will get not only money but Mercedes. Dumas tells the hesitant Maquet that he must decide if he wants to be a major or a minor character. We hear the cawing of ravens and Dumas says, "Good. The ravens are good. Let's keep that."

We hear the sound of a ticking clock as the lights come up on Mercedes. She complains about waiting (and burping) but then sees her lover Dantes, home from the sea. She rushes to greet him just as he opens the door, clunk, smashing her in the face. Dantes thinks she has been hiding and looks at the audience, thanking them for coming on this auspicious occasion. Maquet thrusts the door open, hitting Mercedes in the face again, and, prompted by Dumas, arrests Dantes for treason, taking him off to the dungeon of the Chateau d'If. In the darkness we hear footsteps, an iron door creaking open, Dantes screaming as he is thrown toward the cave mouth, and the sound of the door clanging shut. Dantes describes sounds that the audience also hears and as the lights come up Maquet pushes a bowl of gruel into the cave. Dantes says he is being tortured, and when Dumas asks questions Dantes says that he has imaginary conversations with God or someone like him who smokes cigars and smells of sweat, liquor, and ink. We see Dumas' face as he lights his cigar on the platform above. He asks Dantes for the supreme word in human philosophy, and when the prisoner gives up he tells him it is the word "if." Dumas tells Dantes that he is in prison to further the plot.

Lights come up on Maquet writing as Dumas dictates. Mercedes pleads for mercy for Dantes. Dumas orders Maquet to write that Mercedes' nose has been healed and rips off her bandage, saying, "On to the next chapter. Darkness." Maquet repeats, "Darkness," and the lights go out. Then a dim light comes up on Dantes in prison, talking with Dumas and speaking as the author dictates. Mercedes appears and asks Dantes to help her, saying they are both prisoners in a novel by Alexandre Dumas. Following Dumas' narration, Dantes decides to starve himself to death by throwing his breakfast bowl of gruel out the window. Maquet makes the sound of a rooster crowing and slides a bowl into the circle of light, saying, "Breakfast." Dantes throws the bowl out the window. Lights black out and come up again as Maquet repeats the rooster crow and the bowl action. Again, Dantes throws it out. This sequence is repeated four more times until Dantes collapses and Dumas, speaking from the darkness, tells us that Dantes is hallucinating a mysterious and relentless scraping noise. We hear the scraping noise get louder and louder until Dantes asks if anyone is there and hears the voice of Dumas say that he is number one thirty-seven. Dantes wants to talk and claws at the wall which suddenly gives way and a man tumbles out. It is Dumas in a long white beard, fake nose, and bald wig. Dumas as prisoner says that he has been trying to escape for years but had decided it is impossible. All he can do is write a story about a young man who is falsely accused of treason and thrown into a dungeon. He shows Dantes a drawing he has made on his stomach and describes how the two of them can escape by digging a tunnel. He also shows Dantes a map giving the location of a treasure buried on the island of Monte Cristo. Prisoner Dumas gags, goes into convulsions, and dies. Dantes pushes him back through the hole, replaces the stones, and moves off as the light fades.

We hear birdsong as the lights come up on Mercedes in her garden; Dumas, from the darkness, says that she remains loyal to her beloved. Mercedes, insisting on her loyalty, says that she owes it to herself to consider letting some rich fat guy with a creepy moustache defile her tender young flesh repeatedly. We hear ravens cawing as the light fades on her and comes up on Dantes in prison. Dantes tells us that he plans to take the dead old man's place and be buried in the Cemetery of the Chateau d'If. He crawls under the shroud as Maquet and Dumas come in, carry him up the stairs, and tie a cannon ball to his feet before throwing him off the upstage side of the platform. Maquet expresses gratitude that the sea is the cemetery.

Following Dumas' narration, Dantes, rescued by smugglers, arrives at the Isle of Monte Cristo hoping to find the old man's treasure. Finding it, but exhausted, he falls asleep on the treasure chest and dreams he is back in the dungeon. When Maquet asks for co-author credit, Dumas calls him "a piddling little inky-fingered troglodyte" and decides to have Dantes meet Mercedes in the garden where they vowed undying love. After Dumas tells us that she married a bitter enemy of Dantes, she tells Dantes, whom she apparently does not recognize, that she married because she thought her love was dead. She calls him Edmund but he says he is the Count of Monte Cristo and that she is dead to him. She speaks of how she prayed and wept for him for ten years, and Dumas remarks that "this is good stuff. I really am a tremendous writer." When Maquet says that he wrote that speech, Dumas says that he is hallucinating. They argue over the use of the word "whence" and Dantes tells Mercedes that he has no desire to live after he has been publicly insulted before a theatre full of people.

After Mercedes leaves and Dantes sits holding his head in despair, Dumas and Maquet talk about making cuts because the scene is too long. As they walk off squabbling, Dantes speaks of a voice in his head telling him that nothing that has happened in hundreds of pages is real; it has all been a dream. Maquet makes the rooster noise and slides a bowl of gruel into the light. Dantes throws it out the window and Mercedes asks him if what happened in the garden felt good to him. They remember kissing each other and she says they need to get away from "all this damned plot." She remembers the name Alexandre Dumas, and Dantes says he is leaving to find him.

We hear a foghorn and lights come up on a smoky bar where Dumas and Maquet are drinking. Dumas introduces himself to Dantes as James O'Neill (the actor who played the part of the Count of Monte Cristo for decades). Dumas/O'Neill warns Dantes to stay away from Alexandre Dumas and leaves. Maquet tells Dantes that Dumas is the cause of all his sufferings and is completely insane. Dantes and Maquet resolve to destroy Dumas, and we hear the Chopin *Etude* we heard at the beginning of the play as lights dim on the inn and come up on Dumas at his desk. We hear wind and rain and a part of the *William Tell* Overture as Dumas writes frenetically. He shouts out to cut the music, and the music stops suddenly so that we hear only the sound of a ticking clock. Dumas says that he's lost everything he earned over the years. Dantes appears behind him and says he wants to be in a better novel and that he has come to get revenge on the author. Dumas says Dantes needs to be more angry and that he himself gets revenge by writing novels. He tells Dantes that he can do whatever he wants to him and offers him a glass of lemonade. The lemonade is drugged and Dantes collapses as the lights go to black.

We hear footsteps and the sound of an iron door creaking open, then Dantes screaming as he is hurled into the downstage darkness. Maquet does the rooster noise, announcing breakfast as he slides the bowl of gruel into the light. Reprising the opening scene, Dumas fires questions at Dantes, who says that the mind is a theatre in which memory dances and that his purpose is the conquest of time. The lights fade out as we hear the last measures of the Rossini.

A recent addition to the Pendragon cycle (the other full-length plays are now available from Samuel French, Inc.), *Dreams of a Sinister Castle* requires four men and four women. The setting is a room in the "ancient wreck of a labyrinthine haunted house" in east Ohio. The furniture is covered with cobwebs and sheets and doors lead off in several directions. A stage area also represents a field with a ragged scarecrow outside the house. The time is autumn 1976 and in the darkness we hear an eerie calliope, the roaring of lions, and trumpeting of elephants.

As the lights come up, five characters enter, carrying suitcases. Duncan Rose, 45, plays kings, villains, and "rather stiff heroes" and his brother Duff, 43, plays younger Shakespearean leads. Ally, their sister, 41, June Reedy, 33, and her sister Lorry, 32, complete the entourage. They are all tired and hungry, irritable, but Ally says she feels a spiritual connection with the house, their father's house and the house of the mother of June and Lorry.

Duncan declares that The Pendragon and Rose Theatrical Touring Company has hit rock bottom. The company's costumes and scenery have been confiscated because their show in Pittsburgh failed to attract an audience and bring in the necessary money. As Duncan and Duff squabble, Ally remarks that she dreamed that they all joined a circus, and June thinks they can stay in the house until they figure out how to raise the money to get their sets and costumes back. She says that Aunt Liz will make them all the fried chicken and mashed potatoes they can eat. Duncan says they have seventeen bookings left that they cannot get to, that they have no money, and that the other actors have deserted them.

Ally takes out a huge tangled ball of yarn, saying that knitting is the secret to her serenity. June and Lorry help her untangle the yarn and Ally has the feeling that someone is watching them. Lorry and Duff go out to the kitchen, and Duncan and June leave to use the telephone at Aunt Moll's. Alone, Ally sits on the floor in the lotus position, talking to the spirits of the house, asking for their wisdom. As she speaks, a 20-year-old girl, Molkin, wearing a big false mustache, a tattered old wedding dress, and a stovepipe hat, comes in, takes out a walnut from between her breasts, and places it on top on the yarn. Then she puts the mustache under the walnut and the hat on top of the yarn. She looks at Ally and goes off as the lights fade.

We hear the sounds of crickets and owls, and moonlight through an open window reveals Ally on the sofa, mumbling in her sleep. A dark figure crawls through the window and approaches her. When he (Romeo DeFlores) touches her arm, she screams and sits up. Duff calls from offstage and Romeo leaves. Ally tells Duff she has been talking with the Devil. Lorry comes on wondering what all the yelling is about and tells Duncan and June when they enter that Ally has seen the Devil. Ally insists that the Devil went out through the door, and when Duncan opens the door to disprove her, Romeo is standing there, saying he never actually left because he walked into the broom closet. June tells Ally that Romeo is her father, and Lorry's. The girls want to know what Romeo wants. He tells them he has had a dream that has brought him to the sinister castle (the house). He tells them his son and wife are dead, and he has come in search of his daughters. Reaching out the window he hauls in a large satchel which, he says, contains the insurance money from the fire that destroyed the house of mirrors and his son. He wants them to take the money. He feels guilty because in the past he had talked of burning the hall of mirrors for the insurance money, but he insists that he did not set the fire, although he feels that perhaps his thoughts did. He says he has what is left of the carnival—some old animals and a handful of freaks—are on the other side of the hill. Duff looks in the satchel and Duncan says they could use the money, but Lorry slams the satchel into Romeo's chest and pushes him into the hallway and out the door. Duncan tries to convince Lorry that they can use the money to get their theatre company back in business. Ally says that Romeo is standing in the middle of the yard and it is starting to rain. We hear Romeo howling like a wolf, then barking like a dog. Duncan says they should take the money that Romeo wants to give his daughters and then commit him to a mental asylum. Lorry says that Romeo is conning them and goes off to bed. The lights fade as Romeo howls, Duff drinks, and June and Ally look out the window.

We then see Romeo outside the house, howling at the moon beside a scarecrow. He talks to the scarecrow and says that elephants answer his howling. We hear an elephant trumpeting in the distance. June appears, with Ally, Duncan, and Duff behind her. June wants her father to come inside. When asked about the satchel with money, Romeo says that he buried it. We hear thunder and Romeo tells Duncan that the ghost girl knows where he buried the money. He says she went to tell her father. Duncan is certain he will never see the money again. After June and Ally lead Romeo off, Duff and Duncan sit under the scarecrow and bemoan the loss of their acting company. Duncan wants to try to find the money before the rains come, but Duff has had enough to drink and wants to sleep. Duncan drags him off and Molkin, still in the wedding dress, comes on with the muddy satchel. She opens it and tells the scarecrow that it is full of grief. We see lightning and hear thunder as the light fades on her.

Act Two begins with the sound of crickets as the lights come up on Ally sleeping on the sofa. Molkin comes in with a large "very ugly looking" ax, raises it to strike Ally, and falls over backwards. Ally identifies Molkin as the ghost girl Romeo talked of and asks her what she is doing with the ax. Molkin says she was going to cut Ally's head off because she is going to take her daddy away. John Rose, 88, enters behind her and tells her to put the ax down. Ally recognizes her father, and he introduces her to Molkin as Lorry, Duncan, June, and Duff come on. Ally tells John that their sets and costumes are locked up in Pittsburgh, and John asks why they need "all that moth-eaten crap." He tells Duncan that he gave him the company because he wanted it. Molkin, thinking that Duncan has insulted her, offers to cut his head off, but John takes the ax and sits on the sofa with her and Ally. Molkin tells Ally that John is her real father because he saved her life when she was starving and hearing voices. John says he left the company to come back to the Pendragon house, found Molkin, and stayed. When Ally wants him to rejoin the company, John asks her if the company is sets and costumes. When she says no, he points out that if the company is the actors they have what they need. He tells them the essence of theatre is to use what you have, that no one can prevent them from practicing their craft.

When Romeo enters, Duncan identifies Molkin as the ghost girl he'd mentioned and asks her where the money is buried. She says she burned it. Romeo says he saw them in a play in Pittsburgh and complains that he didn't see an actor exit pursued by a bear the way Shakespeare wrote it. Romeo says that he has a bear where his carnival is camped. Duncan, fed up with Duff's comments, knocks him down and starts strangling him. Ally, June, and Lorry try to pull him off, but he persists until John, in his old actor's voice, orders him to stop.

When John asks what else he has in his carnival, Romeo lists a variety of sideshow artists and animals. Ally says they could call themselves The Pendragon and Rose Shakespearean Theatrical Carnival and use the animals in the forest of Arden and all kinds of places and use the carny people as extras. Lorry says she doesn't have a problem with the idea, but she doesn't think they can trust Romeo. He says he has betrayed everything but never his carnival. The actors vote, four to one (Duncan resisting), to try. Duncan then agrees as long as John is not involved. Molkin wants to go with the actors and John admits that he loved the life of an actor and has missed it. Duncan says he has just learned that his wife has left him and Duff apologizes for sabotaging Duncan's efforts, assuring him that the company needs him and that his wife will come back to him. John tells Duncan to go back to England to straighten things out with his wife. While he is gone, he, John, will take over and help June restage the shows. With the sun coming up, Romeo leads them off to meet the animals.

The Greek Trilogy consists of three interrelated full-length plays—*Iphigenia, Clytemnestra,* and *Electra*—which may be performed independently or as a trilogy done on three successive evenings or on the morning, afternoon, and evening of the same day. The unit set is the same for all three plays: a bench with some tombstones DR and a chair far DL; one step above stage level is the porch with a swing R and, center left, a table and chairs; two steps UL is a study with chair, desk, and books; up another step SR is a bed with night stand and lamp; up three more steps UC is a small landing on either side of which are windows leading UL and UR to a section of roof. Nigro points out that, except for the furniture, the set is not a realistic representation of a house; walls and doors are fragmentary or non-existent. "The flow of action between . . . locations must be easy and unbroken throughout the play, and characters will often be seen in other parts of the stage during scenes in which they do not appear, so that the transition from one scene to the next is often either a moving actor going from one location to another where another actor is already situated, or a change of light from one location to another in which the actors for the next scene are already present. Escape stairs make it easy for actors to enter and exit from any location on the set. There must never be any dead space between scenes or actors scuttling about out of character in the dark. No furniture is ever moved, and there are no set changes."

There are five actors (2m, 3w) in *Iphigenia,* which takes place in Armitage, Ohio, in 1909-1911. In darkness we hear crickets as the lights come up on Lexie, 17, sitting on the porch swing. We can make out Michael, her father, in his study, Carolyn, her mother, in the dining room, Jenna, her older sister, sitting on the bed, and, standing in the DR shadows, Nick Demetrius. Lexie tells Nick she can see him and asks if he has come to ravish her. Nick offers to catch some fireflies and make a necklace for her. She thinks he is a tramp and knows he is a stranger. Nick tells her he wants to see Michael Ryan tonight and asks how many are in the family. Lexie says she has an older sister and a younger brother who is at military boarding school. She tells Nick that her father reads ancient Greek plays in the original language.

Michael comes out on the porch and learns from Nick that he wants to talk about "New York business," that a Mr. Kalkas sent him. Michael tells Lexie to go inside and as she goes up the step she meets Jenna coming down.

Nick tells Michael that when he was a boy he saw something happen in the basement of a New York City pawnshop. Jenna comes out and invites Nick and her father to come inside. Nick tells Jenna that her father has offered him a job at his bank. Jenna suggests the Flowers Boarding Hotel as a place where Nick might stay and he walks to the chair in the shadows DL.

Carolyn enters the study and asks Michael why he doesn't come up to bed. She thinks their daughters are half in love with Nick but will soon be gone and then she and Michael can make love in the afternoons, since they have stopped having sex altogether at night. She wonders why he keeps poring over the same bunch of moldy old plays and he tells her that the stories are inside us and that to know and understand them is all we have. She wonders what myth they are trapped in and wants him to come to bed. She goes up the steps to sit on the bed as the light fades on Michael.

We hear the sound of ticking clocks as Nick looks downstage from the DL chair (the parlor of the Flowers Boarding Hotel) and Michael stands behind him. Nick says he likes staying at the Hotel and assumes Michael has come to kill him. He tells Michael that if an attorney in New York doesn't hear from Nick by a certain day every month, he will send a letter to the police describing what Michael did and where he is. Nick tells Michael that he wants to marry Jenna. Michael says that he can come to dinner and the light fades on the DL area as Nick walks over to the porch to sit on the swing with Jenna and Michael moves to the study.

Jenna tells Nick that she doesn't like him very much and asks what he has done to her father. She goes into the house as Lexie comes out and sits on the porch step with Nick. Nick asks Lexie to help him with her sister. When he asks her if she will dance with him at the wedding, she says she will dance on his grave and smiles at him as the light fades on them and Jenna moves to the study to talk with her father, telling him that she doesn't want to see Nick. She asks Michael why he wants her to marry Nick and asks if something is wrong at the bank and if he is in trouble. She says she will do anything to make him happy. Carolyn comes in and tells Jenna that Nick is leaving. Jenna goes to join Nick and Lexie while Carolyn talks with Michael about Nick and their daughters. Carolyn says that Michael never talks about his past. He kisses her tenderly and holds her as the light fades on them and our attention shifts to Lexie pinning Jenna's wedding dress, telling her sister that Nick is going to make her miserable. Jenna thinks that Lexie likes Nick more than she does because they talk together for hours. Jenna says she has to marry Nick and when Lexie asks, "Why?" Michael comes in. After Lexie leaves, Michael tells Jenna that they can still call off the wedding, but Carolyn enters and says Jenna wants to marry Nick, telling Michael that she didn't want to marry him, but did. Lexie comes back to ask if they are coming, and Jenna tells Michael that it's time to give her away.

The next scene (the wedding night) takes place in the imagined bedroom of the house next door with Nick sitting on the bed waiting for Jenna to come out of the bathroom. She finally enters, barefoot, wearing a white nightgown. He moves toward her and she backs away, saying she doesn't want to be touched. He grabs her and she pokes him in the eye, saying that she married him for her father's sake. She takes a knife from the drawer of the bedstand, but he takes it from her, tossing it upstage and throwing her onto the bed, ripping off her nightgown. She gets away and crawls toward the knife. In the struggle, they knock the lamp over and in the darkness we hear them both scream, ending the act.

Act Two begins on the night of the wedding with Michael drinking on the porch as Carolyn asks if he has seen their squirrel gun. Michael says it sounds as if someone is being killed next door but Carolyn tells him he can't stop it because they are married. Michael tells Carolyn that his name is not Michael Ryan, that he took the name from an envelope in the hand of a dead man in a freight train box car. Michael explains that he was running away because he stole some money and Nick knows what he did and Jenna figured out that Nick was blackmailing him and that's why she married Nick. Carolyn asks Michael if he is so stupid that he believes a woman ever does anything she doesn't want to do. Lexie comes out with a blanket around her shoulders saying that something is seriously wrong next door. She says that Jenna is on the edge of the roof and Michael thinks Nick is going to kill her.

As light fades on them it comes up on Jenna sitting UR on the roof of her house, her nightgown ripped and splattered with blood. We can see Nick in the "gabled upstage attic window." He wants her to come in but she refuses. Michael, Carolyn, and Lexie appear at the window. They try to get Jenna to come in but she threatens to jump if they come out after her. Lexie climbs out and the others leave the window. The sisters talk and Jenna says she left a doll, Sally, on the roof a long time ago. Jenna says the blood on her nightgown is her husband's. She says she bit him and would have made him bleed more if she hadn't dropped the knife. She also hid the squirrel gun in the closet, planning ahead. Lexie urges her to come in from the cold and Jenna notices Loopy Rye, the village idiot, looking up at them from the graveyard DR. The girls sit together with the blanket around them. Jenna says their mother keeps a lot of anger inside and will explode one day like a dirigible. Jenna says she wants her husband dead, slowly, perhaps eaten alive by rats. Lexie says that if Jenna will come in off the roof, she will figure out how to murder her husband. They spit in their hands and then shake hands. Jenna puts her head on Lexie's shoulder and they hold each other as the light fades on them and goes out.

The next scene, six months later, is in the study where Nick and Michael are drinking before dinner. Nick asks how he is doing at the bank and Michael says that everyone thinks he is doing well. When Nick asks about

Jenna, Michael tells him that Jenna goes to the attic when Nick is in the house and stays there until he leaves. Michael says if Nick ever goes near Jenna again he will kill him. Lexie enters and says it's time for supper. Michael leaves and Lexie tells Nick that she promised Jenna that she would help murder him. Lexie says she will tell Jenna that Nick is sorry if Nick tells her what her father did that made him sacrifice his daughter to somebody like Nick. When Lexie asks why Nick wanted Jenna and not her, Nick says that their father loves Jenna more. Lexie says that's a lie, that Nick was terrified of her. He pulls her towards him and kisses her, twice, then pushes her away. She puts the palm of her hand on his chest and, as Carolyn enters, Nick takes a step back. Carolyn sends Nick to the dining room so she can talk with Lexie. She asks Lexie what she is doing with her sister's husband. Lexie says she will stay away from Nick if her mother does.

Lexie moves to Jenna who is sitting on the steps to the attic. Carolyn is in the shadows of the study, drinking, and Michael and Nick are in the dining room shadows, also drinking. Jenna insists that she really wants to kill Nick. Lexie says that Nick never asks about Jenna and suggests that Jenna let Nick do what he wants to her, wait till he goes to sleep, and then cut his throat. Jenna says that Lexie wants Nick for herself. Lexie tells her she can't trust anyone in the house and needs to take charge of her own life. Carolyn crosses to them and Lexie goes to the dining room. Jenna says that Carolyn wants to sleep with Nick, and Carolyn tells her that she has to start living her life again or nobody will care.

Carolyn sits at the dinner table with Michael, Nick, and Lexie as Jenna goes to the study and drinks from the whiskey decanter. Carolyn urges Michael to eat more potatoes and tells Nick that Thomas, her son, likes college very much. Jenna enters the dining room, tells Michael and Nick not to touch her, and orders Nick to pull out her chair. She sits at the table and says everybody who loves her is at the table, excluding Grandpa and the village idiot. She orders those who love her-- her back-stabbing sister, her black-mailing rapist husband, her craven father, and her reptilian mother-- to sit and eat. When Michael tells her she doesn't have to be here if she doesn't want to be, she says she missed her husband who raped her on her wedding night, and her sister who's been lusting desperately after her husband, and her mother who's "got the brain of a cockroach and the morals of a goat," and her father who agreed to sacrifice her body and soul to save himself. She says she has decided to take charge of this human sacrifice and is moving back next door with her husband. She will not hold it against her mother that she's been lusting after Nick since he got here, or against Lexie who was pretending to be her friend while she was rutting with Nick. She will not hold it against her father that he sold her to a pig "to save his wretched, drunken skin." She is going to play out her role in this drama and they are all going to be very nice to her or she will go to the sheriff and tell him that her husband is blackmailing her father for a crime he committed in New York. She says she is going to her bedroom and tells Nick to be there in exactly fifteen minutes. Nick tries to apologize, but she tells him he's not as sorry as he's going to be. She says it is a relief to finally take charge of her own mythological nightmare. She goes out on the porch and then DR. Carolyn says they have to put Jenna in the mental hospital in Massilon because she's clearly not in her right mind. Michael doesn't want to put her in a place like that, but Lexie thinks they might be able to help her there. After a silence, Michael, with a bellow of suppressed rage and despair, lunges at Nick, knocking him to the floor, screaming and punching him repeatedly in the face. Lexie first and then Carolyn manage to pull Michael off, but he jumps back on Nick, strangling him. Carolyn picks up a silver platter from the table and hits Michael over the head five times, stunning him. Lexie helps Nick up and Carolyn says that she'll have the ambulance come to the back door with the siren off. She thinks that they are becoming a family again and while they wait for the ambulance to take Jenna away, they can have dessert—her famous prune upside down cake.

In darkness we hear the sound of murmuring voices and lights come up on Jenna, in a straight jacket, sitting on the floor down center. In the shadows, Nick moves to sit on the bed, Lexie goes up the steps to the UL window looking out over the roof, Carolyn drinks and polishes silver in the dining room, and Michael stands on the porch looking downstage at Jenna. Jenna says she and her sister were always co-conspirators but she is having trouble making sense because of the Greek chorus jabbering in her head and the drugs that cloud her brain. Michael speaks her name and she describes what the other characters are doing. She says, "confess," and Michael tells of two Greek immigrant boys who work for a pawnbroker. Jenna says that her favorite Bible story is about Jephthah's daughter. Michael continues his story of the old man keeping all his money in a safe in his basement, and Jenna says that Jephthah promises to sacrifice the first creature he sees when he gets home. Michael says the boys knock the old man over the head with a board but the old man has a gun and one of the boys is shot in the chest. Jenna tells of Jephthah's daughter being the first creature he sees; he sacrifices her by cutting her throat. Michael's contrapuntal story continues with the other boy pushing the old man against the furnace, cracking his head, and killing him. Seeing his friend is going to die, the boy takes the money and runs away. But the friend's little brother was looking in the window. Jenna speaks lines about there being many possible endings to any story and about the village idiot howling in the graveyard at night. Michael says the killer hopped a freight train to a small town in Ohio, married the banker's beautiful daughter, and has a son and two daughters that he loves deeply, but shame and guilt make it impossible for him to talk to them. As Michael and Jenna have been telling their stories, Lexie has climbed out the window and onto the roof. She finds a tattered old doll, picks it up, and sits on the edge of the roof. Carolyn polishes the silverware and Nick curls up in a ball on the bed. Jenna says she has been constructing her own tragedy, conspiring with the gods who are, of course, insane. Michael asks for her forgiveness. Jenna says at least the village idiot, howling for her in the graveyard, loves. Michael asks again for forgiveness and Jenna's last words are, "Take me, I said to him, on my wedding night, lying naked on the bed. Do it to me. Take me. Take me."

The five characters of *Iphigenia* are ten years older in 1919, the year of the action in *Clytemnestra*, and two additional characters appear—August Ballantyne, 72, and Loopy Rye, 82. As the play begins, Nick and Lexie are drinking on the porch swing at night. Lexie feels guilty for helping to send her sister Jenna to the mental hospital. She tells Nick that she knows he and her mother are carrying on "like pigs wallowing in slop." Nick says that Carolyn showed up in his bed stark naked one night and says that if Lexie sleeps with him he will never touch her mother again. Carolyn comes out asking why they are always on the porch together and we learn that Michael has been in the war in France. Lexie says the war is over but Carolyn thinks both her husband and son Thomas are dead. When Lexie berates her for sleeping with Nick, Carolyn says she loves Michael very deeply. Nick says she was attracted to the guilt she saw in his eyes, that women like men because they are drawn compulsively to danger, despair, futility, cruelty, and violence. Lexie says her talks with Loopy Rye, the village idiot, are the most stimulating conversations she has all day. She says that he draws crayon pictures of her naked on the backs of old envelopes. Nick tells Carolyn that everyone imagines Lexie naked. Carolyn says she doesn't know why Loopy always lurks around their house or why he has begun to howl. Lexie says he misses Jenna. As they bicker, Michael appears in the shadows DR. Carolyn says all men are horrible and that women have to make allowances for them as they do for baboons and other subhuman creatures. She says if Lexie's father were here he could explain it to her, but Michael says he couldn't. Carolyn and Lexie hug him and ask who else is in the shadows. Michael says he has brought Jenna home but, disoriented, she avoids Lexie's attempt to hug her. Michael says he spent a lot of time searching for Thomas, but Carolyn is convinced her son is dead. Jenna says that Thomas is behind enemy lines eating strawberries with two Dutch girls and a cow. Lexie admits to putting a clock under Jenna's bed when they were girls and telling her it was a crocodile. Lexie tells Michael that Grandpa has been calling every day but Carolyn does not pick up the phone and never goes to see her father. Before she goes into the house, Jenna says being home is just like the madhouse, "only more violent." Lexie kisses Michael on the cheek and goes in to make sure Jenna is all right. Michael goes in to take a bath and Carolyn tells Nick that whatever has been going on between them has got to stop, that she wants her husband and she doesn't want Nick sleeping with either of her daughters. Nick says he hears a sound like wings flapping and we hear that sound as the lights fade on the porch and come up on Jenna sitting on the roof as Lexie approaches from the window.

We hear the sound of owls and Jenna says she really missed them and the house and everything but the people. Lexie tells her sister that she is sorry for not coming to see her and sorry for letting them take her to the madhouse. Jenna says she has moved from Hell to one of the warmer suburbs of Purgatory. Lexie swears she never slept with Nick and Jenna puts her head on Lexie's shoulder and tells her a secret: all of them are in a play, a Greek tragedy. Lexie says they're in Ohio, a low comedy at best. Jenna says she used to be Iphigenia but now she is Cassandra.

We hear birds singing as lights come up on August Ballantine sitting in the chair at the Flowers Boarding Hotel DR. He is mumbling as Carolyn tells him he wanted to see her. He says he is going to die and needs to tell her something. He says that he's dead broke, that Carolyn's mother was pregnant when he married her, and that he is not her father. He says that Loopy Rye is Carolyn's father, that her mother was in love with the village idiot. August says he made a business arrangement with Carolyn's grandfather: he agreed to marry Carolyn's mother and was given an excellent position at the bank. Augustus says that Lexie was his, as far as he knows. He says he saw Loopy and Carolyn's mother going at it on a tombstone in the cemetery like there was no tomorrow.

Light comes up on Michael reading in the study as Carolyn crosses to him. Michael says that Aeschylus was as real as they are and that books are all that have kept him from losing his mind. Carolyn is insistent that Michael talk to her and asks what he wants her to do. Lexie enters and asks them to be quieter. Carolyn storms out and Lexie tells her father that Carolyn is a dreadful person, that while Michael was away she was fornicating with her daughter's husband. Michael says that after what happens to you in a war things like that don't seem quite so important. Lexie says she has never understood him and asks him to say anything that isn't a lie. When he does not respond, she leaves and the light fades on the study.

We hear the sound of crows and see Loopy Rye sitting by a tombstone DR as Carolyn approaches with a basket. Loopy says you can learn a lot from watching birds. She says she has brought him fresh bread with butter and strawberry jam. Carolyn says her father told her that Loopy and her mother were rather close. She says she thought it strange that when she comes to visit her mother's tombstone Loopy is always there. Carolyn asks if Loopy forced her mother and he says she was a lonely person so he tried to make her laugh by drawing pictures for her, imitating birds, standing on his head. Carolyn says he loved her but as she is leaving she says she doesn't believe what her father told her about her mother and Loopy. She tells Loopy to stay away from her daughters, especially Jenna. Loopy says Carolyn was always a lost girl and when she says she knows exactly where she is he replies, "In the graveyard."

Act Two begins in the evening and we hear crickets as light comes up on Michael and Nick in the porch swing, drinking. Nick says he finds East Ohio a scary place full of unexpected darkness. He says he had a plan for revenge and getting money, but something "absolutely catastrophic" happened: he got what he wanted and ever since his life has been "a series of increasingly monstrous and obscene nightmares." Michael tells him that if he can work something out with Jenna he won't kill him right away, but there will be no more warnings. When Jenna enters, Nick says he loves her and Michael, leaving, tells Jenna to talk to her husband. Nick tells Jenna that he missed her and will love her even if she doesn't sleep with him. He says he really wants to try to make their marriage work. Jenna says she married a man she hated to save her father. Lexie comes out and Jenna says they should have killed Nick when they had the chance. She leaves to give her father a haircut and suggests she could stab Nick with the scissors. Lexie asks Nick to tell her what he wants so she can be sure not to give it to him. Nick stands up and grabs her, kissing her with passion as Carolyn appears with a large knife in her hand, threatening Nick. Carolyn complains that children hate and devour their parents. She says something is happening in her head, a little storm. She says she is making sandwiches for Loopy Rye and that Michael only takes baths and reads books since he got home. When Lexie asks for the knife, Carolyn stabs it violently into the porch rail and goes into the house, up to the bathroom and then down to the study. Nick suggests that he and Lexie could run away and go to Greece. She says this place is Greece, that "everyplace is Greece. . . .There is no place else." She says they are going to die here, that Greece is inside their heads, everywhere and nowhere, forever. Light fades on them and comes up on Michael in the bath.

In a monologue, Michael says he can't sleep because he dreams he's back in the war. He speaks of the lunacy and horror of war, created by the love of money and imaginary gods. As he is speaking, Jenna comes down from the roof with the scissors, saying he needs a haircut. When she asks him why he let her mother send her to the mental hospital, he says it was despair, and shame, and terror, that people make up reasons why they do things like characters in a play. He says he thought of her locked up in that place every night. Jenna tells him that everything will turn out all right in the end and kisses him on the head. Carolyn enters and asks why Jenna is in the bathroom with her father. Jenna gives Michael the scissors as she leaves to get towels. Carolyn tells Michael that he never left because he was never here and she doesn't know who she is or what she's supposed to do with him. She wants to know why Michael doesn't want anything from her and asks what happened to him in the war. She starts taking off her clothes to join him in the bath but he tells her not to. She asks if there was another woman and he says he met an English girl in France, a nurse, the first woman he could ever talk to. He tells Carolyn she doesn't want him, that she has been sleeping with her daughter's husband. Michael says he needs to give up everything. Carolyn talks about Clytemnestra murdering her husband in the bath and says Michael has made his whole family into a Greek tragedy. She suggests he stick the scissors in his chest and he takes them in both hands and holds them in front of his chest. She tries to grab the scissors and they struggle until the scissors end up plunging into his neck. Jenna enters with the towels and tries to lift Michael out of the water as Lexie and Nick come in. Carolyn says Jenna has lost her mind again and stabbed her father with the scissors. Lexie tells Nick to get the doctor and Carolyn calls after him to call the people at the madhouse to come and get Jenna.

Lights come up on the graveyard DR at night where, in moonlight, Loopy Rye sits by a grave as Carolyn appears. She tells Loopy that they've taken Jenna away for good, that she won't say anything, and that Nick has resumed drinking himself to death. She says her headache has gone away but is afraid it will come back with a monstrous flapping of wings and a great dark thing will tear out her throat. She says her father's dead body was found at the Flowers Boarding Hotel and asks Loopy if he loved her mother very much. Loopy says it's dangerous to love, that someone always dies. When Carolyn says that in her next life she's signing up for comedy, Loopy tells her that you take what they give you and try to play it. He says that Jenna would not have stabbed her father and Carolyn wants to know what happens to Clytemnestra. She says she hasn't read the next play. Loopy tells her that Clytemnestra's son kills her. He says they give him the library books they're going to burn and he finds books at the dump. He says reading random books is better than going to Yale and repeats that Clytemnestra's son comes home from the war and kills her. Carolyn says that won't happen in her case because her son is dead. She asks Loopy if he will hold her and call her his little girl and tell her he loves her. She says she doesn't care if he's lying. He can just pretend he's in a play. He looks at her, but does not move. We hear flapping sounds and the cawing of crows as the light fades on them and goes out.

In *Electra*, the year is 1920 and the cast is composed of Lexie, 28, Carolyn, 47, Jenna, 29, Nick, 40, and Thomas, 27. We hear crows in the darkness as lights come up on Lexie and Thomas in the cemetery DR. She tells

Thomas that their father is buried under "that little mound of earth" and Thomas says he hears a whispering like bees in his head. He doesn't want to answer Lexie's questions about the war and Lexie tells him their mother is a homicidal psychopath who killed their father. She says their mother and Nick were fornicating all over the house while Thomas and their father were off playing soldier. She tells Thomas that she needs his help to kill Nick and their mother, like the script in the Greek plays. She just wants him to play his part; he is Orestes and she is Electra. The whispering he hears in his head is the gods telling him to kill his mother. We hear crows and a faint whispering sound as the light fades on them and comes up on Carolyn sitting on the porch swing.

She speaks about hearing flapping noises and whispering and complains about people not talking to them. She says she dreamed she gave birth to a snake that drew clotted blood and milk from her breasts. She notices Thomas standing in the DR shadows and tells him to sit beside her on the swing. He tells her he doesn't want to work at the bank, that banks made the war and he would rather work in the fields baling hay. He says he doesn't kill any more and the light fades on them and comes up as a shaft of sunlight on Jenna sitting DC. We hear the sounds of moaning, chanting, singing, and chatter as Lexie and Thomas come near. Jenna is speaking nonsequiturs and Lexie tries to get her to recognize their brother. Lexie wants Jenna to tell Thomas what really happened to their father but Jenna says that Thomas should go away from this dangerous place. Lexie leaves, thinking that Jenna may talk with Thomas if they are alone. Jenna tells Thomas she was giving her father a haircut and Thomas asks if the scissors slipped, but Jenna doesn't answer him. She says if this was really a play she'd be dead by now. She asks if he brought her a banana and holds his hand as the light fades on them and comes up on Carolyn and Nick in the kitchen.

Carolyn asks Nick why he doesn't make love to her any more and says even the village idiot won't talk to her. She asks Nick if he would kill the idiot for her. She says she is thinking of taking over her husband's duties at the bank. She thinks Thomas might open up to Nick and orders him to go out on the porch.

As lights fade on the interior, Nick joins Thomas on the porch and hands him a flask, but Thomas says he doesn't like to drink. He suggests that Nick should talk with Jenna. Nick suggests that Thomas and Lexie should leave, but Thomas says he thinks he has something he has to do.

Lexie is sitting at night on the edge of the roof as Carolyn appears in the upstage window, asks Lexie to come in, then climbs out on the roof and moves down to where Lexie is sitting. Carolyn tells Lexie that she knows she was not the best parent, in part because she never got much training from her parents, was never taught how to take care of anything. She says the only real thing is death. Everything else is a "grotesque tangle of vanity, misperception, and self-delusion." She says Thomas will not believe Lexie's lies. She asks if Lexie hears a sound like bats and bees at the same time. When Carolyn tries to crawl back up the roof, Lexie grabs her foot and pulls her back, wanting to see if she can still do "the old swan dive." Carolyn gets free, moves up the roof, and warns Lexie that she is going to end up in the psycho ward next to her sister or in the cemetery next to her father. Lexie says that if anything happens to her, Thomas will get Carolyn because he hates her as much as Lexie does. The light fades on Lexie as Carolyn climbs through the window and down the steps to ask Nick what he is doing in Michael's study.

Nick says that he once thought he was going to be a writer. Carolyn orders him out of the study and asks if he hears a flapping noise. She says she thinks something has to be done about the children. Nick says he doesn't want anyone else to be hurt. He says there are limits to what she can get away with without getting caught or losing her mind. She asks him if he's been reading "those damned Greek plays" and thinks she should burn them in the back yard. Nick says that Michael said that you can deny ancient mythologies but you can't escape from them. Carolyn says if Nick gives her any trouble he'll be seeing Michael in Hell. She leaves as Nick sits drinking.

On the porch swing, Thomas is also drinking, talking to an invisible Loopy Rye he thinks is in the shadows. Carolyn appears to tell Thomas that he is to start working at the bank. Thomas says the military school she sent him to was a breeding ground for homicidal sociopaths. Carolyn agrees, saying all the great men in history have been homicidal sociopaths. They agree they both hear a buzzing sound and Thomas asks her directly if she killed his father. She asks him what he wants and he says he wants it all to have been a dream, a play, and if it is a play then he has to kill her. Carolyn says the dream, the play, would end if a person cut their wrists in a hot bath and bled out into the water. She says his father's razor blades are still in the bathroom cabinet. Thomas says he is going up to take a bath and she urges him to be careful with the razors. Lights fade on her as we hear crows in the darkness.

Lights come up on Carolyn, Nick, and Lexie DR in the cemetery as Carolyn tells Lexie that it is a disgrace that hardly anybody came to her brother's funeral. When Carolyn leaves to put out food, Lexie tells Nick that she will sleep with him if he kills Carolyn. When she starts to leave, he pulls her to him and kisses her and pushes her to the ground. She says she'll scream and he tells her there's nobody to listen but the dead.

We hear crickets and see Carolyn alone on the porch, speaking images from the earlier parts of the trilogy. She wishes the village idiot would come and talk with her and sees a figure in the shadows. Lexie appears, her clothing torn and dirty. Carolyn asks what happened to her and Lexie says that Nick is gone, that he stopped at the bank to pick up a "basket of other people's cash," and that he raped her. Carolyn says no man has ever done anything to her that she didn't want him to do. She says Lexie drove away her only friend on purpose and everything is Lexie's fault. Lexie roars in frustration and fury and knocks Carolyn down and starts hitting and then strangling her. Carolyn gets her hands around Lexie's throat and they roll back and forth. Although she gets the advantage, Carolyn stops and sits next to Lexie. She says she stopped because Lexie is her daughter, the most like her of any of her children. She says Lexie won't kill her because she is terrified of being alone. Lexie picks up a rock and hits Carolyn in the head, drops the rock, and leaves. Carolyn gets up and staggers into the house and up the steps saying that she knows Lexie will be back.

We hear crickets as light comes up on Carolyn sitting on the edge of the roof, looking at an old hat box full of photographs. As Carolyn talks about everything being chaos and throws photographs of her father and grandfather off the roof, Jenna, in white, climbs out the window behind her. Carolyn asks her if she escaped and asks her if she wants to throw photographs off the roof with her. Jenna sits beside her and Carolyn tells her that Loopy Rye was Carolyn's father. Carolyn says she is sorry that she put her away in that place and let people think she killed her father. Carolyn says she is hallucinating and wonders how she can live in this big, empty, haunted house alone. Jenna suggests that she could jump off the roof. They think they see Loopy picking up the photographs and call and wave to him. Jenna empties the box over the edge of the roof. Carolyn calls down to Loopy to pick up the pictures. Jenna picks up Sally, the tattered old doll, and Carolyn asks if Jenna wants to see her swan dive. Carolyn stands on the edge of the roof as Jenna waves the doll's arm, saying, "Bye bye, Mama." She asks Carolyn what she is waiting for. "Nothing," Carolyn says. "I'm waiting for nothing. Look, Papa. See how I can jump." Light fades on them and goes out.

The unit set for *Jules Verne Eats a Rhinoceros* represents the offices of the New York *World* and *Journal*, a restaurant in Paris, a bar in New York, a bench in the park, German headquarters on the Austrian front, a hotel room in Toledo, a madhouse on Blackwell's Island, a battlefield in Cuba, and "various other locations, real and imaginary . . . between 1887 and 1922." Above the middle of the three upstage doors is the gondola of a balloon with steps leading up to it on either side. Four women, three playing multiple parts, and six men, three playing multiple parts, make up the cast. The story concerns the journalistic career of Nellie Bly and the nature of American journalism before and after World War I.

The show begins with the sounds of Offenbach's cancan music from *Orpheus in the Underworld* as the house lights go down and then the sounds of ocean and gulls as lights come up on Nellie sitting on a wooden chair in a small circle of light center stage. From out of the darkness we hear the Doctor's voice, questioning Nellie about what she remembers. Although she cannot remember her name or birthplace, she does remember Jules Verne eating a rhinoceros. The Doctor says he is going to send her to an island where there are people who can help her.

As the light fades on Nellie we are jolted by the "rather overwhelming" Offenbach cancan music, and the entire stage is suddenly full of people in a French restaurant, moving to the rhythm of the music. A waiter sets out plates and silverware at the DR table as Joseph Pulitzer, William Randolph Hearst, and McGonigle sit at an upstage desk that doubles as a table while John Rhys (pronounced "rice") Pendragon and the three Giggle Sisters sit at the DL table. Jules Verne, in full beard, shakes hands with Pulitzer and Hearst, flirts with the Giggle Sisters, touches Rhys on the shoulder, and moves to the DR table as the music comes to a climax and the waiter brings Nellie from her chair to the same table. Nellie tells Verne that it is a tremendous honor to be granted an interview with him, and Verne says that creation is lunacy and that farce is the most realistic art form, telling Nellie that theatre is a place where everyone can go happily to the Devil together. Verne says that he has to keep writing if only to perpetuate the illusion of significance and asks Nellie if she has ever eaten a rhinoceros. He says there is no food in Paris because the Germans have surrounded the city, but the Waiter enters with a large covered pan on a platter and takes the lid off the pan to reveal the cooked head of a rhinoceros.

Cancan music plays as the lights dim on the DR table and come up on the table DL to the laughter of the Giggle Sisters. The other actors have left the stage during the music and McGonigle is moving down to join Rhys and the Sisters. Rhys, who never tries to be funny, is making them laugh with his deadpan remarks. He introduces McGonigle to them and McGonigle tells Rhys he has bad news: Nellie Bly is dead, of pneumonia, and Hearst wants Rhys to write the obituary.

McGonigle recalls the first time he saw Nellie, in the old *World* offices, and the lights fade on the table and come up on the upstage doors as McGonigle moves upstage towards his old desk and Nellie is shoved out from an inner office. When she tries to go back in, the door is slammed in her face. Furious, Nellie tells McGonigle that she has been in New York four months and cannot get a job as a reporter because she is a woman. McGonigle gives her half of his corned beef sandwich and a bottle of root beer which she devours ravenously. She tells McGonigle that she is a great reporter and just needs a chance. She says looking innocent is a big advantage and allows her to write the truth. McGonigle, smitten, takes out an old trumpet and blows a "very loud, horrendous, brassfart, moose-bellow noise." He blows twice more and Pulitzer storms out of the central door. (He speaks English with a Hungarian/Germanic accent all his own.) Nellie tells him that she will be a famous reporter if he will just give her a chance, but Pulitzer rejects her arguments and tries to go back to his office. She blocks his way and tells him he should think how sorry he's going to be if he turns her away and she ends up becoming the most famous reporter in the world. He admits that she has a bucket load of chutzpa but he doesn't know what to do with her. When she suggests that she be sent to France to interview Jules Verne, he tells her that Jules Verne eating a cabbage is not a story, but Jules Verne eating a rhinoceros *is* a story. Nellie offers to come back from France in steerage and do a series on what it is like to be an immigrant, like Pulitzer himself. She offers to get herself admitted to a madhouse to write about life there, but Pulitzer thinks it is too dangerous for a woman. She pleads that she has loved his paper because he champions the underdog, the oppressed, and that if he sends a man to write about life in a madhouse he would have a cabbage, but if he sends an innocent-looking girl like her, it's a huge rhinoceros. Pulitzer agrees to ten days and goes back in his office as the lights go to black.

We hear the "earsplitting sound" of a woman screaming horribly and a babble of voices, monkey chatter, panther growls, elephants trumpeting, and a rhinoceros snorting, under which an eerie player piano version of the can-can music plays quietly. As the babble subsides, lights come up on Verne writing at a table and Nellie standing lost and bewildered. Three Madwomen wander about; Theodore Roosevelt runs across the stage shouting "Charrrrrrrrrrge!"; Verne narrates his story; Roosevelt again, then a Barbary ape runs off with 2nd Madwoman over his shoulder as she screams and 1st Madwoman follows them screaming. Pulitzer comes out of his office to chase after a rhinoceros and the News Hawker shouts headlines as Roosevelt runs back on to snatch up 3rd Madwoman and run off with her. In a slight pause in this madcap action, Nellie asks Verne why she has run into him in a madhouse. She thinks it is a remarkable coincidence, but he says it is not a coincidence, it is a play. The Barbary Ape chases Roosevelt across the stage, both screaming, and Verne insists they are trapped in a play, explaining that he is writing a novel in which Nellie is trapped in a madhouse inside a play. Shouting "Charrrrrrrrge!" Verne runs out the center door, slamming it behind him and we hear birds singing as Nellie joins Rhys on the park bench.

Nellie tells him that the men decide who is and who is not crazy, and Rhys says his mother kept piglets in a box under her bed and talked to them as if they were her dead triplets. He tells her that the woman he loved married his father, set herself on fire, and drowned in a pond. Nellie says that the whole idea of romantic love escapes her, but Rhys tells her she is just protecting herself. She says she treats all marriage proposals as jokes. She and Rhys kiss and she leaves, telling him that she has to feed her monkey and write a story about her adventures impersonating a prostitute.

As she sits at McGonigle's desk in the upstage shadows, Verne joins Rhys on the bench and speaks of the rhinoceros, saying that the play is progressing rather well. When Rhys wonders what play, Verne responds, "Exactly!" and we hear the cancan music "loud and uproarious" as the lights fade on them and come up on the three upstage doors, and the stage is suddenly full of people running about in and out of the doors, "a manic French farce," while the News Hawker shouts out headlines and Roosevelt, Pulitzer, 2nd and 3rd Madwomen, Verne, and Barbary Ape chase Nellie and each other around the stage with lights flickering and the sounds of elephants, horses, cows, monkeys, and jungle birds creating a cacophony. As the music comes to an end, all the characters except Nellie exit through the doors, slamming them as they go.

McGonigle sits at his desk and Pulitzer emerges from his office, slamming the door to the last note of the music, and rushes to Nellie, who is close to collapsing. He tells her to go to the prison to interview Emma Goldman. He says some "rich son of a pitch named Hearst" is trying to buy a paper with his mother's money and wipe out competition. Pulitzer, who is losing his sight, runs into the door as he tries to go into his office. He exits after telling Nellie that if there is one thing he doesn't like about anarchy, it's chaos. He slams the door, signaling a reprise of the cancan as people start running in and out of doors and chasing each other madly across the stage. Nellie moves downstage and "the final note of the music is simultaneous with the slamming of the left and right doors and a blackout."

The lights then come up on a small prison cell where Emma Goldman is sitting on a chair by the DL table. (The year is 1893.) Verne is writing in the shadows on the DR table. Emma is familiar with Nellie's story about the madhouse and her writing on other subjects. She says she has been put in jail for telling the truth about the government, and when Nellie suggests that, although flawed, the government is "rather wonderful," Emma replies that it is good for white Protestant rich men, but not for the poor, the sick and old, people of color, immigrants, and women. A capitalist oligarchy controlled by obscenely rich men and gigantic obscene monopolies, she says, is not a paradise for the poor. She says that Pulitzer will throw Nellie out like garbage when she gets older and is not so pretty, and she urges her to leave the paper. Verne says (in a note to himself) that his heroine is carried off by insane puppets, commenting, "Brilliant!" as the lights fade on the jail cell and we hear a calliope version of the cancan music.

A spotlight shines on the gondola and we see two handpuppets, Mr. Punch and the Ghost of his wife Judy, whom he has murdered. They speak in high, squeaky voices as Nellie moves upstage to join 3rd Madwoman, Hearst, Pulitzer, and Captain Nemo. Judy's Ghost tells Punch that, if he doesn't mend his ways, he will be eaten by the Crocodile. Punch scoffs at the notion, but the Crocodile puppet appears behind him and swallows him. The onlookers applaud and the puppets disappear inside the gondola. Nellie walks downstage with Captain Nemo, "a suave looking older man," who asks her to suppose that he is a manufacturer of barrel hoops and not the captain of a submarine. Nellie says her negative image of marriage was created by a Punch and Judy show she saw as a child. The lights fade on them and a "ghostly light" comes up on Punch and Judy in the gondola. Punch asks Judy to marry him, saying that the journey through the guts of the crocodile has changed him, and he promises never to murder her again. They kiss; Nellie and Captain Nemo kiss; and Crocodile tells the audience that puppet love is a good thing because it makes more food for crocodiles.

The lights fade and we hear sinister music as Nellie crosses to sit with Rhys on the park bench. (It is 1895; Rhys is 25, Nellie is 28.) Upstage lurking in the shadows is Hearst. Nellie tells Rhys that he is a wonderful writer and that she has heard that Hearst is trying to steal him away from Pulitzer. She says she is getting married to an extremely successful manufacturer of barrel hoops and that she is tired of rushing madly around the world and craves stability. She says she is the most famous reporter in the world and has had some wonderful times but that she has had enough. Rhys thinks marriage is a big mistake and says he will not come to the wedding, although he promises to visit her later on. She hugs him and runs off. Rhys watches her, then drinks from a flask as Hearst moves toward him. We hear crows and the wind blows an old newspaper across the stage. Hearst asks Rhys if he is ready to come to work for him, offering to double his salary. Rhys says he will stick with Pulitzer. Hearst says Pulitzer's time is over, that he is nearly blind, and it's time for a new generation. He offers to triple Rhys' salary and let him write whatever he wants. Rhys says that Hearst manufactures news to sell papers, and Hearst responds that nothing is news until he prints it.

The light fades on them and we hear calliope music and the strange gabblings of the mad and wild animal noises as lights come up on Nellie, barefoot, in a madwoman's white frock and straightjacket, on a chair center stage. Verne is writing at his table DR while Doctor observes Nellie closely and the three Madwomen wander, talking to themselves. Nellie questions Verne about why his heroine would marry an elderly manufacturer of barrel hoops when she loved the young man from Ohio (Rhys). Verne says if she needs a reason she should make one up, that we are trapped in our heads, not knowing much of anything, in a madhouse farce written by a demented playwright deity. Doctor tells Nellie that her case is the most puzzling of his career but he hopes to solve it. Barbary Ape carries a large tub onto the stage and Nellie tells Doctor that the women have been locked up in the madhouse because they speak Portuguese and are not crazy at all. Barbary Ape picks Nellie up, puts her in the tub, and empties a bucket of water over her head, then another. Doctor explains that the ice water treatment is to shock her into a more socially acceptable perception of reality. Verne narrates that his heroine, trapped in a madhouse, finds herself more and more disoriented. Doctor and Barbary Ape hold hands and skip offstage together, humming the cancan music. The Madwomen try to console Nellie, saying that the water treatment is a kind of initiation ceremony, "like losing your virginity to a gorilla." Nellie protests that they don't understand, that she doesn't belong there, that it is just a story. They tell her that tomorrow is enema day. Verne exults and says that he needs a big finish for the first act: "Salacious dancing!" Cancan music comes up very loudly as the Madwomen do the cancan with Barbary Ape, Pulitzer, Hearst, Doctor, and Verne. Nellie looks across at Rhys who is standing by the park bench looking at her. Music and dance end. Blackout.

As the intermission ends, we hear cancan music in the darkness and then the sound of a clock ticking slowly as lights come up on Nellie and Rhys in the Wax Museum. The actors, frozen in place, are arranged around the stage and in the gondola: Pulitzer, Hearst, Verne, Doctor, Captain Nemo, 1st and 2nd Suffragettes, and Susan B. Anthony. Rhys tells Nellie that McGonigle has gone to work for Hearst, and she tells him that marriage is a nightmare, worse than the madhouse, and her husband is having her followed. Rhys suggests she come back to the paper, but Captain Nemo (a wax manikin coming to life) says he has caught her with another man. Nellie screams, tells him she is going back to work at the newspaper, and goes off. Rhys advises Captain Nemo to love whoever Nellie is at any given moment, but Nemo says he never should have left his submarine. He exits as lights fade on Rhys, and Pulitzer comes to life and rushes down the steps, groping blindly, shouting for "Mickgoonicle." Rhys tells him McGonigle has gone to work for Hearst, and Nellie enters saying she has been filing her story on the Elephants' Burial Ground. Pulitzer says they have to beat Hearst and wants Nellie to get on top of another elephant. Nellie says she first wants to cover the Convention for the Rights of Working Women and meet Susan B. Anthony. Pulitzer objects but concedes when she tells him that Hearst is doing a two-page spread on the Convention. She leaves after kissing him on the cheek, and Rhys tells Pulitzer that many of his reporters left, not because of money but because he screamed at and tried to manipulate them. Pulitzer is outraged, tells Rhys that the truth is what he says it is, and Rhys is fired. Pulitzer goes to his office door, runs into the wall, finds the door knob, and slams the door behind him. As the lights fade on Rhys the 1st and 2nd Suffragettes come alive and raise signs (FEMALE EMANCIPATION and MAKE YOUR OWN DAMNED FLAPJACKS), then chase Hearst and Verne around the stage and off, beating them over the head with the signs.

Lights come up on Nellie and Anthony on the park bench. Anthony says she has been in love many times but finds marriage generally horrifying and a recipe for disaster for the woman. There is a huge explosion and everything goes dark. We hear screams of agony and News Hawker's voice shouting about the battleship *Maine* being blown up in Havana Harbor. Lights come up on Rhys and McGonigle in 1898 at the offices of the *Journal*. Hearst bursts through the center door, very excited about the battleship being blown up because it means there's going to be a war to liberate the oppressed people of Cuba from enslavement to the Spanish Empire and he is going to sell "one goddamned shitload of papers and destroy that son of a bitch Joe Pulitzer once and for all." He tells Rhys to get to Cuba and write some heart-wrenching stories about the poor, oppressed Cuban people. Rhys worries that Pulitzer may send Nellie, but McGonigle tells him that she has reconciled with her husband. After they leave, Hearst and Pulitzer have an altercation, and Hearst leaves, warning Pulitzer not to step in horse shit. Pulitzer yells after him that he will defeat him, then goes into his office, running into the door, and slamming it behind him.

In a blackout we hear sounds of gunfire and explosions and the voice of News Hawker shouting headlines about Cuba, Dewey taking Manila, America annexing Hawaii, and Roosevelt charging up San Juan Hill. Lights come up on Rhys, sitting on the ground, his arm bleeding. Hearst, in a pith helmet, comes downstage and tells Rhys that he is tired of rewriting his dispatches. Rhys grabs him by the lapels and tells him that if he changes one word Rhys will put a number 2 pencil through his eyesocket to the back of his skull. Hearst fires him and, when Rhys asks for a doctor, leaves. There is a large explosion, blackout, and News Hawker's voice shouting headlines about victory in Cuba, McKinley being assassinated, Emma Goldman being arrested, Teddy Roosevelt becoming President, Rhys Pendragon joining the *Times*, and Nellie Bly's husband dying.

We hear birdsong as lights come up on Nellie and Rhys walking in the park (perhaps 1907). Pulitzer is on the bench, his hands on a cane. Rhys tells Nellie that he will not get into an automobile that she is driving. She says she took over her husband's business and has expanded it, putting management into the hands of "a wonderful man." Rhys warns her that business is inherently corrupt and that if money is appearing and disappearing in the accounts then the man is a crook. She thinks Rhys needs a wife and learns that he is still in love with the woman in Ohio. Nellie says Rhys needs someone very like her, but not so restless, to be his anchor when he is adrift at sea. We hear ocean and gull sounds as the lights fade.

Two dim pools of light—one on Pulitzer and Rhys (Pulitzer's yacht in 1911), the other on Nellie and Captain Nemo (another ship in 1914)—set the scene for the alternating dialogue of the duos. We learn that Rhys has married and has a baby girl, and when Nemo tells Nellie that Pulitzer and Rhys loved her she says that Rhys is married and Pulitzer has been dead for three years. Nellie says she is going to Vienna and doesn't think there will be a war in Europe. Pulitzer tells Rhys that he finally figured out that McGonigle was the one blowing the trumpet. We hear the sound of explosions as the two spotlights fade out.

Lights come up on Nellie in a chair center stage being interrogated by Bismark, who is convinced she is a spy. Doctor enters to treat Bismark's bleeding buttock wound and recognizes Nellie as the now-famous reporter he treated in an insane asylum many years earlier. Bismark wants someone to shoot Nellie, but there is a loud explosion and the three fall to the ground in the blackout. News Hawker shouts headlines about the Germans surrendering, Plank winning the Nobel Prize for quantum theory, Prohibition beginning the next year, and Jack Dempsey going to fight Jess Willard in Toledo.

Lights come up on a hotel room in Toledo, Ohio (1919) that has been turned into a press room. Nellie tells Rhys that it took the senseless horror of war to let her discover who she is. One of the upstage doors bursts open and Ring Lardner, Damon Runyon, and Grantland Rice rush in, having had a bit to drink. They talk about the war, Hearst, and Pulitzer, bemoan the lack of a ready liquor supply, and are joined by the Giggle Sisters who have booze and invite them to a party in their room. After they leave, Nellie tells Rhys she was sorry to hear his wife died in the influenza pandemic. She says she remembers the first time she met Rhys, and McGonigle appears, corned beef sandwich in hand, and moves to his desk as we hear a "slow, sad, eerie version of the Offenbach played on an old piano." Nellie asks Rhys if he remembers how exciting it all was then, and as they look at each other the light fades and we hear a jauntier version of the Offenbach.

The lights come up on the offices of the *World* in autumn, 1888. Nellie asks McGonigle about the mail and Rhys enters with a burlap sack full of letters and one letter in his hand which he gives to McGonigle. The sack of letters, plus three other sacks downstairs, are for Nellie. Rhys says he wants to be a reporter and Nellie says he has to meet Pulitzer. Nellie pleads with McGonigle to blow his trumpet again. He blows two loud blasts and Pulitzer storms out of his office. Nellie introduces Rhys and asks that he be hired as her assistant. She wants to travel the world in 80 days and send back reports and interview Jules Verne when she is in France. Pulitzer finally agrees and hires Rhys as a reporter. Nellie congratulates him and says they are going to have great adventures. The scene ends as McGonigle blows the trumpet very loudly, lights go to black, and the orchestral version of the Offenbach plays quietly.

In the last scene, the lights come up on Nellie talking to Rhys in Toledo, but Rhys is not there and she wonders where he is. Verne appears out of the darkness behind her and tells her that the hot air balloon is ready to depart. They are going to see the elephant. He leads her up the stairs to the gondola as the cancan music swells and characters gather from all parts of the stage to see them off. Verne and Nellie throw cabbages out of the gondola to lighten the ballast. As the balloon begins to rise, Nellie calls and waves goodbye to her friends. The music thunders to a conclusion while the people wave goodbye to the disappearing gondola and the lights fade to darkness as the music comes to "a rousing, magnificent finish."

In *Lost Generation*, three characters—Ernest Hemingway, Scott Fitzgerald, and Zelda, his wife—perform on a unit set with a table and some chairs, a sofa, an armchair, a bed, a Victrola with some'78' records, a practical window with a weight-supporting ledge, and a closet door. Time and space are fluid with no blackouts or set changes. After we have listened to assorted sound effects, the lights come up on Ernest writing at the table. Scott enters from the upstage shadows, drink in hand, apologizing for his drunken behavior. The men talk about writing and Ernest tells Scott that Zelda deliberately drives him crazy so that he won't be able to write. Scott tells him that Zelda says his penis is too small and offers to show it to Ernest. Ernest opens the door and tells Scott to go in so that Ernest can look at his penis, but instead of following Scott through the doorway, Ernest slams it shut.

Zelda enters, asking for Scott, and telling Ernest that he uses people then throws them away and writes mean things about them. Ernest says that's what writers do and thinks it's a shame she isn't stupid because, being so beautiful, she would be happier if she were. She says that he likes to kill things and is the world's greatest authority on "pseudo-masculine sadomasochistic bullshit." She says that none of his fictional women are real and that *A Farewell to Arms* is "just a parlor trick." She puts on a record of "Swan Lake" and begins dancing. Suddenly, we hear the sound of an airplane, close and very loud. She explains that it is her French lover buzzing the house to express his devotion to her.

Scott emerges from the closet with a shotgun and watches Zelda, now dizzy, fall face first on the sofa. We hear the airplane again and Ernest puts a nail through the hole in the record and nails it to the wall. Scott tells Zelda that she has to keep walking because that's what they do in the movies when someone has taken too many pills. He says that she is his muse and Ernest his artistic conscience. Ernest says a writer has to be a bastard and anger is necessary for creation. Zelda tells him his work is that of a terrified man and she doesn't like it, although she thought his book about Popeye (*To Have and Have Not*) was very funny. Ernest gathers his papers and pen and goes into the closet, closing the door.

Scott tells Zelda that he writes to make money so that she can buy things. He says that when she is with him he can't work, and when she's not with him he misses her and wonders what man she is with. She accuses him of stealing her diaries and letters and putting them in his novels. She says she doesn't enjoy sex with him and wants to go out drinking. He says he has to finish writing something so that they are not poor, and if he goes drinking with her he will get drunk and won't write anything. She doesn't understand why he makes such a fuss over other writers and she climbs onto the window ledge as she imitates Scott worshipping Joyce and offering to throw himself out the window unless Mrs. Joyce declares she is desperately and hopelessly in love with him. Scott pulls her down and sits on the couch with her. She says that Gertrude Stein is the "Empress Dowager of Bullshit" who makes "incomprehensible, incredibly tedious, self-indulgent literary cow-flop." As they talk we hear the airplane again, very loud, then a huge crash. Zelda goes out, hoping that the Frenchman had a parachute.

Scott, pouring a drink as Ernest comes out of the closet, asks if Ernest thinks he is a hack. Ernest says that Scott writes a great story and then eliminates the ambiguity and gives it a happy ending so he can sell it to the *Saturday Evening Post*. He defiles his work for money, and that is the definition of a hack. Scott says he can't afford to create masterpieces right now, but Ernest suggests that Scott learn to tell what happened and then take most of it out. Ernest thinks he hears a gun shot; Scott asks him why he wants to kill things. Ernest says that Scott and Zelda have to stop banging on his door at four in the morning, drunk and screaming.

Zelda enters, in tears, announcing that the French aviator has flown into the side of a mountain because he couldn't have her. Ernest says he did have her and dumped her and then flew into a mountain. Scott asks Ernest if he has ever thought of suicide. Ernest says he's thinking of it right now. After Scott brings drinks for Ernest and Zelda, the two men toast the dead pilot. When Zelda tells Ernest that he really wants Scott dead, Ernest says that everything is war. Scott thinks writers should help each other and then he tries to stand on his head. His third unsuccessful attempt lands him flat on his back, saying that writing is like dying. Ernest says that writing is what you do while you're dying and that nothing else matters. Announcing that he has to urinate, Scott leaves.

As they drink, Zelda asks Ernest if he really wishes he were dead, telling him that he is a sentimental liar pretending to be a tough guy. She says that when he runs out of friends to kill he will find himself alone in a room with a gun. He tells her she is going to bleed Scott dry and eventually murder him. She says Ernest is terrified of women and worships violence, again calling him a liar. He says it is easy to write the truth if you are a great liar, that every story is a lie and all writing is betrayal. He grabs her and kisses her violently, knocking her backwards onto the bed. He says he hears something stalking them. We hear "an ominous roaring in the distance" as Scott enters and lights fade out,

Act Two begins where Act One ended as Scott asks Zelda what she said to John Dos Passos on the ferris wheel. She replies that she likes to watch men squirm, but she thinks they are in Delaware because crows have been following her everywhere. Scott is worried about her trying to strangle herself and throw herself under a train. She says she was just playing and asks him if he is going to hit her or cry. Scott asks Ernest if he wants to fight, but

Zelda punches Ernest in the nose, knocking him backward over a chair. She says she is tired of playing a character called Zelda and exits, looking for a plot.

Ernest tells Scott that she is insane and should be committed before she destroys him. When Scott says he loves her, Ernest tells him that the illusion of love is fine unless it hurts his work. He says that he and Scott are writers and the world is trying to kill them. He advises Scott to write the best he can, every day, and never compromise, never give in. Anyone who gets in the way, wife or not, is expendable.

Zelda returns with a telegram for Ernest. He says that his father has died; Scott offers him money to go home for the funeral. Ernest takes the money and, leaving, tells them that his father shot himself in the head. Zelda, humming "Swan Lake," dances and speaks a rambling monologue about ballerinas and rain and mirrors and imaginary hypotheses. Scott tells her to stop dancing and says that she needs to go to a nice, quiet place where people can help her. He says he will write a great book and try not to drink himself to death. She says she does want him to write a great book and admits it is exhausting trying to be charming and funny and beautiful all the time.

After Scott leaves, she speaks another rambling monologue about burning and mirrors and *Alice Through the Looking Glass* and flowers and writing a book. Scott returns with a fat manuscript and asks Zelda (now in the madhouse) what it is. He asks her why she would write a novel about their lives when she knew he was doing the same thing. She suggests that perhaps she could be the writer and Scott could be the ballerina. She tells him she married him because she took pity on him. When he says he just wants her to get better, she says that beauty and love are temporary, but madness is not. She tells him to go to Hollywood and write movies, then leaves. Scott tells himself that he can write, he can.

Ernest enters and tosses a book at Scott. Scott asks him if he read it and what he thought of it. Ernest says he liked parts of it, but not other parts. Scott says that Ernest's book is full of sneers, made up "almost entirely of resentments," of hate. Scott thinks that great art comes, ultimately, from love. Ernest disagrees and says that criticism and critics are "shit." When Scott defends Virginia Woolf, Ernest asks how Zelda is doing in the nut house and tells Scott that he hates him for being a better writer and a better man. When Ernest tells Scott that he is done as a writer, Scott says that Ernest is next. Ernest agrees and says that he fucked Scott's wife.

Zelda comes in with a telegram for Scott, who doesn't want to open it. Ernest, sitting by the shotgun, wonders how fools can write great books like *Gatsby* and *The Good Soldier*. He says there is a hyena out there in the dark that has been following him for years. Scott says that Ernest was right to choose writing over love. Ernest says that he can't sleep at night without a light in the room. Scott thinks he can still do good work, that the book he's working on may be the best he's ever done. Ernest takes out two shotgun shells from a box and Zelda opens the telegram, reading that Scott Fitzgerald died sitting in a chair in Hollywood. Scott says he just needs another twenty-five years and he'll do incredible things, but the light blacks out on him. Ernest opens the shotgun and puts in the shells and Zelda announces, "on a lighter note," that Ernest Hemingway died of a self-inflicted gunshot wound in Idaho. Ernest says he left things out until he'd left out everything. He snaps the gun shut and the light blacks out on him. Zelda closes the play by saying that Zelda Fitzgerald died in her bed in the attic of an asylum, during a fire. She says she used to know a girl with that name who swam naked for boys and lived in the mirror. She says they've asked her to dance at the funeral.

The unit set for *The Ogre* (6m, 2w), "some old furniture scattered about," represents Brede Place, a damp, haunted mansion in the south of England, 1899-1900 "and occasionally elsewhere." We hear the sound of wind as lights come up on a young woman (Marthe) talking to herself of crows, owls, witches, and a prohibition against touching as Ford (Ford Maddox Hueffer), sitting in a chair, speaks, years later, to an invisible friend about "an extraordinary collection of remarkable writers"—Rudyard Kipling, Joseph Conrad, Henry James, H. G. Wells, and Stephen Crane—all living close together in Sussex in 1899. Marthe speaks of her fear of "a creature" that follows her and, from the darkness, we hear a voice (Sir Goddard Oxenbridge) speaking to her. Stephen and Cora (Taylor) enter, exploring the mansion but noticing neither Marthe nor Ford. Although Stephen thinks the house is damp, Cora plans to rent it. Marthe says that the man and woman who have come into the house will be destroyed. We hear wind and crows as Marthe moves into darkness, Ford remains in his chair, and Stephen and Cora walk into the downstage light. They talk about renting the huge, damp, haunted place, and although Stephen has misgivings Cora has plans of inviting artists, intellectuals, and orphans. She tells Stephen that Moreton, the landlord, said that a girl was hanged in the garden and that years ago they dug up the skeleton of a priest in the chapel. Hearing a flapping noise, Cora thinks there are bats in the house and, hearing a shuffling noise, goes off to the kitchen, leaving Stephen staring into the darkness above as lights fade and we again hear crows and wind.

Lights come up on Ford as Conrad and Wells talk about Ford helping Conrad with English. Conrad thinks that perhaps he should write in German. We hear a thunderstorm and a girl crying as Stephen enters with a lamp. Seeing Marthe, he asks if he can help. She wonders if he's a ghost and tells him that she is a servant to The Ogre. She says that she was hanged from an oak tree in the back yard during the reign of Henry the Eighth. She runs into the shadows and we hear birds singing, children laughing, and dogs barking. Lights come up on Stephen writing as Cora walks toward him carrying a muddy wood and metal box. Stephen shakes the box and suggests it's full of bones. Cora thinks their place is lovely; he says it is a madhouse. She tells him the Conrads have accepted her invitation to join them for the weekend even though Stephen spent the last evening they were there jabbering with their baby. Stephen says he wouldn't mind if he and Cora had a baby or two, but she doesn't want to have children. She kisses him before she leaves and Stephen shakes the box as the light on him fades. In the darkness we hear crickets and see moonlight as Stephen approaches Marthe sitting on a bench. He tells her he has been thinking about her. She says something unspeakably evil is close and tells him that he will find out soon enough if the evil thing is after him.

The lights fade and we hear wind and birds as lights come up on Conrad and Ford walking. Ford tells Conrad that that Cora was one of the first female war correspondents and once ran a brothel in Jacksonville, Florida, the Hotel de Dream, where she and Stephen first met. As we hear the sounds of screaming children, barking dogs, and clattering cans, Ford rushes off and Wells, riding a bicycle, almost runs into Conrad and disappears offstage with a loud squawk and a crash. Stephen and James join Conrad as Cora crosses the stage reprimanding offstage children. James wonders how Stephen can get any writing done in such chaos and, after the writers discuss ambiguity, truth, art, and futility, Wells crosses the stage again on his bicycle, followed by Cora who tells Stephen he must write a play for the party they are going to have over the Christmas holidays. We hear the bicycle horn, a cow mooing, dogs barking, children screaming, and cans clattering as the lights fade.

We then hear birds as the lights come up on Stephen writing in his notebook. Cora brings him a plate of toast and picks up the pen he has dropped. She wonders why he leaves her alone in bed at night and why he talks in his sleep. He says he was dreaming of the Black Forest and a red fog. They speak of Ford and Conrad collaborating and the light fades on them and comes up on Ford, "on a previous afternoon," talking with Stephen about Kipling's notion of a daemon who tells him what to write. Stephen thinks this daemon is a "kind of personal Ogre," but Ford insists that writing is putting down what the mad voices inside say. Ford thinks the damp house is affecting Stephen's health (tuberculosis). Stephen crosses to Cora as the light fades on Ford.

Stephen tells Cora of a local legend about an Ogre who ate the children of families who came to live in the house until the children got the Ogre drunk and sawed him in half. Cora says she has a better story about a beautiful, naked sorceress ravished by her slave. She kisses him erotically and beckons to him as she moves into the darkness. We hear Marthe screaming and

Stephen lights a lamp as she runs to hide behind him. She is followed by Oxenbridge, "a large formidable man in rather faded sixteenth century garments," who demands to know why she is afraid of him. He apologizes for disturbing Stephen's sleep and says that the girl who accuses him of being a monster was hanged for murder. She blames him for allowing the hanging to be carried out and wants Stephen to kill Oxenbridge. Oxenbridge says his soul is eternally divided until she forgives him. He asks Stephen if he is playing his part well tonight and thinks Stephen is a person who has loved deeply. He tells Stephen to save himself by fleeing the house. Light fades on them as we hear crows in the darkness, ending the first act.

To the sounds of birds singing, lights come up on Stephen and James playing chess. James asks about seeing a "large, morose looking man in moth eaten clothing and a rather pretty, pale young girl," and after asking James if he believes in ghosts, Stephen says that he is going to write a play about the house. James shares his negative experiences in theatre and, as the men talk about writing, a woman in gypsy attire, her face partly veiled in scarves, enters to ask if they would like to have her read their fortune. Calling herself Madame Zipango, she pours champagne into James' hat and puts it on his head. James stomps off and Cora takes off her scarves and black wig, giggling. She tells Stephen that when she looked out their bedroom window the previous night she saw him sitting on the terrace and she thought she saw somebody or something in the shadows behind him. He says it was probably a crow, but she says that he had been talking in his sleep to some woman about an oak tree. They talk about writing and she kisses him passionately as the lights fade.

We hear crickets and see Marthe in the moonlight as Stephen asks her why she has been avoiding him. She tells him that she and the monster are very angry that he has been writing a play about them, betraying her trust. Oxenbridge offers to help with some amusing anecdotes and Marthe runs off sobbing. Stephen takes a drink from Oxenbridge's flask and Oxenbridge tells him the "old story" of a young housemaid giving birth alone in the garden and burying the new-born infant in a box under an apple tree. Father John, the local priest, insisted that she be hanged for murder and refused to bury the body in consecrated ground, so Oxenbridge buried it again. Cora calls to Stephen and enters as Oxenbridge moves into the darkness. Stephen tells her they cannot do the play because it offends the ghosts. Cora tells him there are no ghosts and asks him if he still loves her. Stephen agrees to do the play and goes off to bed as Cora turns downstage, asking if anyone is there, telling them that she will not let them take Stephen away from her, that he is hers forever.

We hear music, children's laughter, and guests jabbering as the lights come up on the party in late December, 1899. While Wells and, later, Ford gallop on broomsticks upstage, Stephen, Cora, and James talk downstage of the writing of Wells and Conrad. Cora insists that James doesn't like her, but he suggests that she may be sensing his envy of someone who has lived her life when he has not lived his. Wells offers to introduce James to some pretty women, and Stephen tells Cora that James is a genuine artist while he is "a moderately interesting but temporary irrelevance." He says that he and Cora are 'the inevitable result of an enigmatic congruence of absurd causes."

As the lights dim we hear upbeat music introducing the play and lights then come up on Wells in a pith helmet playing Dr. Moreau and Conrad playing Kurtz. The men speak of investigating supernatural manifestations at Brede Place and step back as Stephen and Cora enter, playing Quint and Miss Jessel. Stephen/Quint tells Cora/Miss Jessel that there are much darker spirits lurking and we hear Oxenbridge howling offstage, then entering, mouth dripping with blood, bemoaning the hunger he cannot quench with the blood of a thousand innocents. When he says he must devour Miss Jessel, Wells/Moreau invites her to his island, where humans and beasts live in harmony, but Conrad/Kurtz invites her to the depths of the jungle. Oxenbridge says the woman is the true monster and lights go out on them to the sound of applause. Wells, Conad, Stephen, and Cora acknowledge the applause and Ford raves about the performance of James as the Ogre. Cora tells Stephen that he is the best living writer in the English language, but when she leaves Ford tells Stephen that she is a killer and he should get away from her before it's too late. Stephen says that if Ford ever speaks of Cora that way again he will beat the living shit out of him. Ford drinks from his flask and wobbles off to urinate. Cora comes back and tells Stephen that he is her life. When he offers to show Cora the truth, a 'great burst of bright red blood" pours out of his mouth. Cora calls for help as the lights fade.

In the next scene, Ford tells Conrad that Cora is taking Stephen to the Black Forest for his health and we then hear gulls and a ship's horn as lights come up on Wells seeing Stephen and Cora off. Cora again insists that Stephen is a better writer than anyone, and Wells says that "the great thing is to do your work and everything else be damned." The lights fade and come back up on Cora speaking a letter she is writing to James describing Stephen's health. Shivering in a blanket, Stephen speaks as in a delirium, asking Cora where she got the money to pay for their trip to Germany. He wonders how kind she was to their landlord, Moreton, in persuading him to give the money. She says she is not going to let Stephen die, that she will do absolutely anything. She sobs; he comforts her and says, "What a terrible thing it is to be loved."

Having had supper, Wells, James, Conrad, and Ford sit talking again about art and life. Ford, who has been reading the paper, tells them that Stephen is dead. Light fades on them and it is night with the sound of owls. Stephen and Oxenbridge talk and Marthe joins them, recognizing Stephen as one of the dead. Cora, in mourning, followed by Ford, walks on, not seeing the others. She rails against James for refusing to see her and tells Ford that she loved Stephen and he loved her. Stephen tells Oxenbridge that Cora didn't kill him, and Cora leaves with Ford, saying she will never come back to this evil place. Stephen asks Marthe to forgive him, but she says there is no forgiveness and no touching in this place. They are sitting on the bench and Oxenbridge watches as Stephen lifts his hand and lets it hover just above Marthe's. They look at each other and we hear crows as the lights fade and go out.

Phantoms, the most recent play about British detective John Ruffing, takes place in 1903 with flashback scenes from earlier years. The three-level unit set has multiple stairs for entrances and exits, and Nigro notes that the ten actors (6m, 4w) may appear and disappear at any time from anywhere. In an endnote to the script he writes: "There are more stage directions in this text than usual, because they seemed necessary to indicate properly the complex labyrinth of movement which is essential here, a kind of objective correlative to what's going on in Ruffing's brain. In most cases the stage direction indicates when a movement should begin. It doesn't mean the dialogue of the other character stops while the movement takes place. The movement usually continues through the dialogue. American directors often have trouble with simultaneous action, and it's true that if you don't do it right you can draw focus away from essential business. But done right, what you have is a wonderfully complex organism in which every moving part is intimately connected to every other part. It can generate astonishing beauty and richness when you trust it. But you must commit to it. It will make the moments of stillness and isolation all that much more powerful."

The play begins with a cacophony of music and voices as if from the pier at Brighton, and we see Ruffing enter DL to sit at a table with bottle, glasses, and a deck of cards. Overlapping with the voices of a barker and an oyster woman, we hear a newsgirl shouting headlines about a poisoning, a beautiful young wife, and a possible murder or suicide. Florence and Charles Reno enter UL across the gallery and come down the CR steps as Jane Nix and Dr. Bull move from UR across the gallery and down the far left steps to the left landing, while Captain Fortune appears from the DR wings with a bottle, singing, and bumps into Derby, a detective, before going out through the center arch. Derby moves to Ruffing at the table as the music and voices fade. Derby tells Ruffing he was the first investigator of the Reno case and knows that Florence murdered her husband. Fortune appears in the gallery above saying that one should never drink the contents of a small green bottle. Derby offers Ruffing a drink, saying that he heard Ruffing was a bigger souse than he was. Ruffing tells Derby not to speak of his dead wife, and

Derby says Florence's first husband, Fortune, didn't die of drink but of antimony poisoning. As Ruffing leaves, Derby tells him not to drink any wine that Florence may offer him.

On the sofa DR Florence complains to Ruffing about having to answer the same moronic questions again. She tells Ruffing that she and Charles had been married less than a year and that her first husband died three years ago. As they speak, other characters move about the stage, occasionally making remarks not connected directly to the dialogue. Jane, for example, repeats Fortune's warning about drinking the contents of a small green bottle. In response to Ruffing's question, Florence describes her first marriage an "an increasingly grotesque nightmare of drunkenness and brutality," and Ruffing goes up the steps to the left landing and watches as Fortune moves down to Florence asking what she has done with his sword. He is drunk, falling down, and sends Rowan, a servant, to get another pair of trousers. Fortune then charges up the staircase, disappears, and we hear a thud, a crash, and discordant accordion noises. Dr. Bull tells Florence that her husband has died.

Florence tells Ruffing that, except at the end, her second marriage was happier than the first. Charles, calling for Florence, moves upstage of the bed to vomit violently out the window. Florence explains that Jane, who had come from Jamaica after the death of her husband and was housekeeper to Dr. Bull, became her live-in companion and had known Charles as a child in Jamaica. We hear the sounds of Brighton again as Charles, Florence, and Jane talk on the pier. Jane excuses herself so they can be alone, and Florence tells Ruffing that, when her husband died unexpectedly, she married Charles, following her instincts, choosing a good, solid man over a good-looking, exciting one, but learning quickly to renounce romantic, childish dreams. The mother of Charles, Old Mrs. Reno, with an ear trumpet, sits at the table playing cards as Ruffing sits at the top of the UR stairs to watch Charles move to his mother. As they talk about Florence, Rowan helps Fortune UL and off. Charles' mother says he is too good for Florence and wanders off DL calling for cockatoos as Ruffing resumes his questioning of Florence, and Jane repeats the warning about the contents of a small green bottle.

Florence complains to Charles that someone has been opening her mail, and Charles suggests that Jane should return to her job with Dr. Bull. As Charles vomits out the window again, Tabby, a servant girl, tells Florence that he is very sick. Charles falls on the floor by the bed. Jane massages his chest, but he dies. Florence sends Rowan for Dr. Bull, and Jane says that Charles whispered to her that he had taken poison and she was not to tell Florence. Ruffing questions Jane, who adds that Charles might have said that he had taken poison because he was jealous of Dr. Bull's relationship with Florence. Dr. Bull enters to examine Charles and sends Rowan to collect a sample of the vomit for analysis. Florence tells Ruffing that she does not know who poisoned her husband, but that Charles had become jealous of Dr. Bull after her second miscarriage.

As Ruffing watches, Florence moves to the desk where Fortune is drinking and accusing her of an affair with Dr. Bull. When Fortune leaves and Dr. Bull enters, Florence tells him that she has physical relations with her husband when he is not too drunk. Fortune, drunk, tries to take Tabby to his bed but Rowan intervenes. Florence asks Dr. Bull if he ever thinks of Bad Kissingen. Charles gets up from the bed and Florence says she will answer any questions he has about her past but that she will not sleep with him. She says that when Charles saw her talking with Dr. Bull they were discussing the waters of Bad Kissingen. She says that Charles' mother doesn't like her but she doesn't care. Old Mrs. Reno, appearing in the UL gallery, says that Florence is an appealing little slut who won't sleep with Charles so she won't infect him with a venereal disease. She tells her son to be careful and never drink the contents of a small green bottle. Charles tells Florence that his name was changed from Nix to Reno when his mother remarried. Charles' brother married Jane. Florence tells Charles that he may come to her bed later, for company, and then talks with Jane about her marriage and living in Jamaica. Jane says that every house she has lived in has been haunted. Ruffing questions Jane and Florence about separate bedrooms, pointing out that both of Florence's marriages had the same trajectory—a happy beginning, a miscarriage, indisposition on her part, and an increasingly frustrated husband who then died. He asks if she slept with either husband and, when she says she had two miscarriages, points out that she hasn't answered his question. She says she will not be insulted by a drunk police inspector and adds that Jane slept with her when she was ill.

Ruffing moves up the steps to the right landing as Charles, entering from the left landing, asks Florence why she can sleep with Jane and not with him. He says he understands why her first husband drank himself to death. She says he is not the only person who wishes he was dead. Dr. Bull gets up from the desk and asks Florence how she liked Bad Kissingen. She replies, as a young girl, that she feels grown up and Dr. Bull says that he would do anything for her, die for her, kill for her. Lights fade as the first act ends.

The second act begins with the same eerie lights and cacophonous sounds of the pier at Brighton. Derby talks with Ruffing about Florence killing Charles, but Ruffing doesn't think she did it and thinks the servants know more than they're telling. Ruffing questions Rowan, who observed both of Florence's marriages. After saying Charles was secretive and suspicious, Rowan moves to speak with Charles at an earlier time as Jane moves to the sofa beside Dr. Bull and Ruffing watches from the inner steps of the right landing. Charles tells Rowan to join him in a drink and asks if he has ever been in love. Rowan says his wife died but that he loved her and tried unsuccessfully to hang himself after her death. Charles asks if Rowan thinks that Florence loves him. Rowan says he doesn't know the truth but he thinks we are all in love with phantoms. Charles says his wife is not sleeping with him, congratulates Rowan on his affair with Tabby, and asks if he ever observed any irregularities between Dr. Bull and Florence. Rowan says he did not and moves away as Florence speaks with Ruffing, saying that nothing unusual happened the day Charles died. She says she couldn't sleep with Charles after her miscarriage, and Jane repeats that Charles was not murdered but took poison. She says that when Charles returned from riding his horse he seemed disheveled and upset. Charles enters through the center arch at an earlier time complaining that the horse threw him again. He tells Florence he has always been miserable. Florence says he has always had a peculiar body odor and goes to prepare his bath.

Ruffing continues questioning Tabby and Rowan about wine consumption. Tabby says that Florence seemed sad or haunted; she tells Ruffing that Charles was mumbling to himself and then went into Florence's bedroom. When he came out he was telling Florence that she drank too much. Florence asks Tabby if she is seeing anyone and tells Tabby that she loved a man she couldn't marry, married a man she didn't love only to discover that she did love him and then lost him, married a man she didn't love thinking she could learn to love him, couldn't, but thought it was safer, although it was not.

After Tabby leaves, Ruffing asks Florence about the night Charles died. He tells her that antimony poisoning suggest malicious intent. He says he once considered suicide, and Florence says he is still grieving over the loss of his wife. She says there might have been an intimacy between herself and Dr. Bull, whom she met when she was twelve. Dr. Bull enters and he and Florence, now 18, talk about love being an illusion. He tells her he married an older woman for her money, a woman now in her late nineties. He tells Florence she needs someone closer to her own age to love and says that he will introduce her to Captain Fortune. She tells Dr. Bull she wants him and they kiss.

As Dr. Bull turns away, Ruffing speaks to Florence in the present and she tells him her marriage to Fortune deteriorated after he somehow found out about her relationship with Dr. Bull. Ruffing tells her that Fortune and Jane had an affair in Jamaica; Jane says it ended a long time ago and there seemed no point in telling Florence about it. Fortune comments that his life has been "a series of unfortunate juxtapositions and grotesque incongruities." He and Jane re-enact the scene in England when he tells her that he is engaged to Florence. Dr. Bull advises Florence not to marry Charles and not to tell him about their relationship.

Florence tells Ruffing that Dr. Bull was right, that she shouldn't have married Charles. Jane admits to sleeping with Charles, once, before Florence met him. Old Mrs. Reno, entering on the UL gallery, looks down at Charles, says that she would think Charles an idiot child left on the doorstep if she hadn't given birth to him. Ruffing observes Tabby and Charles talking by the bed as he asks her to put her hand on top of his hand. She kneels and does so, but Jane moves to the bed and sends Tabby to the kitchen. Jane tells Charles not to touch Tabby again because it would hurt Florence. Charles says he has nightmares about Jamaica and wants Jane to leave his house. She says the house belongs to Florence and if he hurts her she will see that he never hurts anyone again. Charles storms out through the center arch and Jane explains to Florence that people were not telling her everything because they loved her. When Florence leaves, Jane turns on Ruffing and asks him if he sees what he's done with all his stupid questions.

Ruffing crosses to Derby at the table and learns that Derby had Fortune's body dug up and determined that he had been poisoned with antimony, like Charles. Ruffing says that might be proof the same person murdered both men, but it is not who Derby thinks. Ruffing turns to Dr. Bull, informing him that Fortune was poisoned with antimony. Fortune enters and replays a scene in which Dr. Bull tells him that he needs to stop drinking. Fortune asks him how long he has been molesting Florence and leaves to get more wine. Ruffing tells Dr. Bull that either he or Florence poisoned both husbands, or perhaps they did it together. Dr. Bull says that when he looks at people he sees nothing but shadows, phantoms. He staggers and admits to poisoning both men with antimony but says he poisoned himself with something else. He goes into the garden to collapse and not make a mess for the servants. Ruffing tells Florence that Dr. Bull confessed that he killed her husbands because he wanted her for himself. But, Ruffing says, he lied to protect her because he thought she killed them both. Florence says she thought Jane had poisoned them. As Fortune enters to the desk to drink, Jane looks at him and remembers that the night he died Charles came to see him. Charles and Fortune re-enact the scene where Charles tells Fortune that he wants to marry Florence. When Fortune leaves, Charles takes out a small green bottle, pours the contents into the wine, and goes off. Jane says Fortune was found dead the next morning. She adds that either Charles poisoned himself out of re-morse or it really was Dr. Bull. Florence says she doesn't know anything, and Jane replies that all she knows for sure is that she loves Florence. Ruffing says the investigation is closed and goes to the UR gallery as Tabby and Rowan, in a flashback to an earlier time, talk and hug but are surprised by Old Mrs. Reno entering DL. She asks if the wine bottles are for dinner and sends the two servants off. She takes out a small green bottle and pours it into the wine that she thinks Florence drinks. "There," she says, "that'll fix the bitch." And we know how Charles was poisoned. Blackout.

Phoenix, set in the Arizona city in the summer of 1961, requires five men and four women on a simple unit set representing all locations, but "all we need to see are a piano and a few tables, chairs, and benches." There are three couples: Kermit, 48, a piano player who runs an accordion school, and Mona, 38, his second wife; Rutger, 40, a German who owns a bowling alley, and his wife Doris; Ned, who manages the bowling alley, and his wife Lea. The other characters are Tanya, 19, Kermit's daughter by his first wife; Mickey, 52, "big and beefy," who teaches accordion; and Ray, 26, "rather small," who also teaches accordion.

In darkness we hear the sound of an accordion playing "La Golondrina," and when the lights come up all the characters except Ned and Tanya are on stage at a picnic area by a lake. Kermit thinks that he remembers Mickey from Chicago, but Mickey denies ever having been there. Tanya, giggling and squealing, wearing a two-piece bathing suit, runs in chased by Ned, also in a bathing suit, who catches her and picks her up from behind, but she manages to escape and runs off. Lea, Ned's wife, leaves, unhappy, and Doris follows her. Kermit moves to the piano and the action shifts without break to his living room where he plays an "elegantly sad old whorehouse piano version of 'When You Were Sweet Sixteen'" as Mona complains about their smoking and drinking. He stops playing only when Mona calls Tanya a slut. When Mona goes (after telling Kermit to be afraid), he closes the piano lid and our attention shifts to a short scene with Tanya and Ray. Tanya says how much she likes to go to the movies but when Ray asks her to go with him she says she is busy.

The light fades on them and comes up on Ned and Lea in their bedroom. Ned denies any involvement with Tanya and tries to console Lea as the lights fade on them and come up on Rutger and Doris on their back patio drinking with Kermit, Mona, and Mickey. Rutger and Kermit are having a discussion about truth possibly being a woman, while Doris keeps asking if anyone wants more avocado or bean dip. Doris describes how she met Rutger at the dog races and how her first husband died after being kicked in the head by a horse. She inherited the bowling alley that Rutger saved with his business acumen. The scene shifts to Tanya and Ray talking in the bowling alley lounge late at night. She tells Ray that she named her breasts Ladmo and Wallace after her favorite characters on a children's tv show. She says her life is like being stuck on a rock from which she cannot descend, that almost everybody in Phoenix is from some other place. Ray kisses her, twice, and she says she has to leave. He asks her what she sees in Ned, reminding her several times that Ned is married. Lea comes in saying that she wants to close the alley and Tanya leaves. Ray asks Lea if she is lonely because her husband won't be home when she gets there, and Lea asks him if he wants to join her, leaving the keys on the table for him to lock up.

Our attention shifts to Kermit, Rutger, and Mickey drinking on Rutger's patio as Kermit explains his theory that Rutger and Mickey are both trying to blend in, pretending that they are just ordinary people, Rutger, well educated, running a bowling alley, and Mickey teaching accordion when it is clear that music has not been central to his life. After Kermit leaves, Rutger tells Mickey that he has done some research on him and wonders if his old acquaintances in Chicago would like to know where he is. Rutger suggests that perhaps Mickey could arrange to have the bowling alley burn down for the insurance money. Mickey says he has to give an accordion lesson and after he leaves Rutger takes out a lighter and lights a cigar.

Then, in Lea's living room, she, Mona, Tanya, and Doris are drinking coffee and talking about the men in their lives. Ned enters to ask Lea to lock up the bowling alley because he has things to do. He tells her not to wait up for him, kisses her, and leaves. Mona is impressed by Ned's kissing, but Lea says that Judas was also a good kisser. The lights fade on them and we hear "stripper music" and see Mickey and Ray at a table in the Carnival Room, drinking and watching a stripper downstage (we don't see her). Ray wants Mickey to give him some tips on how to appear more dangerous to Tanya. Mickey says he knows nothing about women and suggests a hooker, then a trip to the Virgin Islands. Before finishing his drink and leaving, Mickey tells Ray that if he wants to love he should get a dog.

In their living room, Doris tries to get Rutger to tell her about himself. She wonders why, when she mentions the war, he always changes the subject. He says the memories are too painful and suggests that she be grateful for what she has and enjoy life while she can. He tells her that she is the dearest thing in the world to him and asks her to make some sausages. The other characters, drinking on Kermit's patio, listen to Ned and Lea bicker until she leaves. Ray and Tanya follow her, and, after Ned says he thinks he could be a tough guy, Mickey leaves and Kermit tells Ned that he knows what he is capable of.

In the last scene of the first act, Rutger and Mickey wonder if they might find it difficult to start over in another place. Mickey remarks that a fire in which no one was hurt might be a possibility. But Rutger has decided that he wants the bowling alley and his wife Doris both to disappear. With the insurance money, after compensating Mickey, he would retire to a banana plantation in the Virgin Islands. When Mickey says he just wants to be left alone, Rutger says that he has discovered that Mickey has a daughter in Vermont. Mickey puts a hand around Rutger's throat, choking him, but Rutger explains that people die every day and it's not as if Mickey hasn't done this kind of work before. When Mickey lets go, Rutger assumes that they have a deal and that he will be receiving some very bad news in the near future. Mickey says he can always count on bad news and leaves. Rutger says he thinks he has an erection and the lights fade, ending the act.

The second act opens with Doris sitting on a park bench at night. Mickey comes up behind her and she asks him to sit down, saying that she knows he has been following her. She says she loves the park, although the word lagoon makes her think of the movie about the Creature with gills who lived in a black lagoon and dragged people into the water. She tells Mickey that she thinks people who don't talk very much and people who talk all the time are both trying to hide. She tells him if he is going to do "it," then he should go ahead and do it. Mickey is not sure what she means but she says that if he wants to kiss her, then he should kiss her. She says she is going to close her eyes and count to three and then he should do "it." She counts, Mickey looks at his hands, then at Doris, and the light fades on them and comes up on Tanya and Ray walking at night.

Tanya talks about loving the Japanese gardens, about everyone being lost in Phoenix trying to be reborn, about a plague of grasshoppers, and about God being a serial killer. When Ray says he wants to kiss her, she tells him that will never happen, but she allows him to hold her as long as he doesn't touch her boobs. The light fades on them and comes up on Rutger in the kitchen drinking coffee and rehearsing the speech he will give to the police, telling them of Doris not coming home the previous night. He spills coffee on himself when Doris walks in with a bag of groceries, explaining that he had fallen asleep on the sofa and she didn't want to wake him when she came in late. She got up early and walked to the store to get waffles and sausages for his breakfast.

In the next scene, Mickey is in a coffee shop when Rutger approaches him, asking when Mickey plans to complete the "business" they talked about. Mickey says it may take a couple of weeks to find the right opportunity, but Rutger gives him three days before he makes phone calls to Chicago. Then, in the bowling alley lounge, Tanya asks Ned about dangerous people he knows in New Jersey, saying that she's always been attracted to dangerous people. When he suggests that they go someplace and do something a little dangerous together, she says she has to leave, that she is a girl who goes away. Ned calls her a tease and she says that to call a girl a tease is a "terrible, terrible insult." She says she is very complex and that Ned has hurt her feelings. He holds her from behind and kisses her neck as Lea walks in and demands to know what is going on. She threatens Tanya, accusing her of teasing her husband, but Tanya says that Lea should talk to Ned and that she sees Lea with Ray all the time. Ned and Lea argue and Tanya leaves. When Ned goes to see if she is all right, Ray enters and asks Lea what all the yelling was about. He says that Tanya is not sleeping with Ned, and Lea says she would leave if she had someplace to go and someone to go with. She asks Ray if he would like to go away with her, but Ray says that Ned is his friend. Lea leaves and the scene shifts to the park bench.

Doris tells Mickey that he has scars on his soul, but she knows how sensitive he is and, though he looks dangerous, he has the soul of a poet. She wants him to walk with her by the lagoon and says she trusts him to protect her from the Creature, but Mickey says that he is the Creature from the Black Lagoon. In the bowling alley lounge Ray asks Ned if Tanya is all right and tells Ned that he has a nice wife in Lea and that Tanya is mixed up and vulnerable and it would be dangerous to all concerned if she were hurt. When Ned asks Ray if he is threatening him, Ray says that New Jersey "sucks elephant dick," a disparaging comment on his home state that Ned says he will overlook this time but, if Ray says anything about New Jersey again, Ned will shove an entire accordion orchestra up his ass until it comes out his mouth.

Kermit is playing the piano as Mona, "a bit wobbly and disheveled," comes in and tells him she fell into a drainage ditch by an orange grove and couldn't get out. She asks him if he would care if he knew she had been with someone else. She slams down the piano lid and he tells her if she ever touches the piano again he will strangle her and throw her corpse in a drainage ditch. Turning to go, she trips and falls to her hands and knees. Tanya, also a bit tipsy, enters as Mona crawls off. Tanya talks about wanting to kill the men who cut down a big old cottonwood tree next to their house years earlier. Tanya says she dreams her dead mother is telling her to go away and that Mona is a pig, screwing half the men in Phoenix. Kermit knocks her down, but immediately apologizes. Tanya leaves, saying he could never hurt her.

She sits on the park bench and accuses Ray of following her. He says he is worried about her because she is vulnerable. He notices a bruise on her face and assumes Ned has hit her. She tells Ray that she is never going to want him and will call the police if he doesn't leave her alone. She leaves and Ray goes to a table in the strip joint where Mickey is nursing a drink. Ray wants Mickey to help him get rid of Ned. Mickey tells him that Ned is bigger, used to box, and will tear him to pieces. When Ray still wants advice, Mickey punches him in the stomach, telling him not to mess with anybody when he doesn't know what they're capable of.

In the penultimate scene, Rutger, commenting that he thinks Mickey has run out on their business arrangement, wonders if Ned would be interested in a lucrative "piece of work," a "grave matter." Ned says that he is interested and accepts Rutger's offer of a cigar, saying that he smells something. Rutger says he hasn't been able to smell anything since he was a boy and flicks the lighter. The lights black out as we hear simultaneously the sound of a huge explosion, "very loud."

Then we hear bird sounds as the lights come up on the rest of the cast dressed in black at the cemetery. Tanya asks Ray if she can talk to him later, but Ray says he is helping Lea take care of some things. After Ray and Lea leave, Mona tells Tonya that they will be "naked, going at it like a couple of dogs" before the last shovelful of dirt hits the coffin. After Kermit takes Mona home, Tanya tells Doris that she has to get away, gives her a hug, and goes. Doris tells Mickey she doesn't know what to do with all the insurance money, that she didn't ever like Rutger although she loved him, but she thinks she transferred her love for her first husband to Rutger. Mickey asks her if she has ever been to the Virgin Islands and we hear an accordion playing the last few bars of "La Golondrina" as the lights fade and go out.

Nigro describes the "default setting" for *Pushkin* as an "ongoing surreal ball" created by lights and music with actors moving in and out of focus and no breaks in the action. Otherwise, a small desk and chair DR; a large potted plant DRC; an empty oval picture frame RC; an empty doorway UC; a small sofa L; a round wooden table with chairs DL; and enough room for couples to dance C. The play requires five men (two playing two parts, one playing three) and three women (two playing two parts). All eight actors are onstage as the pre-show Chopin piano music ends.

We hear wind blowing as lights come up on the stage and Gogol, in the UC doorway, looks at Pushkin at the desk and describes Pushkin waiting to duel with the man he believes is his wife's lover. We hear crows cawing and then Pushkin's wife, Natalya, standing with her sisters Katya and Alexandra upstage of the sofa, says that none of this is real, that it happened quite differently and could not have been so foolish. Pushkin tells her that she has no guilt in the matter, and Gogol repeats the sentence. We hear a gun shot and crows cawing and flapping their wings. Pushkin turns to his desk and begins writing as we hear Chopin's 19th Etude, Opus 25, Number 7, in C sharp minor.

D'Anthes and VanHeeckeren join the three women in quiet conversation and Gogol watches the scene and gradually moves to sit at the table DL. Benckendorf, who has been standing inside the oval frame, tells Pushkin that everything he writes must be adjudicated by the Secret Police. Snatching the manuscript, Benckendorf says that just as Pushkin gets pleasure from writing, so he gets pleasure from spying on people. He leaves, and our focus shifts to D'Anthes who has just told a funny story to Natalya and Katya, who are laughing. Alexandra talks to Pushkin, who says that Natalya is the most beautiful woman in Petersburg. VanHeeckeren (whom Alexandra calls "the old gargoyle") leads D'Anthes off left, telling him it's bed time. Alexandra urges Pushkin to talk with Natalya and pulls Katya off-stage.

Natalya says that dancing is the only really satisfying form of intimacy. Pushkin says he has a bad knee and Natalya says that she is fickle and has no dowry. She hurries off to avoid dancing with Benckendorf, who tells Pushkin that the Tsar wants him to turn his play into a novel. Pushkin says he can't change what he has written and Benckendorf tells him that from now on he has to submit everything he writes directly to him before publication can be permitted. The sounds of the dance are overtaken by "eerie gypsy carnival music."

During Carnival, Gogol and Pushkin walk in the gypsy camp. Death (a man in a black cloak with a skeleton mask), Leopard Girl (scantily clad in a leopard mask and long tail), Maniac, and Gorilla run on and off. A gypsy who looks like the Queen of Spades tells Pushkin that he will marry a beautiful woman and live in exile in a cold and remote place. Love will be the cause of his death. She tells Gogol that he will die insane with leeches on his nose, burning his life's work. Immediately, from another time and place, Natalya speaks to Pushkin who turns to her as Gogol and the gypsy fade into the shadows. Natalya tells Pushkin that she can't marry him and goes to the sofa to talk to her sisters. Benckendorf tells Pushkin he's better off without her as the light fades on them and comes up on VanHeeckeren telling D'Anthes to watch out for Benckendorf and to come home soon so he won't be thrown in the brig for missing roll call again. As music plays, Alexandra tells Katya that the handsome Baron D'Anthes is looking at her. Katya says that he is looking at Natalya. Gogol asks Natalya to dance; she refuses, but accepts immediately when D'Anthes asks her.

Lights come back up on Pushkin and Benckendorf, who has some suggestions for improving *Eugene Onegin* and wonders why women are so attracted to Pushkin despite the fact that his great-grandfather came from Africa. Pushkin suggests that the Tsar could use him on a diplomatic mission outside of Russia, but Benckendorf says that Pushkin isn't going anywhere. Pushkin says he just wants to be left alone and we hear the sound of a violin playing Paganini's 24th Caprice and see Goncharov, the girls' father, playing. He stops when Natalya asks him what he wanted to see her about since all he wants to do is torture the violin and play chess with the dog. Goncharov tells her that he can't afford to feed his daughters any more, and she should marry Pushkin. Natalya walks to Pushkin and tells him that she has been instructed by her father to accept the marriage proposal, warning Pushkin that his happiness will end after his first ejaculation. As she goes to tell her family of their engagement, Pushkin wonders why getting what one has desperately wanted feels as if one has begun to die. Benckendorf appears to congratulate Pushkin and Pushkin says he needs a letter for his mother-in-law stating that he is not suspected of any criminal activity. Benckendorf sits at the desk to write the letter as the lights fade on them.

We hear the sounds of owls and a ticking clock as Pushkin asks Natalya if she is a virgin. She thinks the question is cretinous and tells Pushkin if she falls asleep he is not to wake her but to go ahead on his own. She walks into the darkness and Pushkin follows her. We hear Natalya moaning in pleasure as the lights come up on Katya knitting and Alexandra reading on the sofa. They wonder what Pushkin is doing to make Natalya utter such sounds. The sounds stop but then begin again and the girls walk off to go to bed. We hear music and are back again at the ball as Pushkin and Natalya come in, speaking about losing the child that Natalya was carrying. She says she is not going to let him touch her any more, that he taught her to feel sexual pleasure and the result of that mad animal ecstasy has been the death of a child. She sends him for punch and asks "pretty boy" D'Anthes what he's looking at and sends him away. Katya tells her sister she is very attracted to D'Anthes and Pushkin tells Natalya that all the men in St. Petersburg, including the Tsar, are lusting after her. Gogol asks to kiss Natalya's hand but she refuses and goes off to dance with D'Anthes.

Benckendorf tells Pushkin that the Tsar has offered him the position of Imperial Archivist so he can write and Natalya can attend the Imperial balls. Benckendorf implies that the beauty of Pushkin's wife may have saved his life and suggests that Pushkin have the mole on his right buttock removed. As Natalya giggles with her sisters, D'Anthes tells VanHeeckeren that he is madly in love with her, an emotion the older man finds juvenile and absurd. Natalya tells Pushkin not to be jealous because men look at her and "storms over" to D'Anthes and VanHeeckeren. Beckendorf offers to spy on her and he and Pushkin stand behind the oval frame as Natalya tells D'Anthes that her husband is insanely jealous although she has done nothing wrong and could never betray him. They dance as Pushkin tells Beckendorf that he wants to kill D'Anthes, and the lights begin changing to the cold blue of the show's beginning and we hear wind. Gogol describes the "etiquette" of the duel, the cold, dark afternoon with knee-deep snow, and Pushkin rushing forward to get as close as he can before he shoots. We hear the sounds of a gunshot and crows scattering as the lights go to black.

As the second act begins, all the characters except Natalya are on stage "like mourners in the shadows." Gogol begins recapitulating the duel but says he can't get it right, that creation, like love, is suicide. We hear crows flapping and cawing as Natalya enters, late from the ball, to find Pushkin at his desk. She says she thinks D'Anthes is in love with her but wants Pushkin to leave her alone. Lights fade on them and come up on D'Anthes moaning and pulling his hair over his desire for Natalya. VanHeeckeren thinks they should take a vacation to Venice but accedes to D'Anthes' request that he talk with Natalya, saying that he hopes that once D'Anthes has fornicated with her the two men can be close again, as they used to be. As VanHeeckeren talks with Natalya we learn from her that other people, even her children, seem pointless. VanHeeckeren tells her that he has taken steps to adopt D'Anthes so that he will inherit a fortune and asks her to give D'Anthes "just a bit of tenderness." He says there will be terrible consequences if she does not see D'Anthes. Natalya crosses to the Baron and tells him that she can't run away with him. He pulls out a pistol and threatens to kill himself, but she says she will consider letting him "take certain liberties."

Our attention shifts to Alexandra telling Pushkin he should have married her but was blinded by Natalya's beauty. She asks him if he would like to have sexual intercourse with her, and when he says that women are exactly like men she says that if they were they'd all be morons. Katya brings D'Anthes a message from Natalya that she will meet him in the arbor by the stream, but she cannot remember the time. Katya begins to cry and D'Anthes sits beside her and puts his arm around her shoulder to comfort her. Then, as Pushkin, Alexandra, and Gogol are walking at the Goncharov's, D'Anthes leaves Katya and feigns interest in the potted plant. Gogol says that Benckendorf wants him to submit his work to the censor, like Pushkin, who, Gogol adds, always goes too far. Alexandra greets D'Anthes, who says he is very fond of Katya. Alexandra calls Katya over to tell her this good news and pulls Pushkin and Gogol away from "the lovebirds." Katya tells D'Anthes that she loves him and that he should pretend to love her so that Pushkin will not shoot him for chasing Natalya.

Benckendorf tells Pushkin that he has some suggestions for improving his story about the Queen of Spades, states that he and the author are very much alike, and reads a letter addressed to Pushkin that asserts that Pushkin is a cuckhold and that Natalya has been fucking D'Anthes in the gazebo. When Pushkin wants to know who wrote the letter, Benckendorf tells him that it is anonymous, "although the handwriting does look familiar." He says that copies have been sent to everyone Pushkin knows. Natalya asks why Alexandra's gold cross was found in the sofa in Pushkin's bedroom. When told of the letter, she calls her relationship with D'Anthes a "harmless flirtation" and accuses Pushkin of "wallowing in filth" with her sister. Both deny the alleged involvements but Pushkin says he is going to resolve the situation once and for all.

VanHeeckeren tells Pushkin that he intercepted Pushkin's letter challenging D'Anthes to a duel and asks Pushkin to forgive, urging him to wait two weeks. Pushkin agrees and leaves as D'Anthes asks what business VanHeeckeren has with Pushkin. VanHeeckeren says that Pushkin has challenged D'Anthes to a duel. He urges D'Anthes to settle things amicably, but D'Anthes says he will give Pushkin two weeks to "back down" and then he is going to shoot him in the stomach and watch him die. Katya tells Alexandra and Pushkin that she is pregnant and Alexandra manipulates D'Anthes into agreeing to marry Katya. They tell Natalya the good news and Katya drags D'Anthes off to plan for the wedding.

As Pushkin sits drinking, VanHeeckeren brings in papers stating that Pushkin withdraws his challenge, and that D'Anthes will marry Katya. Natalya wonders if D'Anthes is marrying Katya to protect Natalya's good name, and she tells Pushkin that no one knows or loves her, that she is nothing.

Katya tells D'Anthes that she will do anything to make him happy, that love is "total enslavement . . . death." She says she will be waiting in bed for him but he sits and drinks, mirrored by Pushkin at his desk, also drinking. Gogol wonders aloud why D'Anthes married Katya, and Benckendorf tells Pushkin he admires a man who trusts his wife. Natalya asks Pushkin why he is drinking so much, and Pushkin is disturbed that she has been talking with D'Anthes. He tries to insult the Baron but D'Anthes refuses to be offended. When VanHeeckeren enters, Pushkin tells him that he is "a ridiculous old woman, a loathsome, grotesque, walking piece of excrement," and accuses him of writing the letters proclaiming Pushkin a cuckhold. He knocks the older man down, kicking him in the buttocks and VanHeeckeren "scuttles away."

D'Anthes, seeing VanHeeckeren's clothes are dirty and his nose is bleeding, learns that Pushkin is responsible but still thinks VanHeeckeren wrote the letters. VanHeeckeren pleads with him, but D'Anthes is determined to kill Pushkin. VanHeeckeren urges Natalya to stop the duel, but she says she is powerless, that the world would be a better place if all the men killed each other. After the older man leaves, Alexandra tells Natalya that she always thought a woman had written the letters.

"Eerie blue light" comes up on Pushkin DR and D'Anthes UL as we hear the sound of wind and the other characters take the positions they had at the beginning of the play. VanHeeckeren has provided the men with pistols and D'Anthes tells Pushkin that even God wants to sleep with Natalya. Pushkin says he'll just have to kill God and that to love any mortal creature is always fatal. They stand, motionless, as Gogol moves DL describing Pushkin rushing toward D'Anthes who shoots, hitting Pushkin in the stomach. Pushkin fires from the ground and D'Anthes falls. But the bullet was deflected by a button and D'Anthes lives "a long and full life." Pushkin suffers "unspeakably" and dies the next day. Gogol says he cannot write about this, that all writing is absolute futility. The actors are frozen as Benckendorf strolls to the center doorway and says that Pushkin's death "over a few stupid letters" is a horrible tragedy for all of Russia. He says that perhaps now he can screw Pushkin's wife.

Armitage, the small town in eastern Ohio that is the home of the Pendragon clan, is the nominal geographic location of *Runes*, a play for four men and three women. The unit set is created with "a few wooden chairs and benches, a bed, a small desk, . . . wooden tables . . . a counter . . . with an old dark mirror behind it," and steps leading to an upstage level. We hear the sound of wind blowing as the lights come up on Vonnie Wolf, 16, sitting in jail casting small, flat stones onto the table in front of her. In the shadows upstage is Matt Armitage, 48, the town lawyer. Arthur Wolf, 39, sits behind the counter of Love's General Store, with Evangeline Love Wolf, 36, at the desk in the storeroom above, and Nancy Wolf, 18, on the upper level bed. Jonas Wolf, 17, and Harry MacBeth, 47, sit at a table in the Flowers Boarding Hotel DL. Vonnie talks about the casting of runes and Matt tells her the Sheriff is going to charge her with the murder of her father, Arthur.

Then, at an earlier time, Arthur asks Vonnie what is wrong with her, saying that she has been worse since she performed in *Romeo and Juliet*. Matt, at the jail, asks Vonnie if the baby she is carrying had anything to do with what happened to her father. The action shifts to Jonas telling Harry how Doc McGort took him on house calls. Harry tells Jonas to go away to medical school, and Matt steps into their light telling Jonas that he needs his help to save his sister, Vonnie. Jonas insists that Vonnie didn't kill anyone. Harry tells Matt that Jonas has been seeing Margery Frost every night for months. Matt asks if they know who the father of Vonnie's baby could be.

Arthur comes out of the shadows of the store to order his son to stay away from the Frost girl. He tells Jonas he doesn't need to go to college to run the store and warns him about women, saying that he can't get Jonas' mother out of his head. The mother, Evangeline, moves into the light, reprising an old quarrel as Jonas moves into the shadows. She tells Arthur that he only married her to get her father's store. He agrees, saying that she was pregnant with someone else's child, Nancy, who is a simpleton. Vonnie enters their space, agreeing that everybody hates Arthur. As she moves upstage her parents continue quarreling, Evangeline pleading with Arthur to make some sort of contact with their children before it is too late.

The light fades on Evangeline and we see Nancy folding laundry in the bedroom above as Matt, Jonas, and Harry continue talking about the murder. Jonas says that Nancy heard the shot, discovered the body, and ran to get the doctor. Vonnie asks Nancy why she does everything Arthur wants since he treats her like a slave. Nancy says that Arthur misses their mother badly and talks to her at night as he drinks in the store. She says that Arthur just needs to be loved, and Vonnie tells her that if he hurts her she will kill him. Matt, Jonas, and Harry talk about Arthur prowling the store at night with a lantern and a shotgun, and Vonnie talks with Arthur who says he keeps hearing something moving around in the store at night. He tells her he doesn't understand her and says that we love people who make us suffer the most. Harry goes up the stairs to the bedroom where Nancy is lying on the bed as Jonas tells Matt that Harry wants to own the store. Matt asks Jonas if he knows why his mother left after so many years.

In the storeroom Vonnie asks Evangeline why she is afraid to be alone in the storeroom at night. Evangeline says that years ago she heard the bell ringing above the door of the store and heard footsteps as an intruder came towards her in the dark. He pushed her down on the bolts of cloth and raped her, a memory that does not go away. Vonnie thinks that Nancy should be told that her father was not a handsome Bible salesman who loved her mother. But Evangeline says that people need lies to believe or they go crazy. She wants Vonnie to promise to protect Nancy. We hear the bell ringing above the store door and the lights fade out, ending the first act.

Act Two begins with the sound of wind and a ticking clock as we see Harry standing by the bed where Nancy is lying. Matt and Jonas are DL in shadows. Vonnie sits C in the jail; Arthur is at the counter and Evangeline upstage in the storeroom. Harry tells Nancy that Matt needs to talk with her about Vonnie. Nancy tells Matt that she was having a bad dream when she was awakened by a gunshot. She went downstairs and found Vonnie covered in blood holding Arthur in her arms, crying and telling her to run to get the doctor. Nancy says she doesn't know anyone that Vonnie could be protecting, and the scene shifts to Vonnie and Arthur talking about her playing Juliet. He doesn't understand why she enjoys pretending to be other people. Nancy comes down the stairs asking them to stop arguing. When Jonas enters the four of them, under Arthur's prodding, talk about their belief and nonbelief in God and life after death.

Our attention shifts to Matt coming down the stairs to the Hotel area where Harry is drinking. Matt says he doesn't think Vonnie killed anyone and Harry says he better get her off before the Sheriff charges her. Matt moves into the light of the jail area with Vonnie and Jonas. Vonnie tells Matt that he is trying to make sense out of the irrational, that she likes runes because they show her how desperate people are to make sense out of meaningless events because that's how their minds work. Matt asks if Arthur was ever violent with them and why their mother ran off. Harry enters their space to tell Matt that Loopy Rye, the village idiot, has something important to say to him about the mother, Evangeline.

At night in the store, Arthur wanders, drinking. The shotgun is on the counter. Nancy comes down the steps saying she thought she heard someone crying and realizes it was Arthur. He tells her to go back to bed but she says he was crying for Evangeline. She tries to comfort him, holding his head to her breasts as if he were a child. The bell above the store door rings and Jonas enters, asking Arthur what he is doing. Nancy goes up the steps to lie down on the bed. Arthur warns Jonas about being trapped into marriage by the Frost girl, and Jonas tells him to stay from Nancy. Vonnie moves into their light, telling Jonas to leave, and asks Arthur why he stays up every night drinking. She asks him if he killed Evangeline. He says that she ran off, that she had run off before when the children were younger and that he brought her back so the children would have at least one parent to love. He tells her he never knew what was going on in Evangeline's head. Vonnie gets dizzy and he helps her to sit. She says she is pregnant but Arthur doesn't believe her at first. She refuses to tell him who the father is and says she is not going to marry anyone. Arthur tells her he tried to be a good father, particularly to Nancy, but her mother's rape always got in the way. He says he always loved Evangeline, but she only settled for him after she was pregnant and desperate.

Lights come up on the DL area, now a farmhouse kitchen where Evangeline sits sewing a quilt. Matt tells her that Loopy Rye told him she as at the Naim farm. Matt asks her if she was at the store the previous night. She says she still has a key and likes to walk around the store at night, except in that room in the back where something terrible happened. She tells him to ask Harry, that Harry knows about the bell above the door.

In the jail Matt tells Harry that he has just had an enlightening conversation with Evangeline and that Harry is going to put Jonas through college and medical school, set up a trust fund for Vonnie and Nancy, and bribe the Sheriff to declare Arthur's death an accident. If not, Matt says, he will tell Harry's wife, Evangeline's sister, that Harry raped Evangeline. Harry will also see to it that Evangeline is taken to a place where she can be helped. Vonnie comes in and learns that she is going to be released. Matt tells her he had a conversation with her mother and knows what Vonnie saw and why she lied. She tells Matt that his son, David, is not the father of her baby.

In the last scene, Evangeline is at the table in the Naim farmhouse and Arthur is across the stage at the store counter. Evangeline says that although she loved her children, sometimes she had to get away, but she couldn't bear the thought of having left them with Arthur. He says, "I know." She says he was a monster for loving her after what she had done, after what had happened to her. To love her after that was unforgivable. She says she came home, found the shotgun on the counter with Arthur asleep at the table. Waking, he looked at her with tears running down his face because he was so glad to see her. She raised the gun, she says, and pulled the trigger.

Seduction, in two acts, is set in Copenhagen in the 19th century. Three men and two women make up the cast. A two-level unit set represents all locations. The play begins in darkness as we hear Regine playing Chopin's Minute Waltz on a piano in the upstage shadows as lights come up on a desk DR where Kirkegaard reads aloud from a diary and Johannes appears in the center arch, then Cordelia in the right arch. She sits on a sofa as Edvard enters through the left arch and sits on the window seat. Johannas moves downstage, asking Kirkegaard what he is reading. Kirkegaard admits to reading from Johannes' diary and says he thinks he knows the girl in the diary. Johannes claims that the diary is a work of fiction, and both men look at Cordelia as she walks to the edge of the stage, looking out.

We hear footsteps on cobbles, a flapping of wings, and a dog barking as Cordelia and Johannes speak antiphonally, she about a feeling of being followed, he describing her actions. Regine plays the waltz again as Johannes questions Kirkegaard about his relationship with her. Johannes tells Kirkegaard that people laugh at him in the street and says that if he neglects Regine someone might take her. Kirkegaard tells Regine that they have been acquainted for years but do not know each other. He says he has been devoted to her since she was fourteen and he was twenty-five. They talk about what their marriage might be like and she says she needs to know if he wants her or not. She takes roses out of a vase, throws water in his face, replaces the roses and leaves. Kirkegaard follows her and we hear the sound of a calliope playing circus music. Cordelia, from the upper level, looks out her window as Johannes looks up at her and Edvard watches from the right window. Cordelia says she imagines a shy man who loves her deeply standing in the courtyard below. Johannes says he had made discreet inquiries and found out that Cordelia is the daughter of a dead sea captain forced to live with a widowed aunt.

Kirkegaard bursts in as Regine is playing the waltz, saying that he can't stop thinking about her, that he wants to marry her. He says that the proposal would have been better if he had written it, because he would then have had an umbrella. We hear the sound of thunder and rain as Edvard, a newspaper over his head, rushes across the upper level past Johannes, who enters with an unopened umbrella. Johannes tells us he has followed Cordelia for weeks and one day she found herself on an empty street in a downpour without an umbrella. He joins Cordelia in the center arch and, after a short conversation, opens his umbrella and they run off DL.

Regine approaches Kirkegaard at his desk and says nothing he says makes any sense to her. He tells her it would be wrong for him to marry her. She thinks there must be someone else and he says her name is Cordelia. Cordelia moves to the edge of the stage, speaking of the man who is following her. Johannes, behind her, says he must control the pace at which things develop, that he must get into her house and that he has acquainted himself with her stupid cousins who have invited him to their home. He speaks to Cordelia and she invites him to join her on the sofa, but he stands and speaks with Kirkegaard.

Regine gets up from the piano and comes downstage to Kirkegaard as Johannes watches from the window seat. Regine accuses Kirkegaard of avoiding her and chasing after the mysterious Cordelia. She says he is insane and she doesn't want to play games. He goes off and she bangs on the piano, startling Edvard who falls into a half-open umbrella which closes over his head. As he tries to deal with the umbrella, Cordelia tells Johannes that she has invited Edvard, a childhood friend, to her aunt's house. Johannes tells Kirkegaard that Edvard is hopelessly in love with Cordelia and that a rival is very helpful. He says that the conquest of a woman should be a work of art. Edvard and Johannes introduce themselves and talk of Cordelia, Johannes trying to convince Edvard that Cordelia is in love with him. Johannes tells Kirkegaard that Edvard has the intellectual capacity of a field mouse and suggests to Edvard that he take Cordelia to the theatre. Edvard wants Johanns to come with them to help keep the conversation going and Johannes agrees to find a date.

Edvard asks Cordelia if she would like to go to the theatre with both of them and Johannes' lady friend, Regine, if her aunt approves. We hear the sounds of a crowd babbling in the lobby of a theatre at intermission. Regine tells Cordelia that she agreed to go to the theatre with Johannes to try to drive Kirkegaard mad but that Johannes wants Cordelia. The men enter to go back to the play, but Regine sits at the piano and plays the waltz, stopping as Kirkegaard approaches. He tells her that he used to wait in a pastry shop to see her when she was a schoolgirl. He tells her that to avoid regretting everything one should embrace fiction, not love. He warns her that Johannes is not what he seems. Regine says she is teaching Cordelia to play the piano, but Kirkegaard says that Cordelia is entirely fictional, that he made her up, or Johannes made her up, or perhaps he made Johannes up, or perhaps he made Regine up. We hear the piano playing the waltz as the lights fade.

As the second act begins, Kirkegaard is at the desk, Johannes in the right archway, Edvard on the sofa, and Regine and Cordelia at the piano with Regine explaining octaves and key signatures. Cordelia wants to know why Kirkegaard broke up with Regine. Cordelia says Johannes frightens her and wonders if it is necessary to murder someone to be certain they are real, or you are real. Regine goes out the center arch and Edvard exits DL as Cordelia picks out the Minute Waltz on the piano and sees Johannes. They talk but are interrupted by Edvard returning with a plate of muffins. Cordelia sits on the sofa with him and they speak of Johannes as Kirkegaard and Johannes watch them. Johannes crosses to them and Cordelia asks Edvard to get her a glass of water. She and Johannes seem about to kiss when Edvard returns. Cordelia excuses herself and goes up the left steps of the bed to lie down. Edvard tells Johannes that when Cordelia is near him he can't think and when she's gone he can think of nothing else. He decides he will give her a dog, hugs Johannes, and goes out the center arch.

Kirkegaard asks Johannes if he feels guilty about manipulating Cordelia and Edvard, and Johannes says that stupid people should be eaten. He says he wants to grab Cordelia and kiss her violently in front of everybody. He supposes that he can kill Edvard. Johannes tells Regine when she enters that she is the only real thing in Kirkegaard's life. After Johannes leaves, Regine tells Kirkegaard that she has decided to marry Schlegel, her childhood tutor. Kirkegaard says that he chooses to behave as if he were happy for her. She kisses him passionately then pulls away. Kirkegaard says he hopes she'll be very happy and leaves. After saying that somebody should kill that demented son of a bitch, she goes out.

In the right archway, Johannes says that ambiguity is the seducer's best friend, that to make one's self a poem in a girl's soul is an art and to extricate one's self from the poem is a masterpiece. Cordelia sits up in bed and says she has been having strange dreams. Johannes tells us that at night he stands outside Cordelia's house in the rain. He thinks she lusts after the dangerous and degrading and starts climbing the trellis. When she moves to the window, he ducks under the sill until she exits. Edvard enters announcing that he is going to ask her tonight. Johannes jumps from the trellis and tells Kirkegaard that he feels he must get to Cordelia first. He tells Edvard that he is in love and Edvard assumes he means Regine, although Johannes will not say the girl's name. Edvard tells Cordelia that Johannes is in love, perhaps already engaged. Edvard heads off to get some of his aunt's brownies and Regine, looking down at Cordelia on the sofa, tells her to get away while she can. Johannes says that what he plans to do with Cordelia must be as ambiguous as possible. He wants her to say yes but for reasons she will not be able to explain. Cordelia tells Johannes that Edvard has told her that he is engaged. Johannes says that is not true and that he has come to ask for her hand in marriage. She thinks he is teasing but he insists he loves her and urges her to say yes because it's in the script he wrote in his head when he imagined this moment. Cordelia says she must consult her aunt but when Edvard enters with brownies Johannes tells him that Cordelia has agreed to marry him. Edvard thinks it is a joke. Johannes says he is willing to stand aside if Cordelia prefers Edvard. She asks Edvard if he wants to marry her and, not getting an answer, storms out. Johannes goes after her and Edvard follows with the brownies.

Kirkegaard moves about uneasily, telling us that he walks all over the city, his brain on fire, going to the theatre in the evening to lurk in the crowd, then going home and writing all night. Before dawn, he says, he sleeps for a few hours but has bad dreams and gets up and does the whole thing over again. Johannes comes in saying that Kirkegaard has not congratulated him on his engagement, that the aunt is very excited and Cordelia bewildered. Kirkegaard asks what she will do when she realizes he has no intention of marrying her, and Johannes replies that it's one of God's ironclad rules that if the man does not deceive the woman, the woman must inevitably deceive the man. When Kirkegaard says that is monstrous, Johannes says that Kirkegaard led on a poor girl for years and then broke off the engagement. He, Johannes, is at least honest and, unlike Kirkegaard, is actually going to fuck his girl. Kirkegaard says he is absolutely right.

Johannes and Cordelia sit on the sofa speaking their thoughts aloud. Johannes says that the person she believes she is falling in love with is a fictional construction they both have created out of her desire to love someone and the pleasure he takes in helping her delude herself. She wonders aloud why he doesn't just jump on her. Regine, from above, tells Cordelia to get away, that he's going to kill her. Saying she will simply have faith, Cordelia rests her head on his shoulder. We hear birds singing as Edvard enters, talking to himself about Johannes violating Cordelia's flesh. He tells Regine it is dangerous for her to be alone in the woods at night. When he says Johannes and Cordelia are to be married, Regine tells him she is going to marry a man she doesn't love. Edvard says his brain is on fire trying to understand how women think and why they do things. He says for years and years he tried to be kind and patient with Cordelia but then suddenly she gave herself to a person he thought was his friend. He thinks he is very, very stupid, and Regine tells him that in matters of love everyone is completely selfish and utterly ruthless. He starts crying and puts his head in her lap as she strokes his hair tenderly and says that in matters of love everybody here is imaginary.

We hear bird song and see leaf shadows as Johannes and Cordelia walk as if on a path by the woods. Cordelia rejects his attempt to kiss her and wonders what Edvard is doing with his head in Regine's lap. Johannes says they are just animals fumbling about in the woods. He says he releases her from their engagement and goes down the steps to Kirkegaard at his desk. Johannes says that he has given Cordelia the privilege of suffering so that her pleasure will be intensified when she gives herself to him completely. He tells Kirkegaard that Edvard had his face buried in Regine's lap. Regine gets up and leaves but Edvard stays with his head resting on the bench. Kirkegaard starts drinking from a bottle and Johannes watches Cordelia come down the steps and go to the edge of the lake DC saying that she can't stop thinking of Johannes and has been following him as he moves all over the city. She asks Johannes if he will be satisfied if she gives herself to him. She puts his hands on her breasts and kisses him passionately, starting to take off her clothes. Johannes tells her that making love is not necessary, that knowing she is willing is enough. The game is over. He says he has taught her a lesson, but she says he is not even real, spits in his face, and runs blindly, bumping into Edvard, then offstage. Johannes wipes his face with a handkerchief and tells us that is how a seduction is accomplished, that the absurd and meaningless act of animal copulation is unnecessary, pointless, and vulgar. But he says he still physically desires her and wonders if he has done a decent thing and might love her.

Making the sound of a wounded, enraged animal, Edvard grabs Johannes' neck from behind, strangling him. Johannes' neck snaps and Edvard drops him to the ground and goes out. Kirkegaard rises from his desk and climbs the trellis, looking in the window and calling for Regine. She helps him through the window and they sit on the edge of the bed. He says that he has been hearing voices and seeing things, suspecting that everything in his life is an illusion. He says that Johannes is dead and that he, Kirkegaard, is not a man but a whole crowd of men, rattling off a list of the pen-names he uses. Cordelia and Edvard come through the center arch separately and sit on the sofa without touching. Kirkegaard tells Regine that he killed Johannes, that he created him and then destroyed him. Kirkegaard kisses Regine as Cordelia goes to the piano and starts playing the Chopin waltz. Kirkegaard climbs down the trellis, goes to his desk, and starts writing in the diary as the lights fade to darkness.

Another five-character play (2m, 3w), set in London (1932), Munich (1923), and Prague (1913) is entitled *The Shadows*. Nigro includes a set diagram that could be used for a number of his plays. Benches are placed DR and DL, desks right and left, a couch center, five sets of steps lead to an upstage platform with a bed UR, a bathtub UC, and a table with chairs UL. As we hear the sound of a ticking clock, the lights come up on Hannah, 19, in London 1932, on the couch. We can see Rath at the bench DL, Quinn on the bench DR, Maya sitting on the bed, and Sophie writing at the table. Each character voices thoughts that occur in the play like leitmotifs.

We hear birds singing as Hannah walks to Rath, her father, asking him if he is all right, that he seems troubled. He asks her where she goes when she is out alone exploring London. Maya enters their space, asking if Rath, her husband, wants meat for dinner. She says that Rath used to dream of his father committing suicide by stepping out an attic window. Hannah leaves to get some lamb for dinner and Rath asks Maya who Hannah is seeing. Maya tells Rath that he should be grateful that Quinn got him a teaching job in London and asks him if he wants to see Sophie. The scene ends as Quinn and Sophie speak their thoughts.

Maya moves toward Sophie who descends the steps and they talk about when they were friends in Munich. Maya wants Sophie to come to see Rath. Their conversation is interspersed with comments on life and love from Quinn and Rath. Sophie joins Quinn feeding pigeons on the bench and Maya watches them from the couch. Rath moves to his desk and begins writing. Sophie tells Quinn that Maya is worried about Rath. Quinn tells Sophie that she is doing very well, getting published, her work taken seriously. He says it will kill her to see Rath again. Sophie describes waiting in the rain in Prague outside Rath's office, then going inside to knock on his door.

As Hannah speaks in 1932 from the bench DL of her dreams of being a young girl in Prague during the war, Sophie moves to Rath's desk. It is 1923. He puts a blanket around her and they sit on the couch. Hannah speaks in 1932 of the first time she met Sophie, when her father brought her home for dinner, and how she loved her from the moment she saw her. Maya moves

toward the couch (Munich, 1923) and tells Sophie that she is always interested in her husband's students. The women talk about children and Sophie
says she probably won't have any. Hannah crosses to Quinn on the DR bench
and they speak of tragedy and their time in Munich. Maya crosses to the UL
table as Hannah asks Quinn if he thinks her father is going mad. Sophie and
Rath eat lunch at his desk and Hannah moves to join Maya at the table.
Sophie and Rath talk about writing and Rath tells her a story of David Hume
being overwhelmed by the terror of solipsism. She says she is real, flesh and
blood, and she wants him to touch her. Rath gets up to leave but returns when
Sophie starts crying and kisses her as the light fades.

As Hannah and Maya start talking (London 1932) at the table, Sophie
moves to the DR bench to sit with Quinn. Hannah says she thinks the shadows have gotten into her father's head. Maya tells her that she went to see
Sophie and asked her to visit. Quinn has moved to his desk and he and Rath
(Munich 1923) talk about their theories of art and love. Rath admits to
betraying his wife with Sophie. Angry, Quinn leaves to teach a class and
Maya and Sophie on the bench DR talk about university politics and how
Quinn has been able to protect Rath. Sophie moves up to Rath on the bed,
takes off her dress, and sits in her slip at the foot of the bed. She tells how her
parents died when she was a teenager and how her aunt took her to an
orphanage because her uncle wanted to sleep with her, and how the mother
superior recognized her intelligence and got her into the university. Rath tells
her that she is better than he is and it seems impossible that she can love him.
He tells her that Maya was his landlady's daughter when he was a university
student and that one night she came to his room. As he moves to the table,
Maya comes to him from the bench DR and they enact a scene from 1913 in
the rooming house in Prague. She tells him she has been reading his manuscript on labyrinths and tragedy and says that she knows he wants her, that
she is like his muse. She rubs his temples and they kiss as the light fades on
them and Quinn tells a fairy tale of a fool and a wise man. Hannah speaks
from the bench DL of fog everywhere, Maya moans, and Sophie on the bed
speaks of death as lights fade and the act ends.

As the second act opens, we see Rath writing at the table UL (Prague
1913) with Maya behind him. Sophie is on the bed in her slip (Munich 1923)
and Quinn and Hannah are on the benches. Maya tells Rath that she is going
to have his child and Sophie speaks from the bed about Rath marrying Maya
as he moves to the couch. He tells Sophie that his father committed suicide
after finding his younger brother in bed with his wife. Rath says he never
spoke to his mother again. Maya enters Rath's time (1923), crossing to the
couch and suggesting they invite Quinn and Sophie to dinner. She covers her
face with her hands as Rath goes up the steps to lie down with Sophie on the
bed. Hannah speaks from the bench about reading Quinn's book on laby-

rinths in which he says that all art is an exercise in futility, "an elaborate device for becoming hopelessly lost."

Quinn moves from the bench to the couch and Maya (Munich 1923), who tells him that Rath is betraying her with Sophie. She wants Quinn to make love to her; he sits on the couch and she puts her head on his chest. Hannah speaks of Rath bringing Sophie home as Agamemnon brought Cassandra home. On the bed (Munich 1923) Rath warns Sophie about becoming friends with Maya. He tells Sophie that, because of Hannah, he can't see her any more. Sophie suggests that they could kill Maya and tells Rath that he is not re-enacting the manifestation of an archetype but is destroying a person who loves him, giving them both a death sentence because he is afraid. As Rath moves down the steps away from her she says he is making the greatest mistake of his life. She sits at the foot of the bed, her head on her knees.

At their desks (Munich 1923), Quinn tells Rath that he saw "that strange little man," Hitler, in a café. Rath says he has ended the affair with Sophie, that it was the right thing to do. He tells Quinn he should see Sophie. Quinn moves to the upper level as Sophie moves to the bath, speaking of Seneca's recipe for suicide—a razor and a bath of hot water. Quinn sees her with a razor in her hand and turns off the water. He says he has been offered a job as department head at a London university and suggests that Sophie can come with him as his assistant and finish her thesis which he will help get published. He puts a robe around her and holds her as the lights dim.

Maya speaks to Rath at his desk (Munich 1923) about fools marching in the streets. Rath tells her that Quinn is taking Sophie to London with him; Maya says that Hannah will be devastated because she loves both of them. Hannah ends the scene by saying that inflation in Munich that autumn made their money worthless. She moves to touch Rath's back and kiss his hair as he is at his desk, then sits on the steps L. Sophie enters, dressed, speaking to Quinn on the bench (London 1932). She is furious that Quinn has given Rath a job in his department. Quinn says he thought she was over her feelings for Rath. She says she had a crush on Quinn first but decided it was foolish. Then she fell in love with Rath. She decides that she has to see Rath again and moves toward the couch. Hannah greets her and Sophie says that Maya asked her to drop by to see Rath. Hannah says her father has not been the same since Sophie left. She says that one day she visited her father's office and saw him kissing Sophie. That moment changed her life forever. She kisses Sophie on the cheek and sits on the couch as Sophie moves to Rath on the bench DL. We hear birdsong and Sophie tells Rath that Maya asked her to come by to see him. Rath wonders why Maya would invite Sophie. He says that he never knew anything, that he taught because he needed the money. They argue, and Rath says that Maya invited Sophie to push him over the edge. He says he sent Sophie away because she had to live her own life. She says she has a gun and sits on the bench beside him.

Quinn joins Hannah on the couch (London 1932). She says she loves London and she loves him. She asks if he and Sophie are lovers. When he says no, she stands up and kisses him, unbuttons her blouse, puts his hands on her breasts, and kisses him again. She pulls him onto the couch on top of her and they are kissing passionately as Maya walks in. Hannah discovers that Maya and Quinn have been lovers and storms out. Quinn wants to go after her but Maya says that Rath is making love to Sophie and she wants Quinn to hold her.

The light fades on them as Rath and Sophie talk about reality and illusion, of living in shadows that devour them. Sophie calls him a compulsive liar, a monster. They don't see Hannah as she moves to the upper level. Rath says he should have made the wrong choice and done the brave, selfish thing, leaving his wife and daughter for Sophie. But instead he did the decent, cowardly thing and has been a dead man ever since. He tells her if she has a gun she should use it because he can't go on living without her, that she is all he has ever wanted. She says he is horrible but kneels down and puts her head on his knee, facing away from him as he strokes her hair. Hannah looks at them from above and turns on the water in the bathtub. She speaks of Seneca and the need for hot water. She gets the razor, speaks of Iphigenia, and begins undressing as Quinn holds Maya on the couch and Rath strokes Sophie's hair. We hear the sound of running water as the lights fade out.

The unit set for *Strange Case* represents the laboratory of Dr. Jekyll, a tavern, the streets of London, and the Stevenson home in Samoa. There are five actors with the three men playing two and, in one case, three parts. As the lights come up we hear clocks ticking and wind howling and then the voice of Mansfield, an actor, trying different ways to say his lines about a door and a very strange tale. The UC door opens creakily and Jekyll enters. He takes a drink and wonders who he is talking to, saying that his life is a tissue of absurd soliloquies. He feels his face changing and looks in the mirror (actually a long oval frame) and sees Edward Hyde grinning back at him. Hyde says that Jekyll is now under his control and Jekyll backs onto the bed, covering his face with a pillow. Lightning and thunder and then the voice of Mansfield (the same actor who plays Hyde) speaking from the darkness, asking for a bigger thunderclap and giving an example of a much bigger "NOOOOOOOOOOOO" for Jekyll.

The actor playing Jekyll now becomes Stevenson being awakened by Fanny, his wife. She tells him he was having a nightmare and sounded like somebody else. Stevenson says he is going to write down what happened in his dream. Jenny, a former lover, standing at the UR window frame on the second level, says that her letters must have gone astray. Fanny says that bogey tales are cheap and vulgar, but Stevenson says he has to write what the brownies tell him. When Fanny asks him where he was, Stevenson says he was drinking with Henley, and Henley, looking down from the UL level, quotes the opening lines of "Invictus." After Henley staggers into the darkness down the left escape stairs, Stevenson says he will see less of Henley if Fanny lets him write down the dream.

Hyde enters DR and talks about the door that is connected in his mind with a late-night encounter with a little girl who ran into him and whom he trampled, twice, only to be accosted by her shrieking family who demanded money. He says he wrote a check but had to wait with them until the bank opened. He leaves and Fanny, who has been reading the pages as Stevenson finishes writing them, asks why the girl was running. She says Stevenson wants her to be trampled, that he is writing an evil book. He says he must write down what the voices tell him. When she says he has a choice, he throws the manuscript into the fireplace. After Fanny leaves, Jenny looks down at the author drinking and says that she once heard "it" weeping.

Henley enters, asking Stevenson what he is writing. Stevenson replies that he is working on a horrifying tale about a fellow who's been harboring a monster inside and finds a potion that lets the monster out to do whatever it wishes. He says the story brings up disturbing memories of a girl he became attached to and whose letters he stopped answering. From the second level Jenny says she dreamed of a room full of mirrors and ticking clocks and a girl lying dead on the floor. Henley tries to warn Stevenson about women, making comments about Fanny, and Stevenson pushes him out the door. As he turns from the door he sees Hyde in the mirror, but he goes back to his desk to write. Hyde asks what the name of the maidservant, "the little prostitute," was and Jenny pleads with Stevenson not to write the story or tell Hyde her name. But Stevenson does, and Hyde says he should pay Jenny a visit. We hear footsteps growing louder, then the door creaking open as Fanny comes in saying that she met Henley raging on the stairs. She regrets her comments about his bogey tale and notices he has begun writing it again. She goes out the door and Stevenson speaks what he writes about a crime of singular ferocity involving a maidservant as lights come up on a moonlit street.

While Jenny watches and Stevenson writes, Hyde and Sir Danvers Carew (played by the actor who previously played Henley) meet in the street. Danvers talks about Oscar Wilde's story of Dorian Gray, but Hyde, losing his temper, beats Danvers with his walking stick. Danvers crawls off. Jenny screams and runs down the escape stairs. Stevenson is still writing when there is a knock on the door and Jenny comes in. She tells Stevenson that she saw a man murdered in the street by Edward Hyde whom she has seen go in and out of Stevenson's back door. Jenny runs off when Fanny comes in and Stevenson tries to explain her appearance to his wife. As Fanny leaves, the actor playing Stevenson follows her out the door, only to return as Jekyll. Hyde looks out through the mirror, talks to Jekyll, and then steps through the mirror into the room. Jekyll complains that he has to spend most of his time trying to undo the evil that Hyde has done and tells him that he must go away. Hyde says that he is the true man and Jekyll is an artificial construction. Hyde says he is the hero of this particular penny dreadful and is a murderer because all heroes must be proficient in killing and doing monstrous things to women. Hyde says he is very glad to no longer be confined by the mirror. Jekyll says that Hyde is not real, that he, Jekyll, is really Robert Louis Stevenson. Hyde replies that Stevenson is a character in a play he is writing with Henley. Jekyll drinks more of the potion, lights swirl, orchestrion music plays like a mad carnival, and lights fade into fog.

Out of the fog, we hear Long John Silver (played by the actor who does Henley and Danvers) singing the "Fifteen men on a dead man's chest" pirate song. Long John thinks Stevenson is Jim Hawkins and speaks lines for the parrot on his shoulder. When Stevenson thinks he is hallucinating, Long John suggests a vacation in Samoa and offers to help if "Jim" will let him look at the treasure map. He warns Stevenson about mayonnaise and about going into the cellar. Fanny knocks on the door to say that Richard Mansfield, the famous actor, wants to talk to him about making a play out of the bogey tale. Long John walks off into the fog; Stevenson opens the door and a voluble Mansfield enters, followed by Fanny. Jenny has reappeared in the window. Mansfield tells Stevenson that the Jekyll-Hyde story was made for the theatre, although some changes need to be made. The actor says he will play both parts, without tricks or makeup. He promises money that Fanny thinks they could use to go to Samoa and Stevenson reluctantly agrees.

In the darkness we hear the door creaking open as Jenny enters carrying a lantern. She goes to Stevenson's desk and the door creaks shut, revealing Hyde. He wants to show her what is on the other side of the mirror and steps into the frame, pulling her after him. She screams in the darkness. As lights come up on Stevenson and Fanny in Samoa, sitting in chairs DC, we hear tropical bird sounds. Fanny says that she told the movers not to bring the mirror but they sent it anyway. Stevenson goes off to bed and Hyde steps into the moonlight, tells Fanny that he is the one who makes her scream in the dark, and kisses her long and erotically. We hear wind and storm sounds as Fanny pulls away and Stevenson enters. She tells him that the other man is "here" and that he is death. Stevenson says she just dozed off and had a nightmare. She goes in to bed and Hyde steps out of the shadows, telling Stevenson that he can never escape him, that he will always be on the other side of the mirror. Hyde says he wants whatever Stevenson has and tells him that he killed Jenny. Fanny comes back with a shovel and whacks Hyde violently, again and again, calling him a monster. She tells Stevenson to bury the body in the jungle and, singing the pirate chanty, helps him carry the body off as the lights fade.

Lights come up as we hear birdsong and Fanny singing the chanty and making dinner. Stevenson, at his desk, says he feels as if he murdered something inside himself, that some essential part is gone. Fanny asks him to get a bottle of wine from the cellar. As he goes out the door Jenny appears in the mirror, telling Fanny that she shouldn't have sent him to the cellar. Fanny puts a blanket over the mirror, saying she is going to break it into a million pieces and bury them in the back yard. Stevenson comes through the door saying that someone is in the cellar. Fanny says no one is in the cellar and tells him to make mayonnaise for their salad. Stevenson says something is wrong inside his head and pulls the blanket off the mirror. "There's nobody in the mirror," he says and collapses. Fanny holds him in her arms, calling for help, and Mansfield comes through the door saying that was not bad for a first rehearsal. She asks what he was doing in the cellar and tells him to get help. Mansfield gives directions about holding Stevenson so his head lolls back with the mouth open. He praises her energy, suggests more desperation, and thinks that the last bit should be played more downstage. He wants to include the line, "Be careful what you write. It will happen to you." He tells her to save her tears for the audience. Fanny sobs that she wants to wake up as Mansfield rehearses his lines about a door and a strange tale that we heard as the play began.

Traitors is a full-length script for four actors (Hiss, Chambers, Nixon, and Hoover) on a unit set: table and chair DR, steering wheel and front seat of a 1929 Ford roadster UR, an old love seat on a dark oriental rug RC with the empty frame of a Queen Anne mirror further upstage, a desk with a 1920s Woodstock typewriter and chair UC, a dumbwaiter large enough for a man to crawl inside UL, a child's rocking chair sturdy enough for a fat man to sit on CL, and a bench with pumpkins scattered around DL. No set changes and no breaks except for intermission.

The play opens with the sound of birds singing as the reddish light of a sunset comes up on Hiss in a chair DR and Chambers sitting on a bench DL; Nixon at the desk UC is in darkness. "They are all witnesses," Nigro writes, "testifying to us." Hiss quotes from the Bible about gaining the world and losing one's soul, and Chambers says that there are ghosts in his pumpkin patch and that sinister forces are at work everywhere, confusing his memory of events. "Like someone turning on a switch," the lights (a Committee light effect) come up on Nixon as he tells us how proud he is of his work on the Hiss case. Chambers says that he wants to see the President about members of the Communist Party holding influential positions in the government.

Nixon remarks that while some people pity Hiss, he has only contempt for him, and Chambers tells us that once we have heard his story we'll never trust anybody again.

As Nixon stands to speak to Hiss, the lights on Hiss change to the "harsh Committee light," and Hiss speaks a brief summation of his career, denying that he has ever been a member of the Communist Party. When Nixon turns to Chambers, the light on the pumpkin patch changes to the Committee light and Chambers says that Hiss knew him in the Party by his code name, Carl. He says that Hiss and he were close friends, that their wives were friendly, and that he and Hiss went birdwatching together. Nixon then questions Hiss about birdwatching and asks if he recognizes a photograph of Chambers. Hiss stands, turning toward Chambers, and asks to see his teeth, remarking that the man he knew had black and yellow, broken, rotting teeth. He says that Chambers bears a strong resemblance to a man he knew in the mid-thirties, a George Crosley. When Chambers denies being Crosley and asserts that he and Hiss were Communists together, Hiss invites him to make that assertion in public. He calls Chambers a liar. Chambers says that Hiss donated his car to him, to the Communist Party. Nixon asks why Hiss did that, and the light changes to evening and we hear birds singing.

In a scene from the past, Hiss and Chambers talk about the 1929 Ford and Chambers asks if Hiss wants to get rid of it because it will draw rats that can swarm out of the darkness and devour him. Chambers stays seated in the car as Nixon questions Hiss about giving his car to George Crosley. Hiss says he may have included the car with the rent for the apartment Crosley was subletting and that instead of money Crosley gave him a large red rug. Chambers says the rug was a gift from the Communist Party and that he doesn't remember subletting anything, although he spent a great deal of time in the Hiss household because he and Hiss were Communists. Hiss tells Nixon that he befriended Crosley/Chambers out of basic human decency but he now sees him as a very disturbed individual who once stole hundreds of library books by stuffing them in his pants. After telling Nixon that he may once have driven Chambers somewhere, Hiss gets into the car next to Chambers while Nixon stands behind the upstage mirror frame watching them.

As they pretend to drive, Hiss and Chambers talk about prostitutes as capitalists and Hiss points out a farm that he once thought of buying. Chambers says he has always wanted a pumpkin patch because pumpkins, and dumbwaiters, are good places to hide valuables. He says one should always be prepared because people cannot be trusted. He thinks a car is following them, and Hiss says that his father committed suicide by cutting his throat. Chambers says he ran away from home when he was eighteen and bummed around the country changing his name. He thinks Hiss understands him and speaks of his brother killing himself by breathing in gas from the oven. Hiss says that his brother died young, too.

The Committee light comes on again and Nixon continues his questioning of Hiss, accusing him of being a spy for the Russians. Hiss denies the charge as does Chambers, saying that he and Hiss were members of the Party, not spies. Hiss again wants Chambers to make his accusations public so he can sue him. Nixon paces angrily back and forth as Chambers moves into the shadows of the pumpkin patch. Nixon is furious that Chambers refuses to admit to espionage and frantic that Truman may abolish the Committee. J. Edgar Hoover enters from upstage and asks Nixon how the Hiss business is going. When Nixon says that Chambers won't admit to spying, Hoover tells "Dick" that this is their chance to squash Hiss like a cabbage worm and expose the "festering, maggoty underbelly of all this sissy New Deal doodleysquat." He says Dick is the man for the job. He urges Nixon to drive to Chambers' farm in Maryland and persuade him to cooperate. Nixon promises not to let Hoover down and crosses to Chambers in the pumpkin patch as Hoover watches from the upstage shadows.

Chambers tells Nixon that Hiss is suing him and that he could lose everything. Nixon says that although they cannot prosecute Hiss for spying, they can get him for perjury if the espionage can be proven. He wants a confession from Chambers that he and Hiss were spies. After a pause, Chambers agrees, saying that Hiss stole documents that Chambers photographed and gave to his Soviet contacts. Nixon demands hard evidence and Chambers says he may have some and crawls into the dumb waiter.

Committee lights again as Nixon questions Chambers, who sticks his head out of the dumb waiter to shout his answers. Hiss denies being a traitor and asks for proof. Chambers falls out on the floor holding "a small sheaf of about seventy pages," claiming they are documents that Hiss stole from the State Department and retyped before giving them to Chambers. Hiss says he never learned to type, and Chambers says the papers were typed by his wife, who did everything for Hiss. He adds that he has film of secret documents concealed in a pumpkin in his pumpkin patch, and, taking the lid off a pumpkin, he pulls out five spools of film. Seeing the typewriter on the desk, Hiss says that they can compare Chambers' documents to something typed on his old typewriter. When asked by Nixon if he still has the typewriter, Hiss says he thinks he gave it away but they can find it and prove Chambers is lying. Hiss goes out as Chambers shouts after him that the truth will make him free, and the lights go to black.

The second act opens with the sound of a loud swish and thwack in the darkness and the lights come up on Hoover swatting flies on his desk. Nixon is worried about the problem of the typewriter, but Hoover tells him not to worry, that a typewriter has been found that experts will testify is the typewriter that the stolen documents were typed on. Nixon understands that the typewriter evidence is bogus but agrees that the important thing, the American way, is to win, no matter how. He then suggests that perhaps Hiss and Chambers are queers, and Hoover, after giving him a look "that would make birds fall dead from the sky," tells him that there's nothing he hates more than queers. He tells Nixon to stand still and smacks him in the forehead with the fly swatter, saying he got the fly. He tells Nixon he has a file on him as thick as Kate Smith and that Nixon is going to get the grand jury to indict Hiss for the survival of the nation as well as his own. After Nixon exits, Hoover, on the intercom, asks Clyde to pick up his ball gown at the cleaners because he is in the mood for a tango tonight. The scene ends with the lights fading on Hoover as he exits "humming a tango and trying a couple of steps with the fly swatter in his teeth like a rose."

In the next scene, Nixon and Chambers move a table center stage as Nixon preps Chambers for the grand jury, piling huge stacks of paper on the table. Nixon tells Chambers to get out of his light as a bright light shines down, flashbulbs go off, and Nixon examines a bit of film with a magnifying glass. He turns to the invisible throng of reporters downstage and speaks "gravely and earnestly" of the evidence of top-secret documents stolen by the traitor Alger Hiss and retrieved by the repentant Whittaker Chambers. He makes the Nixon raised arms V-fingers sign and smiles mechanically as more flashbulbs go off. Hiss emerges from the shadows and confronts Nixon about the "evidence" as Hoover watches from the upstage frame. Nixon says he has testimony from FBI experts that it is "absolutely, unequivocally impossible" to fabricate the "conclusive" typewriter evidence. Hiss realizes that Chambers has made a deal and says, "This is not my country," as he sits in despair on the love seat.

We hear the sounds of a bleating lamb and birds singing as Nixon and Chambers talk in the pumpkin patch about the relationship between Chambers and Hiss, and Nixon urges Chambers to hang in there for the future of America. As Nixon hurries off, Hiss rises from the love seat and tells Chambers about his relationship with Justice Oliver Wendell Holmes, a man Hiss says he worshipped. Hiss wonders if Chambers is going to pay back the money he owes, and Chambers, tears in his eyes, says that he knows when he's not wanted but that Hiss should beware of reprisals. Very upset, Chambers goes to his pumpkin patch at night and rocks in the child's rocker, speaking confusedly about never wanting to hurt Hiss. He scatters the stacks of paper, tearing some, throwing others, speaking of the voices in his head. He takes a bottle marked XXX out of a pumpkin, drinks the rat poison, and then runs over to a pumpkin, falling on his hands and knees, vomiting loudly as Nixon runs on with a newspaper, gleefully announcing the guilty verdict against Hiss.

We hear a "decadently upbeat" version of "Saint James Infirmary" and the sounds of a wild party offstage as deep red light suffuses the pumpkin patch. Hiss, "like the sophisticated villain in an old thirties movie," smokes a cigarette and asks Chambers what he is doing. Chambers says that he is a martyr, destroying himself for the good of the country. He insists that he is a patriot, that his pumpkin patch will become a National Monument. Hiss says that Nixon and the others are using them to discredit the New Deal, the United Nations, everything they hate and fear. He says that people are decent and rational, but Chambers responds that people are "insane, feeble-minded, cowardly, homicidal monkeys" who will believe anything. He tells Hiss that his reward for behaving decently is a five-year prison sentence and he, Chambers, has won. Suddenly, "The Stars and Stripes Forever" blares loudly and we hear cheers from unseen crowds as Nixon appears, giving victory signs and shaking hands with Chambers. Hoover comes on in a ball gown and tiara, kisses Chambers on both cheeks, and hands Nixon a rubber chicken. After dancing a polka with Hoover, Nixon holds the chicken up and speaks a Jabberwocky-like mish-mash of images from American history. The music gets more grotesque and distorted as the light on Nixon fades to darkness.

We hear bird song and see Hiss seated as he was at the start of the play with shadows of bars across him; Chambers is in the pumpkin patch and Nixon is at the desk in the darkness. Hoover, just out of the light, is standing stiffly in the frame. Hiss tells us that he made some lasting friendships in prison and that what kept him alive was the thought of his wife. The lights come up on Nixon telling us that he regarded the Hiss case as a defining moment in his career and that, as a traitor, Hiss deserved everything he got. Hiss says he lost his wife because she wanted him to change their names and find a quiet life, but he had to prove his innocence. Eventually, Hiss says, he got a job selling office supplies. Chambers says his autobiography made him a quarter of a million dollars and Nixon says that what he learned from the Hiss case was to use the newspapers to destroy your enemies. As lights begin to fade on them all, Hiss says he is at peace, that he knows who he is, but he sometimes feels that the other self who was created to live in "this incredible cathedral of lies" may be more real. Nixon says that faith has sustained him because he knows in his heart that God is on "our" side. Hiss repeats the Bible quote about a man gaining the whole world and losing his soul, and Nixon ends the show with the comment: "And if it should happen to turn out, in the end, that in fact God is actually not on our side, well then—fuck him."

The five characters in *The Winkleigh Murders* are Willy (the gardener's bastard son), Bronwyn (the young heiress of Winkleigh), Imogen (the orphaned ward of Bronwyn's late parents), Charles (a school friend of Bronwyn's late brother Edward), and Cedric (also a friend of the late Edward). The set is "like a psychological collage of the Winkleigh estate" in Devon, overlooking Dartmoor. We can see part of a house with a parlor DR; farther

UR and towards center a garden with a gazebo; C a tall hedgerow broken by a wooden gate; a ruined windmill with a wooden bench or two UL; further DL a stone bench and a broken sundial. Downstage of the hedgerow is a "rather primitive" automobile. When Charles and Cedric are out hunting they use the center and down center part of the stage, "in dappled greenwood shadows to give . . . the feeling of deep and ancient forest." The time is early in the twentieth century.

The five characters are on stage as the lights come up, Charles trying to take a photograph of Imogen and Cedric in the automobile, Willy sitting on the gate of the hedgerow, and Bronwyn observing from a bench in the gazebo. Willy speaks his thoughts which, he says, would get him bludgeoned to death if the other characters could hear him since he is expressing his lust for Imogen's body and his wish that Cedric's pickle be incinerated. Cedric expresses his thoughts about Imogen's desire for him. Imogen, speaking her thoughts, says she misses Edward dreadfully and thinks Cedric lucky to be so stupid. Bronwyn and Charles then speak their thoughts (mostly of sexual desire) in counterpoint with the others until Charles takes the picture. In the blackout we hear the sound of birds, and lights come up on Imogen and Bronwyn in the gazebo.

Imogen tells Bronwyn that she knows the boy (Willy) is watching her and that Charles is "desperately infatuated" with Bronwyn. Bronwyn decides to torment Charles and we hear the sound of crows as the lights fade on the gazebo while she strolls over to Charles reading on the bench by the sundial. She advises Charles against fancying her, saying that Imogen fancies him. Then she kisses him on the cheek and leaves as Cedric, carrying a hunting rifle, approaches Charles who prefers taking photographs to shooting things. Cedric thinks a fellow is defined by what he is trying to kill. Seeing anger in Charles' eyes, Cedric pats him on the back and leaves, saying that he knew Charles had it in him.

Willy is polishing boots on the steps of the gazebo and is puzzled when Bronwyn wants to talk with him. She thinks he is mocking her and tells him she knows he is in love with Imogen. Bronwyn wonders why he isn't in love with her, since everyone else is. Willy says he sees something behind Imogen's eyes and advises Bronwyn to get inside because a storm is coming. Lights fade on the gazebo and the sky darkens with the approaching storm. We hear thunder as the lights come up on all five characters.

Willy is trying to fix a cuckoo clock and Bronwyn wants Imogen to hypnotize him. Imogen swings Charles' pocket watch in front of Willy, telling him to relax and fall into a deep sleep. Cedric pretends to be the one hypnotized, but Bronwyn says she once was someone else and speaks of Zeppelins in the sky pouring down "terrible, corrosive rain," of hearing hunting horns and feeling dogs devouring her. Then, she says, her brother Edward took her in his arms to tell her something horrible. Charles insists that Imogen wake her up. Imogen snaps her fingers, we hear thunder, and the lights go to black.

We hear rain and thunder as a red light comes up on Charles in his photo-developing room down right in the parlor area. His recollections of the dead Edward and the beauty of Bronwyn are interrupted by the sound of a door creaking open and a long rectangle of light falling on him. He asks if anyone is there and the lights go to black. After a last rumble of thunder we hear birds, and lights come up on Cedric, at the automobile, cleaning his gun as Bronwyn watches. She says that she knows her dead brother Edward would have wanted his two best friends to come together and suggests that Cedric take Charles out hunting. She moves to Charles who is reading by the sundial and suggests that he stop reading and go hunting with Cedric. He agrees on condition that she let him photograph her. Bronwyn intimates that she might pose nude for him, and the scene shifts to Cedric and Charles in the woods with guns. Cedric says he will gut Charles like a fish if he finds out that he has been intimate with Imogen. As Cedric raises his gun to shoot, Charles notices that the rabbit is pregnant and lunges toward Charles. We hear a loud bang, simultaneous with a blackout.

A cuckoo clock strikes four as the lights come up on Bronwyn and Imogen in the parlor. When Bronwyn refers to Edward's death as an accident, Imogen reminds her that Edward put a gun in his mouth and pulled the trigger. Cedric stomps in, covered in mud, followed by Charles (not covered in mud). Cedric says he could kill Charles for pushing him down a ravine to save a rabbit, but Bronwyn tells Cedric to get cleaned up and tells Charles to apologize. After she leaves, Imogen asks Charles if he is hopelessly in love with Bronwyn, since everyone else is. Then she asks Charles if he would like to kiss her but, as their lips are about to meet, Bronwyn enters abruptly. She wonders what happened to the book that Edward had been writing, and Charles admits that Edward did leave a letter, asking that the book be destroyed. After saying that their lives are a terrible waste, Imogen runs out and Bronwyn asks Charles if he will tell her what was in Edward's letter if she lets him make love to her. She says she was inexplicably jealous when she saw that Charles and Imogen were about to kiss and thinks violence is "in the end much more satisfying than love." She calls Charles a fool and kisses him on the lips. Charles watches her leave as the lights fade.

We hear the sound of owls as the lights come up on Imogen crying at the windmill. Willy steps out of the shadows to tell her that she shouldn't be out so late. She accuses him of following her about but he says he worries about her and tells her that Cedric is not only stupid but dangerous. Imogen tells him to stay away from her and runs off. Willy sits with his head in his hands as Bronwyn comes in saying he looks like her brother. She says that he loves Imogen who loves Charles who loves Bronwyn. She kisses him, rather erotically, and offers to show him her breasts. She orders him to put his hands on her breasts and when he does she tells him to kiss her. Willy pulls away, but Bronwyn says she wants him to make love to her. When he kisses her she tells him to stop. Then she kisses him and he pushes her onto her back. He takes out a razor, saying that he had come out to the windmill to kill himself. She insists that he make love to her, but he slaps her face, telling her to stop, that she is playing with him like a cat with a mouse. Willy says that he is the bastard son of Bronwyn's father, Edward's half-brother, and Bronwyn's half-brother. He lifts Bronwyn's dress as Imogen enters, tells him to stop, then hits him on the head with a shovel. Realizing that Willy is dead, Bronwyn starts screaming as Cedric enters. He pulls Willy off Bronwyn, Imogen helps her up, and the three look down at Willy as we hear the owls and see the light fade out to end the act.

Act Two begins with the sounds of rain and a ticking clock. As lights come up on the parlor, Charles is quoting Tennyson whom Bronwyn, according to Imogen, "cannot abide." When Charles wonders where Willy is, Cedric suggests that he ran off. When Bronwyn starts speaking of Wooster sausages, Imogen says that it must be a recurrence of her malaria and takes her off stage. But Bronwyn rushes back, followed by Imogen who accuses her of pushing her into a closet. Bronwyn takes Charles out for a walk in the rain and, when Imogen says that Bronwyn is losing her mind, Cedric insists that they will be safer if nothing is said about Willy's fate. He will say nothing if Imogen lets him copulate with her whenever he wants. She is also to persuade Bronwyn to marry him.

The scene switches to Charles and Bronwyn, wet from the rain, in the gazebo. Bronwyn kisses him and they start removing each other's clothing. Imogen enters, Bronwyn runs off, and Charles asks Imogen why Bronwyn is losing her mind. Imogen says that Bronwyn is going to marry Cedric and she and Charles go to look for her. At the windmill, Bronwyn babbles of her mother hanging herself there, and Willy, dead, comes up behind her. Imogen enters but cannot see or hear Willy. Bronwyn accuses her of fornicating with Bronwyn's father, and Imogen admits it. Charles enters, also unable to see or hear Willy. Imogen says that she told Edward about his father; Charles says that Bronwyn could marry him rather than Cedric. Imogen explains that Cedric is blackmailing Bronwyn into marriage and forcing Imogen to be his mistress. If they do not agree, Cedric will tell the authorities that Imogen killed Willy. Charles leaves to talk with Cedric, Imogen cries, and Bronwyn and Willy look at her as the lights fade.

We hear birdsong and see Cedric and Charles in the woods, with guns, talking of Edward at college. Cedric says that Edward loved teen-aged whores, got one of them pregnant, and might have killed his own father. Charles tells Cedric he can't marry Bronwyn because she is not in her right mind. Charles then raises his gun and tells Cedric to say "cheese." We hear the sound of a gunshot simultaneous with a blackout.

With birdsong, lights come up on Imogen, Bronwyn, and Charles in the parlor, talking of Cedric's accidental death. Bronwyn thinks she hears children laughing and says she has been dreaming of unspeakable things. After she leaves, Charles says he thinks Bronwyn should marry him. He asks Imogen to return the watch he gave her when she was hypnotizing Bronwyn. She takes it from her bosom and stomps on it. Bronwyn returns and says she hears a whirring noise. She points to the sky and says she sees a Zeppelin. Imogen says something is falling, and the lights go out as we hear an air raid siren, a bomb falling, a huge explosion, more explosions, then sounds of troops marching, garbled speeches, machine guns, airplanes crashing, people screaming, animals shrieking, all building to a cacophony of "patriotic butchery and frenzied madness."

We hear owls and lights come up on a shadowy set. Bronwyn, bedraggled, says that she has escaped from Bedlam. Cedric, groaning, enters with a bloodstained flour sack over his head. Unable to see, he walks like the Frankenstein monster. After Cedric runs into the rusted automobile and falls to the ground, Willy appears from behind the gazebo and turns Cedric offstage. Willy says he can smell someone coming and Bronwyn hides behind the gazebo as Imogen, in black, leads on Charles in a military uniform and dark glasses. One arm is gone and he walks with a cane. Imogen says the estate is in ruins and that she lives in the potting shed. She tells Charles that his sight and hearing may improve over time and that she will take care of him. Willy says that Imogen is the beautiful one and loves Charles, but Charles is in love with the lunatic. Charles tells Imogen that Edward's suicide note said to burn everything, including his book. Charles says that Edward took him to a whorehouse where an old whore recognized Edward as the squire's son and said she was the mother of Imogen. After they exit, Bronwyn tells Willy that she shot her father in the crotch and threw a dead fox on him so the dogs would eat him alive. She climbs into the car and starts singing "Rule, Brittania" as Cedric stumbles on, moaning, and running into the gazebo. He falls, and Bronwyn says that "you" may now take her photograph. We hear a click and see a blink of lights. Then all lights go out and we hear owls in the darkness.

Chapter Two

Short(er) Plays

The unit set for *Appledorn* (1 man playing two parts, 4 women but parts may be doubled), a part of the Pendragon cycle, consists of a few platforms, some steps, furniture, and a round wooden table DR. The action takes place in Armitage from the early to the late 19th century. In darkness we hear French Annie singing "Au clair de la lune" as lights come up on Blossom Appledorn Wolf, 73, in 1883. Blossom, who becomes younger and then old again in the course of the play, tells us that Appledorn was the name of a "wonderful village" her family came from before they moved to Ohio, but all she can remember is looking down a very steep staircase and her father warning her about falling. She says that people called her simple-minded because of the fever that took her parents and that she was taken in as a five-year-old by French Annie to live in the Indian Caves out by Grim Lake. French Annie continues singing softly as Blossom says that her stepfather, Jonas Grey Wolf moved to the caves when he was old enough because he wasn't comfortable about the half of him that was white. When a trapper came by with Annie, she decided Jonas was the man she wanted and, after watching the trapper beat her, Jonas slit the trapper's throat and took Annie to the caves. Annie keeps singing softly in French as Blossom tells us she got along with their daughters but that the boy, John Paul, who was five years older than she was, wanted her.

She tells us that when she was sixteen she went to pick blackberries on Ghost Hill and was struck by lightning. We see a bright flash and then darkness and a huge thunderclap. She had a vision of Appledorn but then realized she was back in the cave. French Annie says she will not die but will live a long time and do wonderful things. When Blossom started throwing up in the morning and began showing, French Annie told her she was carrying a baby and so she married John Paul on whom she had taken pity once or twice, but she knew the child was not his but was created by the thunderbolt. Her narration is punctuated by Crow repeating the line, "Don't fall down the steps." John Paul didn't want to marry her and never touched her again.

She named her son James Jonas Wolf and when he grew up he married Cally Murphy and they had a son named John Arthur. Blossom's son was killed in the Battle of the Wilderness in 1864 and she grieved until she had a dream about the rain barrel. Crow tells her to look in the rain barrel and when she does she sees her son being shot from behind by a man in a blue coat. She says she was visiting her son's widow and the lights come up on Cally as T. H. Grim (played by the same actor who plays Crow) walks in. Blossom says she knew he was the man who killed her son.

Grim says that Cally's husband died in his arms, making him swear to take care of her. Blossom knows it was his face she saw in the rain barrel and that he shot his friend to get his wife. When Grim leaves, Cally tells Blossom that he asked her to marry him. Blossom tells Cally that she can't marry Grim because he killed her husband. She tells Cally that the crow that whispers in her head since she was struck by lightning told her to look in the rain barrel. Cally gets angry and tells Blossom to get out of her house and stay away, saying she should be locked up in a padded cell.

When Cally leaves, Blossom says that she didn't say anything and that Cally did not marry Grim. Grim approaches her and denies that he killed her son. He says she belongs in a mental institution. Blossom tells us that he gave up on Cally and married Mary Louise Frost whose father had property that Grim wanted. When the father said he would disinherit her if she married Grim, the father was found dead in a field with his neck broken. Cally then tells Blossom that she can see her grandson as long as she doesn't say anything about his father being shot in the back by Grim. Blossom says she agreed but kept close watch on Grim and when he started lusting after a cousin of Arthur's named Mona, she heard the crow whispering to her again to look in the rain barrel.

In the rain barrel Blossom saw Grim doing things in the woods to Mona and looking at his wife sleeping and knew he was going to kill her. Blossom then talks with Grim's wife, Mary Louise, warning her that her husband killed her father, her husband, probably his own parents, and plans to kill her. Mary Louise doesn't believe her and calls her a crazy old woman. Blossom tells Mary Louise to follow her husband to Witch Hollow under the sumac tree where she will find Mona. Mary Louise tells Blossom to get out and walks off. Blossom tells us that Mary Louise followed Grim to Witch Hollow and saw him with Mona.

We hear the sound of a ticking clock as Grim enters and Mary Louise appears with a large bowl of mashed potatoes containing her mother's secret ingredient, love. She puts gravy on the potatoes and agrees with Grim that she put rat poison in them. She sits and eats some potatoes and then, as the light fades on them, Grim begins eating. They remain in shadows as Blossom tells us they were found dead the next morning. She says the whispering stopped but then started again and we hear Crow warning her about falling and French Annie singing. Blossom says she thought she saw Grim following her and she went to the top of the staircase and felt a cold hand push hard on her back and she was falling. Crow and Annie repeat their refrain and Blossom says that she was a young girl again in Appledorn where everything smelled of apples. French Annie sings the last quatrain and the lights fade out.

Another part of the Pendragon cycle, *Andromeda Chained to Her Rock* is a dialogue between Ben Palestrina, 17, and Meredith Cherry, 31, his former babysitter. They are at Grim Lake in Armitage, Ohio, on a summer night in 1967. Meredith suggests that they go swimming, saying that she has seen him naked lots of times. She says that earlier in the day she saw a painting in one of her father's books of Andromeda chained naked to a rock in the fog, remembering making love in the ferns on a hillside. When Ben asks her how she can know what a mythological girl in a painting was thinking, Meredith says that in addition to being insane she is also telepathic. She says that she is Andromeda, waiting as a sacrifice to a sea monster that she pictures as the Creature from the Black Lagoon and reminds Ben that he asked her to marry him when he was five years old and that she said she would if he still wanted to when he was eighteen. Ben is leaving for college the next day and she thanks him for visiting her in the hospital, saying that she would have died without him. He says she is beautiful and that he will always love her. She asks him if he is a virgin and then if he wants to make love with her. It will be her going away present to him. He says she is incredibly attractive but he doesn't want to take advantage of her. She says he either desires her or he doesn't, and when he says he does want her, she tells him to give her "this," then go away and not look back. They kiss, "a long and tender kiss," then look at each other as the light fades and goes out.

The set for *Babylon* is a room "in an old white house" with a big desk, some chairs, and several doors. The five actors wear dark suits and are named Abe, Rummy, Karl, Georgy, and Dick. Rummy is sitting at the desk, rubber-stamping pieces of paper, as Abe enters saying he needs to see Georgy. Rummy offers to help but Abe says he has some concerns about the way things are going, that innocent women and children are being killed. Rummy says they never should have gone after Georgy's Dad and calls Sam a fucking psychopath. He tells Abe not to shit on the carpet and resumes stamping as Karl enters to say that Georgy is coming. Georgy shakes hands with Abe; Rummy tells Georgy that he is doing a terrific job; and Karl takes Georgy out of the room. Abe repeats his desire to talk in private with Georgy and Rummy uses the intercom to ask for Dick. Karl returns with a golf ball for Abe (a gift from Georgy) and Georgy comes back looking for a bathroom, saying that he hasn't seen Abe for a long time. Karl goes with Georgy so he won't get lost on the way to the bathroom. Dick enters wearing dark glasses and holding a cane. He sits where there isn't a chair and falls on his ass. Rummy moves a chair toward Dick as Dick tells Abe that he really isn't one of their group. Georgy comes in, lost again, but Karl takes him out for a meeting. Dick tells Abe that if he really wants to talk with Georgy he should sit next to him that evening at the theatre. Dick orders Rummy to give Abe his tickets. After Abe leaves, Dick tells Rummy that he is going to use Georgy's tickets and take care of the situation with Abe. Georgy returns, is told the meeting is over, and says he has been having nightmares. Dick tells him he should not go to the theatre. Georgy gives him his tickets and Karl comes in to take Georgy home. When Rummy tells Dick to enjoy the show, Dick responds, "Rummy, I am the show."

In *The Baltic Sea*, two old men, Kelso and Mott, are huddled in the dim glow of a small fire in a tunnel deep beneath the city. Kelso talks to Mott about the early tv show, *What's My Line?* Mott articulates a series of surreal images, and Kelso says "they" come up from under the ground like slugs after the rain, using strange passageways under the earth and deep under the Baltic Sea. Mott says the Baltic Sea is a gigantic hoax, perpetrated by the Lithuanians, and inhabited by talking fish. Kelso says he was forced into the sewers by the CIA, and Mott continues his description of bizarre events. Mott offers Kelso a drink from a bottle of the finest New Jersey wine. Kelso says that God told him to emit gas, and Mott says he met God under the roller coaster at Coney Island. Kelso says he knows things that could bring down the government and accuses Mott of being "one of them," telling him he will kill him with a can opener. But Kelso doesn't feel so well and asks what is wrong. Mott says he poisoned him and Kelso falls over dead.

Barbary Fox (3m, 3w), part of the Pendragon cycle, takes place during the last decades of the 19th century and the first decades of the 20th in Armitage, Pendragon County, Ohio. The unit set represents two houses and the yard between them created by a framework of a ruined gazebo and fragments of old houses with an old upright piano and bench DR, a bed DRC, and a round wooden table with chairs DL. There are two window frames UL and UR, a door frame L, an old sofa with a broken grandfather clock behind it C, an old cabinet with liquor LC, and an old lion-footed bathtub on a platform URC. The action moves back and forth in time and space continuously, and the actors enter and exit or remain in character on stage when not involved in a scene.

In darkness we hear the sound of whippoorwills and then, as lights come up, Magenta, wife of Silas Quiller, playing Faure's *Sicilienne* on a slightly out-of-tune piano. Barbary Fox is on the bed; Bert Astor, her husband, stands looking downstage from the UR window frame; Gretchen, Barbary's daughter, is on the sofa; Silas stands by the liquor cabinet; and Rem Astor, Barbary's uncle, is drinking at the table. As Rem, drunk, talks to Barbary at a time when she was a child, Barbary tells Gretchen about her life as a child in the house when her uncle would lock her in the fruit cellar to prevent her from going to the carnival. She says she sat on an old cot in the cellar and read from a trunk full of old books. Gretchen tells us that she married Clyde Quiller, her next door neighbor, although his younger brother Con was so handsome he gave her bad dreams. Margaret, sister of Clyde and Con, was Gretchen's best friend, and their father Silas was the best friend of Bert, Gretchen's father. When Silas asks Magenta why she keeps playing the piano, she asks him if he has been next door again. She wonders why Bert, their next-door neighbor, married "that wretched girl from the dump." As Magenta boasts of her heritage, Rem speaks again to Barbary as a child.

Gretchen tells us that her mother Barbary was haunted by the sound of whippoorwills and memories of being raised by her uncle Rem. Barbary and Rem speak of their reactions to birds and then speak to each other about why he locks her in the cellar. He tells her not to let people know how smart she is. We hear the sound of a grandfather clock ticking loudly and Magenta, who has moved to the sofa, tells us that when she was a little girl she would lie in bed and listen to the owls and the clock. Barbary says that when she was fourteen she hated men for the way they looked at her and talked about her behind her back. She hoped that one day somebody would take her to see the ocean where she would wash away her sins. Gretchen, in a sudden shift to a much later time, asks Magenta why she married Silas. Magenta tells her that she can't remember, that no sane person wants to be touched by any other person. Barbary tells us that she made "an arrangement" with Rem's two sons, Lemuel and Dobbs, to let her out of the cellar at night. Gretchen confesses that she takes small objects from stores and from people's houses and hides them in a box in her closet.

We hear crickets as the lights create a night effect and Rem asks Barbary if she wants to hear a bedtime story. She doesn't, but Rem tells her about a girl who sneaked out of her house at night and got eaten by pigs. When

Barbary tells Rem to leave her alone, Bert, at a later time, tells her that he can't leave her alone. He says he wants to marry her so that no one else will ever touch her. When Barbary refers to herself as the town slut, Bert says he doesn't "give a rat's ass." The scene ends as Rem, from another time and place, tells Barbary she doesn't know anything about love, and Magenta talks of "two damned fools" who tried to put up a lightning rod on the roof during a thunderstorm and got hit and killed by lightning.

Gretchen, sitting at the table and illustrating the family history, tells us about two houses, side by side, with eight people living in them. She married a Clyde who was not her brother, and her friend Margaret married the Clyde who was not her brother, and the women moved into each other's house. Gretchen says she is trapped in the house with her late husband's insane piano-playing mother and that her life is desperately stupid because she killed her own mother. Barbary, in a scene from the past, tells Gretchen that men can't be trusted. When Bert calls to Gretchen to come to him, she says she is taking a bath.

Bert and Silas, drinking, talk about Silas' desire for Barbary. Bert says Silas hasn't slept with her because of friendship; he tells Silas he has permission to sleep with Barbary as long as Bert can sleep with Magenta. Magenta tells Silas that she knows he wants Barbary. When Silas says that Bert has a crush on Magenta, she asks him why he built a house next door for Bert and gave him a job managing the cheese factory. She thinks Silas must have done something awful that Bert knows about. Rem then talks about repairing a broken old doll and Barbary tells us about going back to the deserted house where she grew up and going down into the cellar. She names some of the books she read there and tells Gretchen that her sister Eva ran off with a knife thrower from the carnival and their cousins Lemuel and Dobbs went after her and were never seen again.

Rem tells Barbary that her parents, Rem's brother and his wife Tootsie, died in a bizarre accident when the wagon Rem's brother was driving turned over in a rainstorm and crashed into a ravine. Gretchen tells Silas that she has seen him coming out of her house when her father Bert is not there. Silas tells her that his son Clyde has a crush on her. The action shifts to Rem telling Barbary that people look down on them because they live on Shite Creek by the dump and the fireworks factory and the chicken plucking plant. He says that the cellar is the center of God's brain. Rem then tells Bert that he cannot marry Barbary, that she is not for sale. He threatens Bert with a gun and tells Barbary she doesn't know what love is.

When Magenta asks what happened to Silas, Bert says he could forget about killing people, but Silas could not. Gretchen, from another time and place, says that she and Margaret look out their windows at each other, Margaret looking at the house where Gretchen is trapped with Margaret's mother, and Gretchen looking at the house where she killed her own mother.

Bert tells Barbary a story about giving Lemuel and Dobbs money to kill their father, Rem, and, from the past, Rem gives Barbary a jewelry box he says belonged to the mother. Barbary asks Silas what happened with Bert when the two of them were riding the rails and living in hobo jungles, and Silas tells her to take her daughter Gretchen and run away. He says she knows what Bert is capable of. Barbary tells Gretchen she knows what her father is doing to her and tells Bert that if he touches Gretchen again she will kill him.

Gretchen tells us she should have run away, but now she is trapped forever. Rem tells us he found Barbary holding her sister Eva after the wagon crashed and killed their parents. Gretchen says she found Barbary in the bathtub with her throat cut and the razor in her hand. Magenta wonders why two grown men (Silas and Bert) were putting up lightning rods during a thunderstorm. She says they were both fried like bacon. Barbary tells Magenta that she is not sleeping with Silas, and Magenta tells us that she went into the bathroom while Barbary was taking a bath and pushed her, causing her to fall and hit her head. Magenta then took the razor and cut Barbary's throat. Magenta plays "Sicilienne" again as the lights fade and go out. Playing stops. Whippoorwills in darkness.

In *Borneo*, Harry, a large man of 40 with a deep voice, and Rita, in her 30s, with beautiful long red hair, are sitting in bamboo chairs on a verandah at night. We hear occasional faint jungle bird noises and the sound of a film running through an old projector. Harry speaks of re-editing a film and Rita mentions that she has been learning about poisons, adding that perhaps "he" could be persuaded to walk on to the rotted wharf and fall through the boards, a nail piercing his carotid artery. Harry comments that that has been done before and says he is on the edge of an abyss. Rita says she is afraid to sleep. She says he sits in the dark watching the same scenes over and over. She thinks he should cut the nude scenes and tells him she didn't want to do them. As he speaks of editing the scene in which a jealous husband murders his wife, she tells him that all he cares about is the film, that he worships death. He tells her he is making a movie about a man who lives in Borneo with his beautiful wife but every take seems to have something wrong with it. He begins to wonder if he actually murdered his wife or if he only imagined it, like a scene in a script that was never shot or was left on the cutting room floor. Rita says that everything is devoured in Borneo and he says he is keeping in the nude scenes.

In *Creatrix*, two teen-age girls, Tiffany and Kimberly, in pajamas with their backs against the end of a bed, stare downstage into the eerie light of a tv set. We hear the tape they have been watching rewind as Tiffany says they have watched the movie one hundred and thirty-seven times. Kimberly says the movie makes her happier than anything in the world. Tiffany says that after you watch the movie so many times you feel as if you made it yourself. She says no one understands them and that the movie gives them the power to do unspeakable things to the people who order them around. The girls decide to become the girls in the movie and talk about fantasy lives, deciding that life would be simpler if their mothers were dead. They say they could put a brick in a stocking and beat Kimberly's mother over the head with it. Kimberly thinks this is a beautiful story, but Tiffany wants to do it "for real," to make their own movie. Kimberly thinks a person would need to believe "very much" to make such a movie. Tiffany puts Kimberly's hand on her heart and puts her hand on Kimberly's heart, asking her if she can feel the "great creatrix of the universe throbbing and seething and writhing beneath our flesh." Kimberly wonders where they can get a brick as the light fades and goes out.

The unit set for *Darkpool* (3m, 1w) includes an office with table and chairs, a bench in a rooftop garden, and the balcony of an apartment. Dutch, 37, and Mick, 29, overseas operatives of Darkpool, discuss their responsibility for killing people in a war zone. Mick thinks they will be punished but Dutch assures him they will be protected. Max, 53, introduces the men to Justine, 30, a lawyer with a specialty in public relations. Max tells the men they will be taken care of because working for Darkpool means they are part of God's family and have a special dispensation to take whatever measures become necessary. He says democracy is an illusion, and the military are cannon fodder. Darkpool is the muscle that multi-national corporations use to get and keep power. Max says that when Jesus comes again he is going to be "one of us." After Max walks off, Justine asks Dutch to leave so she can talk with Mick alone.

She invites Mick to dinner at her place as the lights fade and come up on Dutch and Max in the rooftop garden at night. Max says that the Christian community needs to be ready to take back America from the secular liberal conspiracy that's hijacked it. This great crusade will promote the sovereignty of Jesus Christ our Lord and Savior. Max says Dutch is in trouble because he didn't follow his orders to neutralize all the inhabitants of a certain house in a certain village. He warns Dutch about being too arrogant to follow instructions, and the scene shifts to Mick and Justine sitting at night on her balcony. Mick tells her that when he and Dutch were on their way to some little village, Dutch stopped and turned around and headed back, but they got lost and ended up in the middle of a traffic jam, hearing what sounded like hostile fire. He and Dutch started shooting, thinking there might be suicide bombers. Justine says she needs to edit his story to help a potential jury or the public in general to understand it in a way that doesn't shed negative light on him.

In the fourth scene, Mick enters as Dutch is eating breakfast. Dutch says that Justine's job is to make sure that Mick won't say anything that could hurt the company. Light fades on them and comes up on Justine and Max drinking coffee. Justine tells Max that she thinks Mick will be all right and Max warns her to be careful. The scene shifts back to the rooftop garden where Mick tells Justine that, because of a childhood injury, he thinks he hears bees. They talk about watching other people sleep, and Justine tells Mick he must play the character of an innocent man. Justine then talks with Dutch, telling him that she doesn't like him but her job is to help him. He asks her how long it has been since somebody really fucked her, and she slaps him very hard across the face. He grabs her by the neck and kisses her as Mick enters. Justine tells Dutch that if he ever does anything like that again she will shoot him. Mick says that he and Dutch shot real people, women and children and old people. Max enters and tells Mick that there are no innocent people, just degrees of guilt, and that they are not murderers but global stabilization facilitators. After Mick and Justine leave, Max tells Dutch that Mick doesn't know how to play the game and could have an accident. He also tells Dutch that Justine is his daughter and that the cleaner everything is, the closer one is to God. Dutch responds that to worship God is to worship chaos. Dutch suggests that Jesus wants zombies, and Max tells him about staring into a deep, dark pool of water and learning that God is the Devil. He changes the subject by asking Dutch how his daughter is doing in Princeton, pointing out that she would be in financial difficulty if Dutch got sent to prison. Max says he loves the rooftop garden, but it is so high up that someone might fall, or jump. Justine enters to say she can't find Mick, and Max sends Dutch up to the rooftop garden to find him, telling his daughter that everything will be taken care of.

Lights come up on the rooftop garden as Mick tells Dutch that he hopes he can take Justine away to a nice, quiet place where they could settle down and have a couple of kids. Mick says he shot those people because he was scared. Dutch tells him that they will go to prison if he tells the truth. Mick says he has to tell the truth and moves to look over the edge of the garden. Mick says it is a long way down. Mick says he thinks he hears bees, and the light fades and goes out.

Don Giovanni is a long one-act for four men and three women. On the upstage side of the upper platform of the unit set is a balcony reached by a trellis, the bottom of which can be seen through a central arch under the platform. Steps left and right lead to the upper platform. At the top of the SR steps is a door that opens into a bedroom; at the top of the SL steps is a window frame from which Don Giovanni can talk to Leporello in the street below. The lower level is the street and the inside of a house represented by a table and chairs left and a bench right. A trapdoor down center goes to the basement of the house and to Hell. There are escape stairs on the upper platform left and right.

We hear the opening notes of the overture to Mozart's *Don Giovanni* as lights come up and Leporello speaks to the audience about working for Don Giovanni who, he says, is going to hell for sleeping with so many women. Don Giovanni asks him if he has been talking to an invisible friend and says that they have to climb up the trellis to Donna Anna's bedroom. He says that his only sin is that he loves too much. Leporello warns him about Donna Anna's father, the Commendatore, but Don Giovanni puts on a mask and starts climbing the trellis. Complaining to the audience, Leporello follows and we hear the first bars of "La chi darem la mano" as lights come up on the bedroom. Don Giovanni and Leporello are hiding as Donna Anna and her maid Zerlina enter. Donna Anna complains that her father keeps her locked up tighter than an oyster and says that sometimes she prays that a handsome man in a mask will climb up on the balcony, hide behind the curtains, then leap out and make passionate love to her. Don Giovanni says her prayers have been answered, but Leporello warns them that Donna Anna's father has just returned. The Commendatore climbs the steps to the door and pounds on it because Zerlina has locked it. The women tell him they are naked; the father threatens to break open the door. Donna Anna kisses Don Giovanni as the father does break through the door, drawing his sword and chasing Don Giovanni around the room. When the father falls and drops his sword, Don Giovanni grabs it and the Commendatore, lunging toward him, is run through. He vows to come back from the grave and drag Don Giovanni to Hell. The lights fade as Don Giovanni and Leporello climb down the trellis, the Commendatore dies, and we hear "Or sai chi lo'onore."

On the street level, Don Giovanni tells a distraught Leporello that they have to leave. Don Giovanni climbs the steps, telling Leporello to hurry. Leporello tells the audience that he doesn't understand why women fall into bed with Don Giovanni and not with him. He concludes that life is a joke and death is the punch line. Donna Elvira enters and asks him where her husband, Don Giovanni, is. Leporello tells her that the man she thought was a priest was a horse doctor from Barcelona. Donna Elvira shakes Leporello like a rag doll, and he insists that Don Gionvanni is dead. But then Don Giovanni sticks his head out the upstairs window, yelling for Leporello. Donna Elvira runs up the steps and embraces Don Giovanni. Leporello runs up the steps and we hear the sound of an angry mob approaching as he drags Don Giovanni, with Donna Elvira hanging on, to the balcony. The mob sounds get louder as the light fades and we hear "Non mi dir."

In a prison created by light and shadows, we see Don Giovanni, Leporello, and an old man who introduces himself as Casanova. Casanova tells Leporello that men are unsuccessful with women because they do not fully appreciate them. Donna Elvira, having bribed the jailer, comes in and hits Casanova for propositioning her. He looks for his teeth as the others leave and we hear. "Viva la liberta."

The next scene occurs at night with thunder, lightning, and rain. A statue of the Commendatore has been set up in the arch of the cemetery tomb under the platform. Leporello tells Don Giovanni that they are in the Commendatore's tomb as Don Giovanni tries to explain to Leporello that he loves all the women he has encountered. Leporello thinks the statue has moved and Don Giovanni invites the statue to come to dinner with him and his daughter at the next full moon. Don Giovanni turns away and the statue speaks: "As you desire." Leporello screams and as he and Don Giovanni leave the statue slowly lifts an arm with a clenched fist, shouting: "KILL, KILL, KILL, KILLLLL, KILLLLLLLLLLLLL." The lights fade and we hear "Bisogna aver coraggio."

In moonlight, Don Giovanni and Leporello have climbed the trellis to the balcony and are sneaking into Donna Anna's bedroom when they are met by Zerlina who tells them that Donna Anna has been having dreadful nightmares. Don Giovanni finds Donna Anna sitting in a rocking chair, blaming herself for her father's death. Don Giovanni says her father had no right to imprison her, kisses her tenderly, and persuades her to eat some soup. We hear "A cener teco m'invitasti" as the lights fade.

In moonlight we see Donna Elvira climbing up the trellis with a knife and hiding behind the curtains as Leporello enters telling Zerlina that he believes Don Giovanni is a changed man because he is taking care of Donna Anna without having sex with her. Rejecting Leporello's offer of marriage, Zerlina warns him that Donna Anna may remember that Don Giovanni killed her father. Noticing the full moon, Leporello tells Zerlina that the statue of the Commendatore is coming to dinner and will drag Don Giovanni down to Hell. Entering below, Don Giovanni refuses to leave because for the first time in his life he is truly in love. Donna Anna enters with a box of wooden puppets she has carved. Donna Elvira looks down on them from the balcony, noticing how tender Don Giovanni is with Donna Anna but still resolved to kill him. She descends the steps, telling Donna Anna that she is Don Giovanni's wife, twice ruined and abandoned by him. We hear the sound of three hard knocks and Zerlina says that someone is at the back door. Three louder knocks prompt Leporello to urge Don Giovanni to run away. Don Giovanni admits to Donna Anna that he killed her father by accident. He says he is sorry and loves her. Knocking continues as Zerlina goes through the upstage arch and Leporello gets down on the floor trying to locate the trap door. Zerlina screams and runs in saying that the statue is walking. The statue appears as Leporello opens the trap door. Don Giovanni asks forgiveness of the statue and they shake hands, but the statue continues holding Don Giovanni's hand as they descend the steps of the trap where a red glow is shining up. Don Giovanni grabs Leporello and pulls him down the steps as we hear groans of pain and horror mixed with distorted music from the last scene of Mozart's opera. Zerlina slams the trap door shut and drags Donna Elvira away from it. Donna Anna opens the trap saying that there's nothing left but ashes and a little pile of bones. All three women look into the trap. When Donna Elvira asks what they are going to do, Donna Anna says that they can have a puppet show with the naked puppets singing opera. Light fades on them and we hear the last measures of the opera.

Another two-character play from the Pendragon cycle, *Draw a Face, Win a Pig*, takes place in the law office of Jacob Armitage, 49, as Mary Casey, 24, accuses her mother of stealing and eating the pig she won at the county fair for drawing the best picture of George Washington. She wants to sue her mother and father and everyone who ate some of her pig and says she will pay Jacob by allowing him to take certain liberties with her. She says she has seen him looking at her with lust in his eyes and knows he visits a house of prostitution. She says she is a virgin but will allow him to take certain negotiated liberties with her in the name of justice because her pig was like a child to her. She says her father has a barn full of stacked up pianos and that Jacob's father drank himself to death so he knows what it is like to be trapped. Since Jacob will be disbarred if he accepts sexual favors from a woman, she says she will accept his proposal of marriage. He admits he wants to sleep with her and asks, if he marries her, she will forget about the pig. She says she will take that as a yes.

Drury Lane concerns two characters from the Pendragon cycle, James Rumpley, 40, and Jane Armitage, early 20s, on the stage of Garrick's Drury Lane Theatre in the mid-eighteenth century. Jane says she is tired of rehearsing and James says they must get it right or Garrick will dismiss them. He says that she asked for Garrick's help and wonders what she gave him in return. She says, "Nothing," and he grabs her and shouts, "WHAT DID YOU GIVE HIM IN RETURN?" After a slight pause he lets her go and asks if "that" was too much. She says it's always been too much because James has always been a victim of passions beyond his control. She says that Garrick might have saved him, that their child needed his help but that James preferred to turn thief because of pride, drink, and low company. She shouts that he has sacrificed his wife and child to his stupid, self-destructive pride. He agrees that what she says might be the truth but that it sounds too much like a play. When Jane says that the son is in America, James says that he doesn't like the scene and wants to do something else. She says they cannot rewrite the scene; they can only play it. James wants to do the seduction scene and warns Jane of the dangers of a life in the theatre. He kisses her and says they must not do the scene of his deflowering her. Jane says they have begun and might as well finish it. She wants James to deflower her again. He remembers that she said that she wanted to haunt the theatre when she died. He says all theatres are haunted and that "this is a play." He says he was a carnival boy who became an actor and she was an innocent country girl and one night they made love on "this" stage. She got pregnant and he drank what money they had. He hated her when she asked Garrick for help, and he became a thief. He was caught and hanged as she watched with their son. Then she died and the boy went to America and they keep rehearsing the play of their lives again and again, forever. Jane says that she wanted to haunt the theatre when she died and he tells her that she is. She thinks it is a beautiful story and that they might make a play of it. James says, "We might. We have. We will." She thinks their son will be an actor and that she will perhaps forgive James.

There are three characters in *Emotion Memory*—Chekhov, Stanislavsky, and Lyka. The simple unit set has a few pieces of furniture and represents four places: Chekhov's estate at Melikovo, a room in Moscow, the Paradise Theatre in Moscow, and Chekhov's home in Yalta. The time of the action is from 1892 to 1904. We hear Beethoven's "Moonlight Sonata" being played on an old piano as the lights come up on Chekhov and Lyka. It is evening; we see fireflies and hear crickets as the music ends. Lyka tells Chekhov that he is good company but that he is lonely and unhappy. Chekhov tells her of an experience he had with a young peasant girl when he was a young man in Moscow. Lyka thinks the story is sad, but Chekhov insists it is funny. She says that she never knows where she is with him and asks what he means when he says he loves her. She tells him she has been spending time with Potapenko, a married man, and wants to give herself to someone who wants her. Chekhov thinks she should have what she wants and, as she leaves, remarks that the fireflies flash their lights in a complex mating ritual. "I hope they're better at it than you are," Lyka says, leaving as the lights fade.

The second scene takes place in a room in Moscow early in the morning after the first (and disastrous) performance of *The Seagull*. Lyka is sitting in a chair as Chekhov comes in after walking for hours in the snow. He says the theatre is "a monstrous obscenity," the actors "totally incompetent," the audience "moronic," and the critics "cannibalistic orangutans." He wants her to shoot him if he is ever stupid enough to write another play. She tells him that at least the terrible production has brought out his true feelings, deep emotions that he always tries to hide. She says Potapenko's desertion and the death of her child and her suicide attempt were connected to deep emotions, that at least she is honest about what she feels. Chekhov says he is sorry for her suffering and Potapenko is a swine, but he is not going to wear his heart on his sleeve to be destroyed over and over. She says the play is beautiful and that it is about her, the girl who loves the cynical writer who abandons her. She tells him that the play was an act of love and that she is proud of his "amazing gift."

Three years later, at the Paradise Theatre in Moscow, Chekhov and Stanislavsky discuss the latter's production of *The Seagull*, an artistic triumph to everyone but the author. Stanislavsky tries to convince Chekhov that he wants to spend the rest of his life living inside his plays, that it's "the most important thing I could possibly be doing." Chekhov says that even when the play is done right it is still a betrayal of "a poor, lost girl who was my friend and who loved me." "Well," Stanislavsky says, "life is made of betrayal. Art holds up the mirror. Love makes us do it. It's completely insane. Let's do it again."

The last scene takes place at night, with fireflies, at Chekhov's home in Yalta in 1904. Lyka has been drinking and Chekhov tells her that his wife, Olga, makes him very happy. Lyka tells him that he was just using her, the way all writers use people, that his words have infected her brain, that all she wants to do is drink until she can sleep. She says that everybody is dying and that we go to the theatre while we wait. She asks Chekhov if fireflies love, and when he says he doesn't know anything about love she suggests they sit and watch the fireflies "for a little while longer." They watch as the lights fade and go out.

In *Exposition*, two characters from the Victorian period, Haggard and Leaf (whom we have met in earlier Nigro plays), begin conversing as if they were starting a play, but each character knows what the other is going to say, repeating the phrase, "As you well know." They have been providing the exposition for plays since the beginning of time. But when Leaf asks to be reminded of the matter of the dead sheep, Haggard asks, "What sheep?" Leaf asks if they are lost and should start over. The phone on the desk rings and

Leaf eventually picks it up, handing it to Haggard, saying it is for him. Haggard is dubious, but Leaf says it is in the script. Haggard talks into the phone and hangs up saying it was a wrong number. Leaf says that Haggard was having a conversation on the phone and asks if the caller was not General Beauregard telling them about the destruction of his plantation by boll weevils and the imminent arrival of his beautiful and mad daughter Ermengarde who may or may not have murdered her lover, the Satrap of Bangalore. Haggard says it was not General Beauregard but each time the phone rings Leaf insists it is. Haggard tells Leaf that a decision has been made to cut the entire exposition scene, starting the play in the middle. Leaf thinks that is insane, but Haggard tells him that the scene is over and he is leaving. Shaking Leaf's hand, he walks off. Leaf says he can't be left alone, that starting with a monologue is absolute poison. But he tries anyway, talking to a Haggard who is not there, imagining that the phone is ringing, answering it and telling General Beauregard that a decision has been made to cut the exposition. He speaks into the phone, saying that he will have to call back, that the play is apparently starting. "As you well know." Darkness.

In *A Fellow of Infinite Jest* (2m), Will Kempe enters a London tavern late at night in 1599 as Shakespeare sits writing at a table. Kempe complains about Hamlet's advice to the players and learns that Falstaff, a part he enjoyed playing, is not in Henry the Fifth, but, like Yorick, dead. Shakespeare says there will be no more jigs, no more improvisation, from now on they're sticking to the script. Kempe says the script is just a road map, that he is an entertainer, a comedian. He says that he made it possible for Shakespeare to work in theatre. Shakespeare says he is grateful but cannot allow Kempe to ruin his scripts with his old, irrelevant slapstick routines that have nothing to do with the play. Kempe rages that the theatre is not a building or words but flesh and blood and gonads. He says he will be remembered in a hundred years and that Shakespeare is nothing. He storms out but comes back in, and Shakespeare offers to put Falstaff into Henry the Fifth as long as Kempe says the lines as written. Kempe refuses and Shakespeare says that Falstaff is dead. Kempe says he will dance a jig on the smoking ruins of the theatre. He leaves, Shakespeare writes, and the lights go out.

A short play for a man and a woman, *Film Noir* is set in a director's office furnished with a desk, a chair, a smaller chair, and a leather couch. The year is 1939. The director, Hatch, remains seated behind his desk throughout and the couch is necessary even though it is not used. Jane, the actress, in response to Hatch's questions, says that she had a wonderful honeymoon in Cornwall. Hatch says he no longer has sexual relations with his wife because she is afraid he will crush her since he is grotesquely fat. Hatch says that Cornwall, the land of demons, would be a "delightful" place to murder his wife, causing her to fall off a cliff. He says he picked Jane for the role because of her innocence. He says he has a fantasy about living with Jane in a house in Cornwall, joining in a "deep and genuine sensual communion." Jane wants to leave but he orders her to stay. He tells her that the thought of making love with him disgusts and horrifies her. Jane erupts in a tirade, berating him for abusing his position, calling him a fat, disgusting pig. Hatch replies, "Excellent." He says he wants her to remember exactly how she felt when she was shrieking at him and to recreate it in the scene they are shooting tomorrow. Jane says she can recreate what she felt but that what he did was horrible. He says it worked and that's what matters in life and art. She leaves and Hatch bangs his head three times on the desk, calms himself, and says that he must really get a place in Cornwall.

Written in the free-verse form Nigro uses to indicate rhythm to the actors, *Fundevogel* (1m, 1w) opens with birdsong and Fundevogel sitting in a chair looking out a window. Near him is another chair with a large rag doll in it. Lisa enters and asks why Fundevogel is sad and lonely when she is there and will always be there. She talks as if Fundevogel is a bird that her father found in the forest and brought home. She wonders if Fundevogel is afraid that the cook will cut off his head and cook him in boiling water. She tells him to be happy because she and he will run away and, when chased by the cook's three servants, will metamorphose into a rose tree. The servants will be beaten by the cook who will tell them that they should have broken the tree in half and brought back the rose. When they look for them again, he will turn into a chapel and she into a chandelier. Then the cook will come looking for them and this time Fundevogel will become a pond and Lisa a duck. When the cook tries to drink the water in the pond, Lisa will grab her by the neck with her duck's beak and drown her. Lisa grabs the rag doll with her teeth, shaking it, then throwing it down and strangling it. When Fundevogel pulls her away from the doll and holds her tenderly she asks if he is sad because she is insane. He says, "Yes." She picks up the doll, puts it back in the chair, and sits where Fundevogel had been sitting. We hear birdsong again as Fundevogel starts off but stops, turns to Lisa, and asks her why she is sad, saying that he will never leave her.

Further Adventures of Tom and Huck is set in the living room of Tom's brownstone townhouse in New York City in 1876. Tom, very well-dressed, tells a shabbily-dressed Huck how glad he is to see him. Tom and Becky are married, have a cook, a nanny, a maid, and "an English coachman manservant flunky," and Becky drinks a lot. Huck asks for a drink and Tom gives him some Scotch. Huck tries to drink it but chokes and spits, saying that the liquor tastes like embalming fluid. Tom says he made a lot of money during the war. Huck was shot in the head, held as a prisoner, and has bad dreams. Tom tries to get Huck to remember a balloon ride to Europe they took years earlier but Huck denies that there ever was a balloon. Becky enters in a bathrobe and thinks Huck is a bum. Tom says he has to go to the sausage factory to check on his "simple-minded half-brother Sid." When Huck says he came to New York to kill Tom, Becky offers to pay him. She says Tom is a monster, a liar, and a cheat, obsessed with money. As Huck vacillates, Becky offers herself, twice. if Huck kills Tom slowly. She tries to get Huck's pants off and they fall onto the sofa as Tom enters. Huck admits he came to New York to kill Tom because Tom talked him into enlisting in the Confederate Army and then deserted the first time they heard enemy fire, leaving Huck to be wounded and put in a prison camp while Tom went north and got rich. Tom says that war is a great place to do business and that it's the American way. Huck says that his best friend Jim is dead and, after Becky passes out on the sofa, tells Tom that Jim was killed by a gun that exploded in his face, a gun probably supplied by Tom. Tom says it was just "good old American business," but Huck sits on the sofa and cries. Tom asks him if he remembers when they buried a marble in the hope of digging it up again to recover anything they had lost. He says that the spell didn't work, but that he learned that superstition and religion were bullshit, although he still has the notion that somewhere, perhaps in an attic, is everything he has ever lost. He says that what he misses most is going fishing with Huck. He wishes his kids were more like Huck and says they are more like Sid. Becky lifts her head to say they are Sid's kids, not Tom's. Furious, Tom shakes her and starts strangling her, but Huck pulls him off and he and Tom fall onto the floor. Tom says that the country is all about money and that his life isn't worth "a mouthful of ashes." Becky comes back with a large carving knife and chases Tom around the sofa, slashing at him. Huck tries to intervene; Becky trips and plunges the knife in Huck's chest, killing him. Tom assures Becky that no one is going to know what happened, that Huck is a stranger, a nobody, and they're going to roll him up in a rug and run him through the sausage machine. The lights fade as Becky sits beside Tom, who has Huck's head in his lap, crying as he says that he and Huck had some exciting adventures in that balloon, some good times.

In *Funhouse* (2m, 2w) we hear in darkness the sound of a train whistle and the train coming to a stop as lights come up on "a wilderness of funhouse mirrors," with tables and chairs as if parts of a rather nice house had been blended with a small restaurant and the ruins of a funhouse. Julie tells Trista as they sit at a table C that she must have dozed off on a train ride from Long Island into the city and woke up when the train stopped. People were saying that a girl had fallen between the cars and onto the track. She walked away from the crowd toward what looked like a derelict carnival with a funhouse. Standing, looking downstage, seeing the funhouse around her, she says she had an eerie half memory of her father taking her to a labyrinth of funhouse mirrors that smelled of damp old wood, cherry drink, and popcorn. Roman says a 16th century Kabbalist described the ten Sephiroth reflecting light back and forth like a house of mirrors, and Paul moves to stand behind Julie as she describes seeing a girl in the mirror that she could almost remember being in another life. She realizes that a man is standing just behind her, but she cannot see his reflection. Paul says a section of the mirror is missing and that is why he has no reflection. We hear the train whistle and Julie says she needs to go but Paul says they will get something to eat and wait for the next train. Julie says they found a quiet restaurant and she woke up naked in a bed in a little motel.

When Trista reminds her she's getting married in two weeks, Julie says she knew she had made a mistake, wrote a short note begging the man never to try to contact her, walked to the station and caught the next rain home. She did not tell her fiancée Roman because her mother told her that, with men, the best course of action is to behave as if nothing has happened. Besides, Roman's head is full of "quantum philosophical bric-a-brac." She and Trista agree that Roman is not "normal," and Roman speaks of places in a nut garden that might be portals to other dimensions, to interpenetrating realities. He says some people might be able to enter those portals and see a multiplicity of universes which have always been around us.

Julie says that when she got back to the house she saw Roman and Paul, the man she had slept with, in the library. Roman introduces Paul as a squash-playing Princeton classmate, and Trista wonders how Julie could leave while the man she slept with was taking a shower, go right home, and find him talking with her fiancée. Julie says she knows it doesn't make any sense and asks Trista to unbutton her blouse to attract Roman so that she can talk alone with Paul. Roman has been talking to Paul about the possibility that in parallel universes fictional characters are real. When Trista distracts him, Julie asks Paul to stay away from Roman, saying that what happened between them was an aberration and meant nothing. Paul asks her what she is talking about and moves away to have a drink with Trista. Questioning Roman, Julie learns that at Princeton he slept with Paul's fiancée. Julie tells Trista to talk with Roman and accuses Paul of sleeping with her to get revenge on Roman for sleeping with his fiancée. Paul says he doesn't know what she is talking about and Roman and Trista join them. Roman says that a funhouse is "an apt metaphorical representation of the multiverse," finite from the outside but infinite inside, an exact mirror reversal of the infinity of infinities where all possible worlds exist. He argues that the fictional world and characters of *Great Expectations* must exist and that, paradoxically, to tell a lie is to make it true, "in some part of the funhouse."

Julie tells Roman that she slept with Paul; Roman asks Paul; he denies it. Roman says that physically she could not have slept with Paul because he was at his house all day and never out of Roman's sight except to urinate. Roman says that memory is unreliable and that imagining and remembering are the same thing. He says that since fictional characters exist, God, in whom he does not believer, exists as much as Hamlet or Krazy Kat. Trista says there is a newspaper article about a girl who fell between the cars of a train. She says the picture of the girl looks exactly like Julie. Julie says she has to get back to the funhouse and figure this thing out. Roman says she can't go back to the funhouse because "this" is the funhouse. We hear eerie calliope music as the lights fade out.

Set in China a long time ago, *The Gatekeeper* tells the story of Lao Tzu, an old man, knocking on a gate at the edge of the civilized world. The Gatekeeper says he must pay a fee and when Lao Tzu says he has no money, the Gatekeeper says that nobody has ever wanted to go out the gate into barbarism and chaos. Lao Tzu identifies himself and the Gatekeeper invites him into his lodge to warm himself by the fire and have something to drink. The Gatekeeper says he remembers hearing Lao Tzu speak many years earlier. Lao Tzu says he want to go out the gate because he wants to die in a place where there is nothing. The Gatekeeper pours more wine in Lao Tzu's cup and says that he had a dream in which he refused to let Lao Tzu through the gate until he wrote down his wisdom. That, he says, is the fee. Lao Tzu says his writing will be misconstrued and turned into dogma over which people will kill each other. The Gatekeeper says that his teachings make him happy and his words and images are beautiful, but Lao Tzu insists that there is nothing to be gained from writing, nothing to be gained from anything. The Gatekeeper gets pen and ink and tells Lao Tzu he can go out the gate if he writes down his wisdom. Lao Tzu refuses and the Gatekeeper pulls out a trumpet and blows it into Lao Tzu's ear five times, but Lao Tzu refuses to write down his wisdom. They struggle over the trumpet and the Gatekeeper starts whacking Lao Tzu over the head with it until Lao Tzu collapses, dead. The Gatekeeper says he will write down what he remembers of what Lao Tzu said. He continues to write as the lights fade and we hear the sound of wind in the darkness.

In another Pendragon-related play, *Gazebo,* two friends, Margaret and Gretchen, with Margaret's younger brother Con, carry on conversations that took place between 1912 when the women were seventeen and 1938 when they are forty-three, but much of the play occurs in 1928 when the women were thirty-three and Con was twenty-seven. Nigro specifies that the actor playing Con should be no older than that and the women should be in their early thirties.

In darkness we hear a cello version of Faure's "Sicilienne," rain falling, and a distant storm. As in other Nigro scripts, characters sometimes talk to themselves, remembering images of past events, sometimes to each other, and sometimes to the audience. Gretchen begins the dialogue by speaking of storms, of being unable to sleep, of voices whispering in the gazebo, of something leering at her through rotten trelliswork, of "his hands." Margaret matter-of-factly tells the audience that Gretchen has always been her best friend, that they have lived next to each other all of their lives and married each other's brothers. Gretchen speaks of headlights coming toward her in the rain, and Margaret says that Gretchen saved her from drowning at Grim Lake. Con speaks of driving in the rain with Violet and Mary and seeing someone by the side of the road. Margaret says that three people died in the crash.

Gretchen tells us that Margaret had two brothers, Con, and the one she married. Margaret says that three witnesses swore there as a fourth person in the car before it crashed. Con and Gretchen begin talking about the voices Con hears whispering and which Gretchen can't hear because, according to Con, she closes up and never listens. Margaret says that all the girls always loved Con. Gretchen tells Con to stop looking at her, that she doesn't like it, and as they talk Margaret interjects reminiscences of giving Con baths when he was small and of how he likes to fix clocks.

She and Con then talk of clocks and time until Gretchen speaks again of the headlights. She tells Con that she has seen him at the lake with Glynis and Jason. Margaret asks about her mother who lives with Gretchen and suggests that she and Gretchen could simply change houses, a suggestion that Gretchen rejects. Con wonders who his father might have been and tells Gretchen that their fathers knew each other out west, that his dad came back with money and married the Potdorf girl. Then Gretchen's dad showed up, dirt poor, was given a job as foreman of the cheese factory, and lived in the house next door that Con's father built for him. Con says their parents had secrets and offers to share a secret with Gretchen, but she says she doesn't have any secrets. He asks her why she married his brother, tells her she is beautiful, and asks what she saw at the lake when she spied on them. She says she saw three naked people and adds that she hates the water.

Margaret speaks of her husband Clyde who disappeared with Gretchen's husband on a trip to Great Slave Lake. She says Gretchen's brother Clyde and Jason Cornish and Jimmy Casey went to war but Con didn't go because he had a bad heart. Gretchen says that Harry MacBeth arranged to have Con marry his daughter Glynis who loved Jason. She tells Con that he compulsively betrays people and Con says she wouldn't let her husband touch her. As Margaret remembers practicing on the cello, Con reminds Gretchen that she used to babysit him. Margaret remarks that something we believe we hate turns out, after a time, to be something we absolutely cannot do without.

Gretchen mentions the headlights again and Con, now the driver of the car, tells her to get in. Gretchen remembers blood on her dress, between her legs, something crawling out of her in the rain. Con, sitting next to Gretchen on the gazebo steps, says that she taught him more than Chinese Checkers. Margaret remembers the two fathers going up on the roof in a thunderstorm and being struck by lightning as they held on to a lightning rod they were installing.

Gretchen speaks of finding her mother in red water in the bath and remembers seeing her brother kiss Margaret in the gazebo and being filled with fury and later pushing Margaret into the lake where she hit her head on a rock. Gretchen dove in and pulled Margaret out and revived her. She says Margaret didn't remember what had happened but was never the same after her head injury, although her cello playing improved remarkably. Con and Gretchen then speak lines from the time of the car accident when Con pulled over to pick up Gretchen (apparently pregnant with his child). Gretchen was furious with Con and clawed his hands off the wheel of the car. Margaret speaks of a dream she has of driving late at night in a rainstorm and swerving to avoid two red eyes in the dark and then to avoid the oncoming car which spun round and crashed. She sees the two girls, Violet and May Pelly, and her brother Con, dead. She says when she can't sleep she goes out to the ruined gazebo and plays the cello. Con kisses Gretchen "very tenderly" and Margaret begins to play Faure's "Sicilienne" as the lights fade and go out.

A train at night and a Mexican cantina are represented by a unit set in *Ghostland,* a play for four men. In the darkness we hear "Cielito Lindo" played rather eerily by a mariachi band until the music is overcome by the rhythmic clattering of a train, then the scream of the train whistle as lights come up on Ambrose Bierce, 71, sitting in a SR train seat opposite Dr. Hern. (The actor who plays Hern also plays Mark Twain and William Randolph Hearst; another actor plays H. L. Mencken and Jack London; and a fourth actor plays Pancho Villa.) Hern asks Bierce if he is familiar with non-Euclidean geometry or of a space in which it would be possible to turn a rubber ball inside out "without a solution of its continuity." Bierce responds humorously to Hern's description of wormholes and insists the train is heading south. Hern opens the window and leans out to show Bierce the position of the stars and moon as evidence for the northerly direction of the train. Bierce puts his foot on Hern's butt and pushes him screaming out the window. Mencken appears with a large black satchel which, he says, contains the cremated remains of the critic, Pollard. Bierce pulls a long bone out of the satchel, then a ball of string, and then a skull. Mencken recognizes Bierce and tells him he admires his writing. Bierce describes two short scenarios in which people inexplicably disappear into Ghostland, the faery realm of Celtic mythology that is parallel to our own. Mencken says it sounds like malarkey to him and Bierce invites him to take a look out the window. Mencken opens the window, leans out and, like Hern, is kicked screaming from the train. Bierce picks up the satchel as we hear a loud train whistle and the train jolts, throwing Bierce backward as the lights go out. We hear brakes screeching, gunshots, horses, women shrieking, and then the mariachi band playing.

When the lights come up we see Bierce face down under a table in the cantina, his arms around the satchel. Villa sits at the table, drinking, telling Bierce that the train was liberated by the glorious forces of the revolution. Gunfire rips through the cantina and Villa takes out his gun and goes off. Jack London dives under the table with Bierce. They recognize each other and Bierce tells London that his writing stinks and that nothing written in America is worth a bucket of slop. He says Stephen Crane is a "shameless hack," Theodore Dreiser "boring and incompetent," and Henry James "an incomprehensible old woman." London says that Bierce told a woman that he had a suitcase full of documents that would put Hearst in jail for a hundred years. London says he has been sent by Hearst to retrieve the suitcase. He doesn't believe Bierce when he says the satchel is full of bones. We hear wind blowing and the beating of a heart that increases in volume as the stage darkens and pulses with red light, then the piercing scream of a train whistle as the lights go to black and the heartbeat resolves into the clattering of the train.

Lights come up on Bierce in the train sitting opposite Mark Twain. Bierce, saying it is 1913 and Twain died in 1910, rips off Twain's mustache and wig to reveal Hearst. When Hearst tries to grab the satchel, Bierce pulls the emergency cord and tries to climb out the window, saying they have arrived at Owl Creek Bridge. Hearst yanks the satchel away and Bierce falls screaming. We hear a loud splash and Hearst pulls a ball of string, a rubber ball, and a skull from the satchel. As he sticks his head out the window to yell at Bierce, the train lurches forward, and Hearst falls screaming out the window. We hear a loud splash, the sound of the train moving, the mariachi band, and as the lights fade the sound of the train moving farther away, a distant train whistle, and then the hooting of an owl in the darkness.

In *Goat*, a short one-act for a man and a woman, we hear in the darkness the sounds of subway trains passing above and see a flickering fire in front of a man sitting, warming his hands. Lil, with a flashlight, asks the man if his name is Goat. He tells her to go away, but she says she needs him to do something for her. He says there are snakes everywhere, that he kills and eats them and makes boots out of their skins. He asks her why she has come to this lost place and tells her that he is here because he was cast out. Lil says that Goat knows her husband and his brother and their father because the father is also Goat's father. She says things were fine until the second son came along and Goat was replaced in his father's affections and pushed out. The third son was Adam, her husband, the moron. Goat says he dreams of falling into the abyss, and Lil says she dreams about the garden and wants Goat to help her get back at the father by tricking Adam's new wife into breaking the rules and begin a "relentless chain reaction." She says Goat is the only one who can make the father pay for casting them out. He can wear his snakeskin boots, she says, and we hear the sound of "something violent and terrible going by" as the light fades out.

A long play for two women, *Gorgons* uses very short blackouts to separate scenes as in a movie. The simple unit set contains a sofa, a bed, a makeup table with mirrors, a staircase, a few chairs, and a table. Action is continuous and music plays during the blackouts. Ruth and Mildred are actresses who have been in the movie business for a long time. Ruth visits Mildred backstage after a stage performance to offer her a script that Ruth thinks would make a good movie, but she needs Mildred to play opposite her. The women insult each other and agree that they have never been friends, but Mildred says she will read the script that Ruth thinks will put them both "back on top" again. Ruth says that Mildred will play the sister who is the "washed up, psychotic bitch," that the sisters live in an old Gothic mansion, were once a famous tap-dancing act called Enid and Bunny, and that they both loved a handsome, tap-dancing comedian named Bob. When Ruth thinks she sees a rat, Mildred walks over and steps viciously on it. We hear the rat's squeal, and, after a blackout, "rather harrowing Hitchcockian thriller music."

The music ends as the lights come up on Mildred (Bunny) at the top of the Gothic mansion staircase in a fright wig and housecoat. She wonders where Bob is, and Ruth (Enid) comes on in a wheelchair to tell her that Bob sent her a present, in a box in shadows at the top of the stairs. Mildred/Bunny opens the box and discovers Bob's head which she throws down the stairs. Ruth/ Enid asks Nigel, the director of the movie, if they can shoot the scene again because the head didn't bounce the way she wanted. She throws the head back to Mildred/Bunny who reprises the scene, throwing the head more forcefully. But Ruth/Enid is not satisfied and throws the head back up to Mildred/Bunny. Tired, complaining of sore feet, Mildred wants to leave but Ruth persuades her to stay and have a turkey sandwich that she made. The women talk of their unsuccessful relationships with men and their absent children, then resume their work on the scene as the lights go to black and we hear "ominous, harrowing music."

In an eerie moonlight effect in the Gothic mansion, Ruth/Enid wheels on her chair, asking for Bunny. Mildred/Bunny enters, dragging an ax, telling Ruth/Enid that if she is afraid she can get up and run away. Ruth/Enid insists she cannot walk and screams loudly as Mildred/Bunny gets close to her with the upraised ax. The scream is too loud for Mildred, who breaks character and asks Nigel if they can take a break. The women insult each other's acting ability, appearance, and sexual behavior. Mildred thinks that Ruth hates her because Mildred slept with French, one of Ruth's husbands whom she barely remembers. Mildred suggests that they do their work like "the old war-horses" they are and be done with it. She asks that in the baked rat scene Ruth/Enid remember that Mildred has a herniated disk and will need help getting Ruth/Enid out of the bed. We hear ominous music in the blackout.

When lights come up we see Ruth/Enid in the bed, the wheel chair just out of her reach. Mildred/Bunny comes on with a dinner tray with a covered dish on it. Ruth/Enid screams when she lifts the cover and sees a baked rat. Ruth/Enid says she needs to make a phone call and asks for help getting into her wheelchair. As Mildred/Bunny tries to move her, Ruth/Enid makes her body a dead weight and Mildred screams and falls to the floor with Ruth on top of her. Mildred tells Nigel to call an ambulance and we hear the siren in the blackout.

Lights come up on Mildred in bed. Ruth enters with a box of chocolates, apologizing, hoping they can finish the movie. They decide that what they both love is the work, although Mildred prefers the theatre to movies. They start trading insults again but realize they need each other. Ruth says that she likes sex, and Mildred says that sex is horrible. Ruth agrees, but then the insults continue. Ruth says she was born into a large, poor, immigrant family and was unloved. Mildred shares the information that she inherited a Puritan-ical streak from her New England family who disowned her when she said she wanted to be an actress. Ruth helps Mildred out of bed toward the bathroom and, left alone in the light, carries on a conversation with Mildred in the darkness. Ruth regrets the fact that her children loathe her and Mildred says she can't talk to her daughter without hearing her own mother's voice squawking. Ruth asks Mildred to help her finish the movie and we hear the toilet flushing and then in the blackout the sound of a powerful orchestra.

In a spotlight, dressed up and holding an envelope, Mildred announces that the winner of the Best Actress Academy Award is Ruth St. Ives for *Gorgons*. Mildred smiles grotesquely as she gives Ruth the statuette and steps back for Ruth's acceptance speech. In a long litany of people she is thankful to, Ruth mentions her cockatoo and her cat, Mr. Poopy, but not Mildred. The music and applause fade in the blackout and lights come up on Ruth's house.

We hear crickets and a loud banging on the door. Ruth, in a robe, lets in Mildred, still in her gown, rather drunk, furious that Ruth didn't mention her and deliberately humiliated her. She grabs the Oscar and Ruth tries to get it back. They struggle and fall over behind the sofa. We see Mildred's arm, holding the statue, come up and then down, violently, several times and we hear Ruth's screams. After a silence, Mildred stands, spattered with blood, holding the bloody statuette. She praises Ruth for her death scene performance. We hear sirens and Mildred explains that she probably set something off when she climbed over the barbed wire fence. A bright light shines into the room and Mildred takes it for a spotlight and speaks to the Academy, thanking them for the award. She concludes by saying that movies are like life, futile and stupid, but "when they're over, what else have we got?" Lights out.

Three men and one woman comprise the cast of *Grand Cayman*, a one-act in which the beach is represented by three deck chairs and a hotel room by two doors and, probably, a bed and at least one chair. We hear the sound of the ocean as lights come up on Murphy and Antonelli on the deck chairs wearing business suits. They chat about the sun and rain and Ireland and money and lizards and pirates and about the man they have been sent to deal with. Mary, in a bikini, sits in the middle chair, telling them that they have some very serious, potentially dangerous, business on their minds. She says she knows they have been watching the man she is with. Murphy, over Antonelli's abjections, explains his theory that God is Popeye the Sailor. She asks them if they have been paid to kill somebody. She wonders if one of them would kill the other if he were offered an obscene amount of money. Antonelli puts a hand around Mary's neck and asks what she wants. She says that when she was in the mental hospital she met a girl named Mary who told her everything about her life, including two friends of hers who were tough guys. Mary in the bathing suit says she knew about a man who had stolen large sums of money and put them in a private account in the Caribbean. She sent a check to hire the two tough guys to help her get her hands on the money. She says the man they have been following wants to see them. She says they are to make him tell where the money is and how to get it and then kill him and the three of them will split the money. She takes the room key from her bikini bottom, gives it to Antonelli, and leaves. The men are sure she is not in her right mind but agree that she looks like a Mary they used to know.

As light fades on them we hear the sound of waves, then a key turning in a lock. An upstage door opens as dim light streams into the hotel room. Leo tells the men, thinking they are room service bringing him clams, to come in and close the door. Another door opens and Mary comes out in a bathrobe with her hair in a towel. She turns on a lamp and we see Leo, half patrician, half gangster. He tells Murphy and Antonelli that they are nothing, dog shit under his mucklucks. Mary says that Leo is a very great writer and producer who writes under thirty-seven different pseudonyms and has suffered a stroke. Leo asks the men if they came to kill him and says all they want is the seven billion dollars he has in the bank. The three men drink and Leo offers Mary two million dollars to get naked. She goes into the bathroom, slamming the door. Leo offers Murphy and Antonelli seventy-eight thousand dollars to go in the bathroom and kill Mary. Leo talks of Jack Kennedy and the effect of high-fructose corn syrup on the intelligence of children. He says he has seven billion dollars in a tax-free account, but when he says he boinked Martha Washington in the rotunda, Antonelli wants to leave. Leo tells them the story of a movie with two guys who came to a tropical island looking for an obscene amount of money without realizing they are in a trap. Antonelli says that this is about Mary and Murphy and, feeling dizzy, wonders what she put in their drinks. Antonelli staggers into the door and asks Leo who he is, to which Leo responds, like Popeye, "I YAM WHAT I YAM," and orders the lights to be cut. Blackout.

The unit set for *Grim Lake* (6m, 3w), created by tables and chairs, represents all times and places at the Red Rose Inn in Armitage, Ohio, during the years 1791 to 1805, the play moving back and forth in time without set changes and actors remaining on stage. Nigro prefaces the play with the information that, in 1791, Henry and Margaret (Mag) Grim, their son Thomas and his wife Clara Jane, and their daughter Daisy Grim Quiller, all disappeared or were murdered. "There are several stories about what might have happened to them." The play begins in darkness with Jonas Grey Wolf gazing into a fire, speaking of the ubiquitous power of Manitou. As the fire goes out we see Polly Crow, 42, sitting on a wooden chair, staring into a down-stage fire we can't see. George Grim, 19, sits near her and his sister, Mary Grim Armitage, 21, is finishing cleaning. The voice of Robert Armitage is heard from upstairs, telling Mary to come up to bed. Mary wants Polly and George to go to bed. Polly says she is someplace else and George says he has been dreaming of something that happened when he was five, fourteen years ago. George says he sees things and thinks Polly does, too. Mary says she was seven and doesn't remember anything and agrees with Polly that purple berries and bears drive people crazy. Mary says she doesn't want to think about it; they're dead and nothing will bring them back. Polly says it was the Devil, except he looked more like God. George says Polly was twenty-eight at the time and saw what happened. She says the Devil had long white hair and a white beard and a black suit; he had huge hands and his face was red and his eyes were blue. Mary says it was the Indians that killed them, but Polly says she can see Henry, Mag, Thomas, Clara Jane, and Daisy as clearly as if they were still alive. She says she heard whippoorwills.

Lights dim on them and come up on Henry and Mag (in 1791). Mag thinks she hears something besides whippoorwills and Henry asks her if she has been eating the purple berries again. When she calls Henry Enrico, he says his name is Henry. Mag says "he" is close, that he is coming for them. She wants Polly to put the children in the root cellar. They refer to Henry killing a Jesus and Mag says she liked the way Henry walked the tightrope is his costume. She wants him to walk on his hands. When he says he's too old, she says he was walking on his hands the night he killed Jesus. He says Enrico killed Jesus; he is Henry. Mag says that Mephistopheles is here and tells Henry to listen. We hear the sound of whippoorwills as the light fades on them and comes up on George and Jonas.

George tells Jonas he has been having dreams about the massacre. Jonas says the Indians were blamed, that he was blamed because he is half Indian. George says that white people saved him and raised him like their own. Jonas says there is something evil in the lake and that it's always a mistake to love. We hear whippoorwills, and Jonas says he saw George's father and Polly Crow and heard them talking about Jesus as an old man with white hair and beard appeared. Jason says he went into the woods and when he came back they were all gone. He says something came up out of the water and advises George to leave it alone. We hear whippoorwills again as light fades on Jonas and George and comes up on Thomas Grim and Polly Crow (1791).

Thomas tells her that he has been dreaming of a creature living deep in the lake, a creature that came up and started devouring "us." He says he hears voices in the woods, that his wife Clara Jane, whom he met on a ship coming to America, never talks to him. Polly says that Daisy told her that Thomas hasn't talked to her since she married Pete. Thomas says that Polly slept with both Old Man Rose and his son and has had a child by each of them. Thomas thinks his parents are speaking gibberish, but Polly says they are speaking German. Thomas says they can't speak German and that once he saw his father walking on his hands. He says he dreamed that something came up out of the lake. Polly warns him about eating the purple berries and Thomas says he saw Daisy and Clara and his mother and father lying dead by the shore of the lake with blood everywhere and something pulled them into the water. She kisses him on the cheek as the light fades.

She crosses to George, Mary, and her husband Robert Armitage (in 1805). Mary berates George for asking questions about dead people and George says he wants to know what happened to his family. He asks how five people can be killed in such a small town and nobody knows what happened. Robert, who was eleven at the time, says there was blood every-where. Mary says she dreamed that something came out of the water and took them. George asks Polly about the man she thought was the Devil. Polly says the man told her his name was Mephistopheles and she should not be afraid. We hear whippoorwills as lights dim on the others and stay up on Polly, younger, sitting in the woods as Mephistopheles DeFlores comes up behind her.

Polly tells him he looks a little bit like God and they introduce them-selves. Mephistopheles tells her about his twin children, a girl and a boy named Jesus. Polly says Mephistopheles is very angry at his daughter. Me-phistopheles says she married a clown who did somersaults on a tightrope and walked on his hands. He says he can't forgive his daughter because she is responsible for the death of Jesus. Mephistopheles says he has been follow-ing them ever since. Polly says he should forgive his daughter and tells him about being taken by Indians when she was a child and then taking care of other children. She says that Henry and Mag are over by the stand of maple trees. She speaks their surname and Mephistopheles says he has been search-ing for Henry and Margaret Grim for twenty-nine years. When Polly tries to leave, Mephistopheles grabs her by the shoulder and tells her to take the children to a cellar because a storm is coming. He leaves and Thomas enters and learns that Mephistopheles is looking for his parents because they killed Jesus at the carnival. Thomas tells Polly to hide with the children in the root cellar. After Polly leaves, Thomas talks about Revelation as the making known of what has been secret. He leaves to find an ax and lights come up on Mag and Henry.

Mag says that when Henry was Enrico Grimaldi and walked on his hands she loved him but now he is somebody else and they are lost. Mag says she saw him in the woods with Clara Jane, his son's wife, comforting her with his penis. Mephistopheles appears from the upstage shadows, telling them that he came west alone to find them. He reminds Henry that he used to throw knives in the carnival. He says he met Polly who told him to forgive. He says he has pursued them across an ocean and nearly half a continent for almost three decades, but now he is tired and wonders if there's any point to anything since before long everybody alive will be dead. Light fades on them and comes up on George and Polly (in 1805).

Polly is telling George about putting him and Mary in the root cellar and about seeing Clara Jane and Daisy kissing. She says she doesn't know if the old man with white hair and big hands killed them. Polly says she remembers somebody saying, "Don't look in his eyes." Light fades on them and Thomas enters (in 1791) with an ax and sees Henry and Mag huddled together.

Thomas asks where Mephistopheles is and Henry says he must have imagined him, then says that the old man went back into the woods. Mag says that Henry is fornicating with his son's wife. Henry says that Clara Jane also slept with Thomas' sister, that she can't help it, it's just her way of making friends. Mag says something is coming out of the water to kill them. Henry thinks it's just fog, but Thomas says it's retribution for all their sins. Light fades on them and comes up on George, Robert, and Jonas sitting at a fire (in 1805).

George says the past is a puzzle with most of the pieces missing. He doesn't know what the truth is. Robert says we make educated guesses that are illusions to keep us alive long enough to fornicate with a few women. We come from nothing and go to nothing. To find truth, read the tombstones. Jonas says that sometimes the Manitou whispers in a person's head, but the person doesn't always understand. Light fades and we hear the sound of whippoorwills in the darkness.

In *Hagridden*, another Pendragon-related short play, two members of the DeFlores traveling carnival show in the 1920s—Broglio, a strongman in his forties, and Carmelita, his wife, in her thirties—are talking at night. In the darkness we have heard a recording of Chaliapin singing Mephistopheles from Gounod's *Faust,* and as the lights come up we see Broglio, wearing only his trousers, drinking at a table while Carmelita, in her slip, sits on a bed reading a novel by the light of an old lantern. Broglio says he dreams of an enormous moth fluttering behind him and complains of Carmelita reading penny dreadful novels about ridiculous people who do monstrous things to one another. He complains that she is always picking at him, but she says he should read more and then reads aloud a passage from the novel. She thinks the passage is beautiful and says she escapes into fantasy because her life in the carnival is a mind-numbing pandemonium. Speaking his thoughts aloud, Broglio says that in the worst of her books a shirtless man with bulging muscles and wild eyes strangles a woman wearing only a slip. He speaks again of the moth leaving its horrible, choking powder all over him. Carmelita describes the book in which the crazed husband strangles his wife and puts

her body in a trunk which he dumps in a pond. When he returns to his
bedroom the woman is there reading a book to him about a man who strangles his wife and puts her in a trunk. She says the story has a kind of
circularity, an ambiguity, but Broglio says that's not right, that stories should
have endings with certain meanings. Carmelita says the interesting thing is
whether the woman is really dead or not. Perhaps she escaped from the trunk
or perhaps she comes back as a ghost, a figment of his tortured imagination
come back to haunt him because he is torn by guilt and because he still
desires her. Or, she says, perhaps it's a game in which the wife picks at,
teases, the husband to pull him back into the world. She speaks of a strong
man being afraid of a moth and teases Broglio about a former lover. Broglio
tells her to stop and begins waving his arms around as if tormented by moths.
Carmelita says that he strangled his wife Carmelita not for sleeping with
Ulysses DeFlores but for never letting him forget that she allowed Jack
Basileus to deflower her in a hammock when she was a girl. She puts the
book down as Broglio moves toward her and puts his hands around her neck.
Strangling her, he pulls her up and kisses her lips as the light fades and goes
out.

Hologram, Praying Mantis, and *Night* are closely related one-acts that
may be done individually or together. If done together, the order is *Praying
Mantis*, *Night*, and *Hologram*. The trilogy may also be done with the monologues *Entanglement, Telepathy,* and *Uncertainty.* In *Hologram*, Laura sits in
a wooden chair in a circle of light, and Stephen sits in another chair in a
circle of light. They speak as if on the telephone but no telephones are
visible. Laura tells Stephen she's a little drunk, started grad school, is having
a party with friends, and wonders how his book is coming. Stephen says he
isn't writing any more and she doesn't answer his letters. Laura suggests that
the woman in Stephen's book who is obsessed with the praying mantis could
have a daughter who is in love with her stepfather. There is a conspiracy
between them that drives the mother out of her mind and makes her leave.
Stephen says his book isn't about that. Laura asks if he touched her mother.
He says he did but respected her boundaries. In response to her questions,
Stephen says he sits on the porch alone, drinking. He asks Laura what she
wants and if he can help her. She says she doesn't need his fucking help. She
says he can call anytime and leave her a message when she doesn't answer.
She says she wants him to suffer and then die. Or he could drive up and have
"hot, desperate, guilty, screaming sexual intercourse" with her and then she
would eat his head. She says this isn't real, just a dream, or his novel, or a
hologram. She decides it's a hologram and tells him to keep in touch.

The Last of the Dutch Hotel is a shorter script for a man and a woman, Harry Cust and Lady de Grey, both a bit past their prime. They are seated at a table on the terrace of a Dutch seaside resort hotel. It is autumn and we hear the sounds of the ocean and gulls and "an old scratchy recording of 'Au fond du temple saint' from Bizet's *The Pearl Fishers.*" Lady de Grey complains about the sausages they were served for breakfast and notes that some of the guests have disappeared. Harry says that he has tried to talk with the staff but they don't seem to speak English or even Dutch. Lady de Grey doesn't like the way the waiter with an eye patch looks at her. Harry doesn't believe her when she tells him that the summer house where they used to meet has been torn down. Nor does he believe her when she tells him that an entire wing of the hotel has been abandoned. Lady de Grey thinks the handwriting of a note she received resembles Harry's love notes to her years earlier. The note says, "Where were you on the 19 of October?" Neither is sure if that is today. Lady de Grey says she saw a man that is dead walking by the trees. She complains about the incessant rain and cold and Harry notices that the bathing machines and life lines have been removed. Lady de Grey wonders if they have wasted their lives. She notices something, a seal, a walrus, in the water but then thinks that two people are copulating. Harry's vision is failing but he thinks it is a large mass of seaweed moved by the tide. Neither can remember when their affair began and each asks if the other killed Lady de Grey's first husband. Harry looks through his spyglass at the object in the water and discovers that the couple is a young version of Lady de Grey and himself. Taking the spyglass Lady de Grey sees the couple and also a creature moving rapidly toward them. Harry is preoccupied with the waiter staring at them with something in his hand. Lady de Grey screams that the monster is dragging the couple into the ocean. Harry says that the waiter has a meat cleaver. Lady de Grey says that the monster is devouring the couple and Harry tells her that he thinks he knows what's on the menu for lunch.

There are five actors (3m, 2w) in *Le Fanu's Dream* (pronounced LEFF-anew) who enter and disappear on a dark set representing a park and rooms in a house on Merrion Square in Dublin from the 1840s to the 1870s. We hear clocks ticking as lights come up on Susanna, a young woman dressed in white. She tells us that toward the end of his life Joseph Sheridan Le Fanu, "celebrated author of ghost and mystery stories," suffered from nightmares in which he found himself walking in ruins in Phoenix Park. Le Fanu walks on as ravens caw and, facing downstage, looks up at something we can't see.

Susanna says that he hears an ominous creaking noise and sees that the house is going to collapse on him, but he cannot move. We hear the sound of a wall crashing down as the lights go out and ravens caw in the darkness.

In moonlight we see Carmilla, in white, sobbing on a park bench in front of a hedge. Le Fanu asks if he can help, and she says she has been abandoned by a company of actors. He says she can stay in his house and act as his secretary. When she asks if his wife will object, he says his wife is dead, and Susanna appears in the oval mirror frame, looking at them. Carmilla introduces herself as Miss Smith and she and Le Fanu walk into the darkness. Susanna tells us from the oval frame that the young woman proved to be "surprisingly efficient," although Le Fanu still had bad dreams. Susanna sits on the park bench, describing a dream in which two hands come through the hedge and slowly pull a young girl through the hedge, an action that happens to Susanna as the lights fade out.

We hear birds singing and see Carmilla reading theatrical reviews in a newspaper. She tells Le Fanu she loves the house because, like an old theatre, it is full of ghosts. She says she thinks our life on earth is a performance watched by ghosts. Le Fanu tells her of a dream he had about finding a dead girl lying at the foot of a low brick wall and seeing two red eyes staring at him. Carmilla says that a dead girl was found murdered in Phoenix Park at the foot of a low brick wall and all the blood had been drained from her body. When Carmilla asks how his wife died, Le Fanu says her problems began on their wedding night.

We hear owls and see Susanna sitting on the bed, talking of "the unspeakable mad violation in hell," and telling Le Fanu that someone with red eyes is looking at her in the dark. Carmilla moves into the empty oval frame and speaks to Susanna from it. Susanna wants Le Fanu to cover the mirrors and sleep in another room. Carmilla steps out of the frame and Le Fanu remarks on how similar she is to his wife's sister. As they sit at the table with Brother and Susanna, Carmilla transforms into the sister, "bright, bubbly, flirtatious, a little reckless, and a bit wicked." Sister asks how Susanna and Le Fanu slept on their wedding night and assumes that "a successful hymeneal execution has been accomplished." Susanna is upset to learn that Le Fanu and Sister were writing letters to each other before the marriage, referring to Susanna as Miss Smith Bluebeard. Susanna tells Le Fanu that his mind is full of puppets, peopled by a grotesque collection of Swedenborgian doppelgangers. After Susanna storms out, Le Fanu says he can't find her, and Sister says that she and Susanna grew up in the house and know all its secret places.

In the next scene, the sisters are sitting on the park bench, and Susanna says she feels as if something is watching her, something that lives in the mirror. She says Le Fanu talks to imaginary people as he writes, and it is as if his entire life was one great hallucination. She asks if Sister thinks of their father and Sister says she stole Papa's razor from his corpse and Susanna may borrow it if she decides to cut her husband's throat as he sleeps. The light fades on them and comes up on Le Fanu writing late at night, saying he is sometimes visited by his dead great-uncle, the playwright Richard Brindsley Sheridan. Sheridan appears "in all his decayed and cobweb covered late 18th century glory," telling Le Fanu that he disapproves of his unhappiness over his wife's death and asserting his conviction that we are put on this earth to engage in as much copulation as is humanly possible. He says the secret of life is to jump on a willing woman before she changes her mind. Sheridan thinks he hears someone calling him to rehearse a play in Hell because there's always something wrong with the second act. He goes into the darkness as Susanna enters asking Le Fanu why he stays up so late writing and talking to imaginary people. She says that there have been moments when she has not been entirely horrified by his nocturnal violations, but she thinks he intends to murder her. Le Fanu says her dark fantasies are brought on by loneliness and fear and are not real.

Talking with Brother, Le Fanu asks him what he and Susanna talked about when they walked in the garden. Le Fanu watches as Susanna tells Brother that when he husband touches her she feels the "rough, filthy digits of the Evil One." Sister and Le Fanu then congratulate Brother on the upcoming birth of his child. Susanna says her three children are goblins and she doesn't want her husband playing with her teats in bed. At night, we hear a ticking clock, wind, and owls, and see Le Fanu asleep at his desk. Susanna appears in the mirror frame, saying that he has been reading Swedenborg on the multitude of intersecting worlds. Swedenborg, played by the actor who did Sheridan and will later play Papa, crawls out from under the bed and speaks with a Swedish accent about the inner eye that can see oceans of spirits, worlds within worlds. Le Fanu wakes and when Swedenborg asks him what one thing he wants to know above all others, Le Fanu wants to know why his wife sobs uncontrollably when he touches her. Swedenborg munches on a meatball, says his wife is dead, and crawls back under the bed.

We hear a creaking sound and the ticking of clocks as Carmilla, in a white nightgown, steps into the light. She says she keeps hearing voices and wonders in she could be of any assistance to Le Fanu. They look at each other as Susanna watches from the mirror and, after Le Fanu moves into the shadows, goes to the bed. We hear voices whispering as Carmilla steps into the frame, talks with Susanna, and gets into bed with her. Le Fanu moves into the light, apparently not seeing Carmilla, and Susanna tells him that a young woman got into bed with her and held her. Carmilla smiles at Le Fanu as she cuddles with Susanna and when Le Fanu says that the only thing he is certain of is his love for Susanna, Carmilla/Sister tells him everything he is certain of is a lie.

We hear thunder and see lightning as Brother tells Le Fanu that he must come in out of the storm. Le Fanu says that Susanna caught doubt from him and it drove her mad and killed her. Lights come up on Susanna in bed speaking the letter she is writing to God. She says she knows God is insane and is really Satan who lives in the mirror and copulates with the vampire girl. She says there is no love, no salvation, only darkness and fear and something pressing against her in the night. She says she felt a hand clutching her throat until she could not breathe and her senses left her. We hear ticking clocks and see Susanna on the bed, then a door creaking open, and Papa going to the bed. Susanna says she has missed Papa since he died and he says there is room for her to cuddle in his coffin. He asks her why her sister was in bed with her. Susanna says her sister was comforting her the way Papa comforted her. He starts climbing onto the bed and she screams "NOOOOOOOOOOOOOOOOO" as the light goes out on them.

Le Fanu awakens at his desk from a nightmare and is told by Carmilla that his wife was disgusted and horrified by his touch and not because of anything terrible her father did to her. She asks how his wife died and light fades on her and comes up on Susanna in bed screaming. Le Fanu is where Papa was and Susanna says some monstrous, pawing creature was on top of her so that she couldn't breathe. She says Le Fanu writes about men murdering women, and he shakes her, telling her he doesn't want to kill her, but she says sex, death, and writing are all the same thing. Carmilla says he put his hands over her face and raped and smothered her. Le Fanu denies it, but Carmilla says she saw it from inside the mirror. She thinks Le Fanu should cut his throat with a razor.

Le Fanu wanders in the dark as ravens caw and we hear the voices of Susanna and Carmilla reprising the opening lines of the play about Le Fanu's nightmares and the collapse of a debilitated mansion. But Le Fanu says there is no house, no wall; he says he is innocent and is not responsible for his wife's death. He sits on the bench, saying he has conquered the nightmare and no longer has anything to fear. Two hands come out of the hedge and wrap around his neck. He screams and is pulled through the hedge as lights come up on Carmilla and Susanna sitting on the bed. They say they have the house to themselves and can be alone together, forever. Carmilla kisses Susanna's lips, then her neck, then her breasts as the light fades and goes out.

A man, Rupert, and a woman, Senta, sitting on wooden chairs inside a room lit by moonlight, speaking of themselves and of each other in the third person, recall, in *A Legacy for the Mad*, their on-again off-again affair, a recollection that grows increasingly bizarre. Rupert says that her apartment smelled sometimes of cigars and that he could smell her perfume in his room months after she had gone. He speaks of making love with her against a wall of the zoo, the "greatest experience of his life," but says that she then refused to return his phone calls for months. Senta shifts to the first person, saying, "I was in Spain . . . ." When Rupert says that as a boy he gathered mushrooms his mother would cook and serve with lamb and green jello, Senta says that her husband loved mushrooms. Rupert says that "after some years" he felt that she trusted him enough to share her memories, although he was never certain whether she was inventing them. One night she took his hand and told him how her husband had died when a wagon turned over and he struck his head on a stone. She says that he left all his money to an insane asylum, with nothing for her or the children. When Rupert, now speaking directly to her, asks about children, she says she doesn't have any, and Rupert says he doesn't believe anything she's said. Senta says her husband was a Swedish ventriloquist who once made love to her at the zoo, "the greatest experience" of her life. Rupert says he loves her. She says that the owls have come to devour them, and Rupert, reverting to the third person, hopes that the zoo-keepers will be bringing green jello for lunch.

The setting for the four-character (2m, 2w) one-act *Letters from Quebec to Providence in the Rain* represents two old houses, one in Quebec and one in Providence, with some furniture being part of both. We hear whippoor-wills in the darkness and then see Petrus taking some letters from an old book, Drago's *Occult Notebooks*, that he had bought that morning from a girl selling books by the river. Vanessa questions him about his motives, and Petrus tells her that the letters are written to someone named Vanessa by a Jonathan and were mailed from Quebec to Providence.

Lights come up on Jonathan speaking, not writing, a letter to Vanessa about moving into a house in Quebec. Vanessa tells Petrus that she had a brother named Jonathan, now dead. Jonathan speaks of hearing the sounds of a girl talking to herself in the bath, and lights come up on Marianne in the tub, speaking in the third person of Vanessa meeting her roommate, Mari-anne, at Brown University in Providence, Rhode Island. As Petrus and Va-nessa continue their conversation about Vanessa's brother, Jonathan de-scribes how he went up the stairs to the bath and found the water running and the tub about to overflow, but "nobody was there."

Marianne speaks to Petrus, calling him a "wicked boy," and tells him to close the door because he's letting in goblins. She then continues her narra-tion of Vanessa bringing her roommate Marianne home to Quebec to met Vanessa's brother Jonathan who fell hopelessly in love with her. Vanessa tells Petrus that she went to Brown University because she was fascinated by the writer H. P. Lovecraft who lived in Providence. She says she brought her roommate Marianne home with her over Christmas break and corroborates what Marianne said earlier about Jonathan falling in love with her. Marianne says she used to walk by Lovecraft's house at night, and Jonathan, still speaking a letter, asks Vanessa if Marianne ever speaks of him. Marianne asks if Petrus is out there on the staircase.

Then Vanessa narrates an idea for a story about a man who buys a book from a girl by a river and finds some old letters inside. Marianne says that Jonathan wrote her hundreds of love letters but she never wrote back. Petrus says that there is a photograph in the book with "From Marianne, With Love" on the back. He asks Vanessa if she knows the girl in the photograph and Vanessa says she can't be certain, that the time she spent in the mental asylum with the drugs and shock treatments have addled her memory.

Marianne tells Vanessa (in an earlier time) that she has met "a most wonderful young man" named Petrus Van Hoek, an artist who studies the anatomies of young women and is taking photographs of her in the bath. Vanessa (in a later time) tells Petrus that she was jealous and confronted Marianne while she was in the bathtub. Jonathan says he climbed the stairs to the bathroom and found Marianne lying dead in the tub. Vanessa says that "the murderess" was hiding behind the door and hit the intruder in the head with the bulldog door stop, realizing later that it was her brother, who has never been right in the head since.

Vanessa says that "she" began receiving letters from Quebec, written by her brother, and she goes back to confront him but ends up wandering the streets of Quebec, thinking it is Providence. Jonathan says he goes to the house, finds Drago's book, and sees that the name on the inside front cover is Petrus Van Hoek. Vanessa tells Petrus that he was Marianne's lover. She wonders why he came to read to her in the hospital and then took her into his home. He says she knows why and that it is time for her bath. The lights fade and we hear whippoorwills in the darkness.

In *Lightning Rods*, the two fathers that Margaret mentioned in *Gazebo*, Silas Quiller, her father, and Bert Astor, Gretchen's father, both 55, are on a downsloping rooftop in 1919. Silas is putting up lightning rods and Bert is sitting, watching him. We hear the sound of thunder in the distance. Bert says that a storm is coming and that he came up on the roof because he wanted to see a man dumb enough to put up lightning rods in a thunderstorm. He asks if Silas is bothered by people talking about their relationship, of Silas building a house next door for Bert and his wife. When Silas asks Bert to get him a lightning rod, Bert refuses, and Silas gets it himself as Bert warns him to be careful.

Bert talks about his dead wife, Barbary, who had "tits for the ages," who lived in the poorest area in town, and who had a reputation for being the "biggest slut in Pendragon County." Silas, he says, married the petite Pott-dorf girl from a land-poor but respectable old farm family, and he says that if

Silas is bothered by his wife's family then he and Silas could just kill them. He wonders, since the storm is getting closer, if Silas would like to go inside and take turns screwing his wife, or his daughter. Silas tells him to shut up and after a pause Bert remarks that he misses his wife, who got into a tub and cut her throat. He says that Silas actually seemed to like his wife while Bert could never stand her (although he did enjoy fucking her).

Silas asks Bert if he loves his children, and Bert replies that Clyde and Gretchen could be anybody's children. He asks Silas if he loves his children and when Silas says he does Bert wonders which of Silas' children are his. He says Maggie looks like her mother, Con looks like Bert's dead brother, and Clyde looks like a moose. He says neither his son Clyde nor Silas' son Clyde have as much brain as ear wax and asks why Silas named his first-born Clyde. Silas says it was after his mother's father who died in the Battle of the Wilderness.

Silas again asks Bert if he loves his children and Bert says that that is an awfully funny question coming from a man who is putting up lightning bolts with big ass bolts of lightning coming towards them. Silas says that Bert's son is engaged to Silas' daughter and his son is engaged to Bert's daughter. Silas tells Bert that he walked in on his daughter while she was taking a bath and told her to lock the door in the future. Silas says that Bert's daughter is troubled and asks what Bert did to her. Bert says that Silas is feeling remorse for the stealing and raping and killing they did out west and tells Silas he has to turn off that part of his brain that feels bad about it. He says that's the secret of success in America. Silas says the sight of his naked daughter's body in the bath brought it all back to him.

Bert wants to get off the roof before they're both fried like a couple of pork chops. He says he's on the roof because Silas is the only friend he has. Silas asks Bert if he came to where Silas was living to blackmail him about the past. Bert says that Silas is his only friend and that they have things, memories, between them. Silas asks if Bert loves his daughter and Bert says every chance he gets. Silas tells him to come over and help put up the lightning rod. He asks Bert if he loved his wife and if he wants his daughter to end up the same way. He orders Bert to help him.

As we hear the sound of the storm approaching, Bert says his wife was lonesome and lost when he met her and he told her to sleep with Silas, even though she didn't want to, because he was sleeping with Silas' wife, even though he didn't like her. He says his daughter used to trust him but some things you got to put out of your head. Lightning flashes and thunder are very close as Bert moves shakily to Silas, slips, and clutches both hands around the lightning rod as he falls on the wet roof. Silas stands holding the lightning rod and tells Bert when he asks that he is Bert's friend. There is an "enormous lightning bolt and thunderclap" as the lights go to black.

Loopy Rye (3m, 1w), part of the Pendragon cycle, uses a unit set with a chair in the Flowers Boarding Hotel DR, Blaine Plum's desk and chair facing downstage RC, a bench in the cemetery LC and tombstones under an old tree DL. Characters are on stage throughout the play, which begins in 1925 but goes back to events that occurred in 1872 as if remembered by Loopy. We hear the sounds of a ticking clock and an old piano playing Chopin's 13th Prelude as lights come up on Loopy in the DR chair. Blaine Plum, Lavinia's father, is seated at his desk; August Ballantine is on the bench; and Lavinia is sitting with her back against a tombstone.

Loopy as an old man talks about learning to tune pianos, mentioning the names of characters in the Pendragon cycle, and as the lights come up on Lavinia he identifies her as a lost girl. Blaine tells Lavinia that she has to see Doc McGort because she has been vomiting every morning. August tries to converse with Lavinia (in 1872) while Loopy (in 1925) remembers how a family was found dead at Grim Lake. Loopy talks about how people treated him and how he likes rain, china bowls, sparrows, and the smell of horse manure and hay. Blaine tells Lavinia that Augustus has agreed to marry her, but Lavinia says she doesn't even like him.

As they talk Loopy tells us in counterpoint the history of Ghost Hill with herds of buffalo moving through the forest and speaks of the Delaware Indians who lived in the caves. Loopy says he likes to talk to the crows and thinks being the village idiot is a big responsibility because dumb people need someone they can feel superior to. He says he gets uneasy when the Carnival comes to town and he moves to the tombstones to talk to Lavinia (in 1872).

He tells her that she shouldn't come to the cemetery at night, that there are ghosts and a lot of fornication. She asks him what he sees when he looks into people's windows at night. He says just about everything and that he has seen her taking baths. He admits to leaving drawings of her on the back porch. She thinks he couldn't possibly have drawn them and, finding a piece of paper in her pocket, asks him to draw her. As he draws, Blaine tells his daughter that if she doesn't marry Augustus he will throw her out of his house without a penny. She says that Augustus is not the father of her child and says he is so he can marry her and get her father's money. She tells Blaine that Loopy is the father of her child, and her father says he is going to have Loopy locked up in a mental institution. Blaine admits that Augustus told him that he saw Lavinia and Loopy in the cemetery. Lavinia says that her father is paying Augustus to marry her. Blaine says that they are coming this evening to take Loopy to the institution where he will be castrated and lobotomized.

Lavinia looks at Loopy drawing and tells Blaine that if he leaves Loopy alone she will marry Augustus and do whatever Blaine wants. She says if any harm ever comes to Loopy she will take her child and disappear. Blaine accepts her offer on condition that she never speak to Loopy again, never look at him or acknowledge his presence. As we hear, faintly, the Chopin Prelude again, she walks over to the bench and sits next to Augustus. Loopy finishes the drawing, puts it on the tombstone, and goes back to his chair, becoming an old man again. He tells us that Lavinia never said a word to him after that and would pass him in the street as if he wasn't there. He says she knew as she played the piano at night that he was outside her window but she wouldn't look. He says she died young and that he sits by her grave at night. He saw her through the window looking at the drawings. He watched over her little girl and then the little girl's children. He says the best thing about love is that it doesn't make any sense. Like God. And the crows.

As the lights come up on *Marilyn Gets Ice Cream*, a short one-act, Knees, a short, pudgy janitor in his thirties is sitting on a wooden bench in a Tastee-Freeze in Phoenix, Arizona, on an evening in March, 1956, while Jake, in his twenties, is sweeping up. We hear a buzzing sound which Knees attributes to beetles that can't stay away from lights. He tells Jake that the pretty second-grade teacher he liked got fired for inappropriate behavior. Knees tells Jake to call him Arthur and asks if Marilyn Monroe has been back. Knees says that a black limo pulled up to the store and a huge chauffeur got out and ordered two ice-cream cones, saying that Marilyn Monroe and Jackie Gleason were in the back seat. Knees couldn't see through the dark glass of the back window and tells Jake that they're making a movie called *Bus Stop*. But Knees says he will never be absolutely certain he was that close to Marilyn, and that he felt he was possibly close to establishing a relationship with Lou Ann, the teacher. Jake says she would never have anything to do with the janitor at the grade school. Knees says that she might be capable of deep human compassion and tells Jake she was seen screwing some guy in the coat room after school, apparently her fiancé from Nebraska. Knees complains that he can never get close to women, that they either leave like the teacher or are behind dark glass like Marilyn. He goes on to tell of the time when he met a really nice girl in a bar, but when he went to buy her a drink, the bartender looked down at his short stature and asked if he was standing on his knees. Everybody in the bar laughed and now he is "a fucking walking joke." He says he walked into the coat room and saw "the nicest girl you ever met, being fucked like a dog by some shit-kicker from Nebraska." He tells Jake he is going to the rodeo tomorrow and hopes that he will see Marilyn there. He asks Jake if he is going to the rodeo and Jake replies, "I don't think so, Arthur."

Midsummer (1m, 4w) is set in a wood near Athens with lush vegetation and shadows. Puck and four fairy girls—"sweet, pretty, and delicate"--are relaxing. Peaseblossom says that Puck is "absolutely manic," and she doesn't know what to make of his behavior. But, she says, not all fairies are alike. Cobweb, for example, is distracted and complex, Moth is always fluttering around, and Mustardseed is always critical. Mustardseed says everything excites Puck sexually and he's always bragging. Puck says he saw the Great God Pan die because nobody believed in him, but his ghost still haunts the woods. When Puck tells Peaseblossom that pleasure and disgust are closely related, Cobweb mentions Freud's *The Interpretation of Dreams* which, she says, Hermia left in the woods. She says Freud isn't born yet, that all times and places coexist in the forest, including some which are entirely imaginary. When Mustardseed says Puck is a lost, evil little thing, Puck says they are all evil things, all lost. Peaseblossom observes that throughout the woods creatures are kissing, copulating, killing, and devouring each other.

Puck says that long ago they were gods, that the wind moving through the trees is the breath of Pan and the feeling of panic is the awareness of the presence of an ancient god reminding you that you're going to die. Mustardseed says she would rather be a fallen god than a human; Puck says humans are degenerate monkeys. Moth says she is too young to die. Cobweb says that when the last person who believed in you or at least remembered you was gone, you'd be gone too. Peaseblossom says they have to do something so people don't forget them. Puck says that's exactly what he's been doing. They sense something and Cobweb suggests that perhaps Shakespeare is coming with more rewrites, perhaps cutting the scene. Puck says there isn't any wind and urges them to listen. Lights fade out.

Mind the Gap, requiring a man in his late 50s and a woman in her 20s, is set on a wooden bench in an old European train station. (A note says that the writer W. G. Sebald drove into an oncoming lorry and was killed on December 14, 2001. He probably suffered a heart attack driving his daughter home.) As lights come up on the characters sitting on the bench, we hear footsteps and voices echoing in the distance. Max notices that Anna is reading a book by Sebald, a writer Mac finds unusual and rather difficult. They speak of memories, happy and unhappy, and ambiguity in Sebald's work. Max says that he sometimes feels he has written Sebald's work himself, that the numinous symbols of the writer are significant to him as well. He says he was drawn to Anna when he saw her sleeping and knew, although he cannot explain what it was he knew. Anna says that when she was a child her father told her that when a person dies they go to a big room like the one they are in where people wait for trains to take them to unknown destinations. Max says, "Mind the gap," explaining that the sign by the tracks warns of the danger of stepping into the abyss between life and death, two inexplicable realities. Max speaks of one of Sebald's narrators who returns to his village but nobody recognizes him, and he observes life as a spectator, noting coincidences that seem to give meaning to existence. Max begins to remember driving with his daughter and feeling a sudden pressure in his chest and seeing something very large coming directly at them. Anna thinks she remembers driving with her father, and Max tells her that the train that has arrived is for him, not her. Max says she must go through a door back to where she was before she got to where she is. Max takes out a small camera and takes her picture. Anna, leaving, stops and says, "Papa? . . . Mind the gap." He says he will, she goes, and the light fades out.

"The action flows like a dream" in *The Mulberry Tree Variations* (2m, 2w), a long one-act on a unit set representing an old house in London and a prison cell on a South Sea island in the first decade of the 20th century. The set has no walls, with a bed, table, and lamp SR, a wooden table with chairs DL, and a practical door UC. In darkness we hear the sound of an old film projector and gradually see a strobe, flickering a very primitive silent film effect on the door as we hear Bach's 13th Goldberg Variation played on an old piano.

We hear Jack's voice describing a memory of a girl moving through the door into the room as Madchen, in a white dress, moves toward the audience and then off into the down left darkness. The silent film effect ends as the music fades out and Jack and Petra appear in the doorway and move into the room talking about the similarity between the girl in a "cinematograph" Jack has gone to see night after night and a girl he used to know as "the jailer's daughter." In answer to Petra's questions, Jack says that he was in jail, that he murdered someone, and that the room looks uncannily familiar to him. He says he was a sailor on a merchant ship in the South Seas, and as he speaks of that time Madchen appears DL as a waitress putting a tray of food on the round wooden table. She speaks to Jack as he moves into her space, the jail, but Jack keeps explaining to Petra (in a different time) how he accidentally killed another sailor in a bar fight.

Madchen speaks to Jack of love and mortality, and he speaks alternately to her and Petra. Madchen asks about London and says she wishes she were there, voicing a question that appears in several Nigro scripts: "Why is a raven like a writing desk?" She tells Jack that if she dies before she gets to London she will haunt him there. Petra comments on Madchen's mental state as Madchen tells Jack and us about her parents and her love for books. Madchen speaks of her grandfather who taught her never to put mulberries in her pocket. She tells Jack that now would be an excellent time to kiss her, and he does, telling her that if she helps him escape from the jail he will take her to London with him.

Petra intrudes on this past event by telling Jack that he is a horrible person. Madchen wants Jack to make love to her under the mulberry tree and Petra asks him why he is telling her this. He says she asked and thinks that he has to get out of the house that Petra has brought him to. Jack tells Madchen they have to leave or the ship will sail without them, but she exits to get her diary. Jack tells Petra that he had to jump in the water and swim to the ship and didn't see Madchen again until he recognized her on the film. Jack says he keeps a watch that Madchen gave him under the mulberry tree. It was her grandfather's and only runs backwards. Jack can't explain how Madchen could have been on the film but he thinks he recognizes the house and the door.

When Jack says something is on fire in his head, Petra thinks that Madchen is a lie that Jack made up. Jack remembers his father as a horrible man, a scientist who invented a sort of motion picture camera to make a record of his experiments. He asks Petra why she brought him to this place, and she tells him how a man, some sort of doctor, came backstage after every show and talked with her.

Evans, "a distinguished and rather intimidating looking older man," enters and sits in a chair. Jack witnesses this scene as Petra witnessed the scene with Jack and Madchen. When Petra tells Evans she is pregnant by an actor who has gone away, he invites her to stay in his house and have the child there. He says his wife is dead and his son is gone. Having no other options, Petra stayed in the house but dreamed that the dead man's wife warned her to get away before the child was born. But Petra gave birth and was told that the baby she thought was healthy had died during the night. She says she ran away but the man found her and paid her to find his son, Jack, and bring him to this house. Evans tells Petra that Jack had suffered an injury to his head that made him forget things, and that as a child he was prone to violent fits of rage that made it necessary to lock him without food in a small, dark room.

Jack remembers his father finding him with a maid, Jenny. Jack woke up on a merchant steamer and thinks the girl on the island reminded him of the maid. Jack realizes that his father is going to kill both him and Petra because he thinks Jack knows about the older man's experiments in the basement. Madchen enters, speaking a letter she is composing to the mulberry tree, describing her arriving in London and finding the house by the river Thames.

Evans asks her what she is doing in his house and she tells him she is engaged to Jack and is carrying his child. Evans says she can stay and help him with his research in cinematography and vivisection. He leads her off DL and Jack tells Petra that the basement contains large bottles with heads of animals and corpses of infants floating in alcohol.

They hear a door slam and footsteps as Evans enters. Jack accuses him of killing his mother and the maid and Petra's baby, but Evans tells them that he put something in the wine they drank that will make them relax and soon nothing will ever trouble them again. Petra rushes at Evans and he puts the syringe on the table to grab her arms. Jack says he cannot move or see properly and we hear again the sound of Bach's 13th Goldberg Variation and see the flickering movie effect as Evans sits Petra on the bed next to Jack and rolls up Jack's sleeve. Madchen comes in the door as in the beginning of the play and moves downstage to the table, picking up the syringe and plunging it into Evans' neck. He screams and falls to the floor. Madchen tells Jack that he'll be all right when the drug wears off, that the poison was in the syringe. She says Evans let her live because she was carrying Jack's baby. She says she brought some mulberry tree seeds to plant in the back garden and raise a mulberry grove for their child to play in. Petra says that Evans is dead and Madchen says that he will fit "quite nicely" into a large bottle in the basement.

Murder in the Red Barn is a longer one-act (2m, 2w) set inside a large old red barn with light shining through the broken slats, old pieces of furniture in the straw, and fragments of other locations. The place is Suffolk, England, and the time is the late 1820s "or perhaps a dream of that village in that time, dreamed in a more recent time." As the play begins we hear doves cooing and see Maria, 26, sitting in the straw, Will, 30, leaning on a post peeling a hard-boiled egg, Young Stepmother, 29, sitting on a wooden chair, and The Molecatcher, 50, drinking at a table.

Maria says all barns are haunted and that she is going to Ipswich to make a new life. Young Stepmother relates a dream she has every night about something terrible happening in the barn. Young Stepmother asks Maria if she has been out again with Will and warns her that he cannot be trusted. Maria says Young Stepmother loves her father's money, thinking that he had found a bag of Roman coins, but her father is obsessed with moles. The Molecatcher says that moles are tricky and philosophical and that his daughter is smart and imaginative. Maria tells Will that she is pregnant and that he is the father. Will says he took precautions by praying to the Lord before entering her "tabernacle." She says he will marry her or her father will kill him.

Will tells The Molecatcher that Maria has gone to Ipswich, taken a job as a baker's assistant, and is happy. Young Stepmother says that she dreamed that Maria was murdered and put in a sack in the barn and buried in the straw. She wants The Molecatcher to look in the barn. Will asks Young Stepmother why she married the old man and she replies that he was kind to her. Will thinks she would be happier in bed with him. After the lights go to black The Molecatcher appears in the darkness with a lantern and Maria calls to him. He puts the lantern down, looking at the straw, and asks if what he sees is a hand.

We hear birds singing as lights come up on Maria telling Will that he was sent away for stealing pigs. The only reason he came back was because his brother Tom drowned. Will says that being around her makes him happy. The Molecatcher tells Young Stepmother that nobody except the killer knows how Maria died. He says that he knows that horrible unspeakable things are hidden beneath the earth. Will tells us that he opened up a boarding house for young ladies in London, where he does all the cooking. He says that The Molecatcher and two policemen dragged him off to jail. Will tells The Molecatcher that he and Maria had an argument and he remembers finding her in the barn, dead, and burying her. He says thousands come to see him hang and cut up his skin in pieces. He says they are the subject of a penny dreadful and Maria says her picture is on the cover. Will picks up two dolls from the straw, identifying one as the Notorious Red Barn Murderer Doll and the other as the beautiful and tragic Maria doll. Maria speaks of using milk as her beauty secret and dreaming she was drowning, while Will speaks his memories of making love to her.

The Molecatcher talks to Young Stepmother about her dreaming that Maria was buried in the barn. The Molecatcher says that Will is not in his right mind, and Young Stepmother says that all men are murderers. In a previous time Will tells Young Stepmother that he is meeting Maria in the barn so they can run away to Ipswich or London. Young Stepmother tells Maria that her children are dead and Maria describes how people came to the barn to collect souvenirs, leaving just a skeleton, and made up songs and plays about her. She says she had three babies, one by Will's brother Tom, one by the clockmaker who sent money, and one by Will, but all three babies died. The Molecatcher wants people to leave them alone as Young Stepmother tells him to come to bed. Maria says if you dig down far enough you come to the center of the darkness, that all God is, is darkness, but he is famous.

Mysterium (3m) is set on the deck of an ocean liner at night. Freud and Jung are returning to Europe after visiting America. Jung thinks America is "a wonderful place," "intensely numinous," charged with the "tremendous mystery of the uncanny other." Freud says that America is "a pig hole," the "most vulgar sewer on earth," "almost entirely constructed of greed, vulgarity, stupidity, self-congratulation, bigotry, and the worship of violence." When Jung suggests they analyze each other's dreams, Freud refuses to give up what he considers his authority and thinks that Jung may want to kill him. They squabble, which Jung thinks is good, and Freud says that they have to agree on the fundamental doctrine. Jung says there is no doctrine and, when Freud accuses him of escapades with women not his wife, Jung replies that everyone knows that Freud has been sleeping with his wife's sister. They call each other hysterical and Jung cautions Freud about fainting.

A steward enters and asks them to be quiet because some women in the ballroom heard them talking of penises. He suggests that they separate until they have calmed down. Freud says that Jung's theories are "rubbish." He feels the ship may have hit something, an iceberg perhaps. Jung says that Freud is jealous of him because he is younger and stronger and full of ideas. Freud gets angry and faints. When the steward enters again he tells Jung that the ship has hit an iceberg and there are a limited number of life boats and they have room for only one more, Jung himself. Jung says he can't leave Freud but, after the steward leaves, rationalizes that, as a doctor, he could be of help in the lifeboat, which would be an excellent place to study psychological types. He leaves; we hear singing, then gunshots; and Freud wakes up. He sees Jung in the life boat waving up at him and then sees "that great white thing . . . looming up out of the darkness." He thinks he must be dreaming and wonders what it could mean. We hear singing as the lights fade out.

New Year's Eve at the Flowers Boarding Hotel, part of the Pendragon cycle, is a one-act for four men and two women set in Armitage, Ohio, on New Year's Eve in 1899. The unit set represents a comfortable parlor of the hotel. Loopy Rye, the village idiot, is picking out a tune on the piano as James Rose on the sofa looks at his brother Hugh whose wife is having a baby in the doctor's office in an adjoining room. Doc Braine comes in to tell Hugh that his wife is fine and the baby will come when it wants to. He takes out a flask and drinks, telling Hugh that it's New Year's Eve and his hand is steadier with a few drinks. Doc says that Vonnie, his housekeeper and receptionist, is driving him crazy. The men talk about Vonnie being acquitted of killing her father and giving her baby to Odin Grim's wife. Doc wonders when the fireworks will begin and questions the capabilities of the Proctor brothers who run the fireworks factory. Zinnia, the 50-year-old woman who runs the hotel, says Hugh's wife is all right but that the baby doesn't want to come out. Doc goes to check and Zinnia says that Vonnie, who can turn a grown man into a bowl of cranberry sauce, is making the men crazy. Vonnie enters to tell Zinnia that Doc wants her, and Loopy tells Vonnie that James thinks the end of the world is coming at midnight.

After Vonnie leaves, James tells Hugh that he had a vision of the world disappearing and that he has a big sin to confess. He says he fathered Vonnie's baby and that her father went crazy when he found out and Vonnie killed him Hugh says a burglar killed the father and that James is having a mental breakdown. As director of the local theatre group, James says that when he heard Vonnie do Juliet's speech "take him and cut him out in little stars," he fell hopelessly in love with her. When Doc comes in Hugh asks him if Vonnie ever identified her baby's father. Doc says no and Loopy comes in to say that the baby is coming. Doc goes back in; James insists that the world is going to end; Hugh says maybe someday but not now. Vonnie says the baby is a girl, born in the first minute of the new year. Hugh goes in to see the baby and we hear the sound of an explosion as the fireworks start. James apologizes to Vonnie for taking advantage of her. She says she needed somebody to hold her and love her and he was there. She is not sorry and he should not be apologizing. Loopy brings in a bowl of popcorn which he gives to Vonnie before he sits down to play the piano and sing "Hello, My Baby" as the lights fade out.

The set for *Night* is a bedroom upstairs in an old house near a university in 2003 with a telephone on a night stand beside the bed. Laura is showing Stephen where he will sleep and suggests he take his clothes off because he is all wet from standing out in the rain. She asks if she can get him something to eat or drink, but he doesn't want anything. She says she's not sure if she got his letters and tells him there is a party downstairs. Stephen says he came because he was worried by her telephone call. She says he has been drinking and asks if he has taken drugs. He says he is not hallucinating and knows she has called him for some time. She says it must be telemarketers. He says that when he walks at night he feels somebody is following him and he has been hearing sounds in his house at night. Laura suggests raccoons. He says that the last time she called she said she had an idea for his novel. He says she was talking about their relationship in the suggestive way she did the night before she left for college. She says she still has dreams about feeling his hands pulling her from the water when she was drowning. She tells him to lie down and rest and imagine this is a chapter in his novel like the Red King's Dream. She almost touches his face, but doesn't, and leaves. The phone rings; Stephen answers asking if anyone is there. Light fades out.

In a circle of light surrounded by darkness, Lil, a woman in her thirties, is on a couch, and Doc, a man in his fifties, sits in a chair by the head of the couch in the two-character play *Orchard Hill*. Lil says that she is God's wife, that there has been a lot of sexual intercourse, that they were married on Orchard Hill although God said the marriage was never legal and so she married his son, Adam, instead. Eve, she says, was Adam's second wife. She says God was already married to Ashtaroth who went mad "living with that gigantic control freak" and was put in the attic. When Doc asks her about her childhood, Lil says she remembers walking at night on a deserted road in the rain where God picked her up. When Doc says he is there to help her, she wonders what sort of deep neurosis would lead anyone to want to pretend they actually derived pleasure from helping anybody. Lil says when God wanted to get rid of her she went to another son, Lucifer, and persuaded him to seduce Eve on Orchard Hill. Lil says God threw Eve and Adam out because sooner or later everybody disappoints him and he rejects them. When Doc asks Lil what would make her happy, she says she wants Orchard Hill. Doc says it's just down the road, but she says she can't go back because Orchard Hill is a portal to another dimension, another existence. When she tells Doc that he wants her, he says her compulsive sexualizing of her experience is evidence of some terrible trauma in her past. She says the trauma is God who created this nightmare of cannibalism and horror. Existence is a crime, she says, and God is the criminal. Doc says he has a folder with information about a Lillian Knight, who is an assistant professor of literature at the University of Massachusetts. The photograph, he says, looks suspiciously like her. Lil says she has had to assume false identities and that the Lillian Knight who teaches a course on the Brontes and another on the Book of Genesis is a character, but that she, Lil, is real. She says that maybe Doc is God in disguise, trying to persuade her that she is not who she is. She says he cannot kill her because he still desires her. When Doc says their time is up and they will have to continue this discussion in their next session, she tells him to come and touch her, worship her as he wants to. God, she says, is love.

The Owl Was a Baker's Daughter (3m, 4w) is about Charles Lamb and his sister Mary. The time of the action is the late 1790s and early 1800s and for the set Nigro writes that, in addition to a punishment stocks with holes for wrists and ankles, "a few old chairs, one a rocker, and a sofa will do, and a cabinet with silverware." We hear the sound of a ticking clock as lights come up on Charles and Mary sitting by a fire. In the upstage shadows we can see Mother, Father, Aunt Hetty, and Jane, all sitting. Charles says that Coleridge told him that his wife is trying to kill him. Mary tells Charles that she knows she is a terrible burden to him but she is very grateful that he did not put her in Bedlam. She tells him that there is a witch in the parlor with them but Charles says they and the cat are the only ones in the parlor.

He leaves and lights come up on the others. Father speaks of being a butler for Old Mr. Salt; Mother wants the cat; Aunt Hetty has difficulty remembering a parrot's name; Jane talks about ducks; and the conversation becomes a hodge-podge of humorous misunderstandings. But we learn that Coleridge's wife has given birth, although Mother insists that Coleridge cannot be the father because he couldn't stop talking long enough to put it in her. Frustrated, Mary throws a spoon at Jane and then more silverware at the other characters. She grabs a carving knife and stabs Mother in the head, twice, threatening Jane who runs out, bumping into the re-entering Charles. He takes the knife from Mary and, as the lights go to black, we hear the sounds of moans and shrieks, a madhouse cacophony.

The lights come up on Charles visiting Mary, who is in a straight jacket. She asks if they are going to hang her, but Charles tells her the verdict was lunacy and that she will stay in the madhouse until she is better and can be brought home. Mary says she is sorry for hitting Father in the head with a fork but that putting a knife in Mother's heart was the only joy she has felt. Charles says he remembers his own temporary insanity fondly and swears he will never leave Mary.

As he goes off, lights go to black, we hear the madhouse cacophony again, and then lights come up on Charles, slightly drunk, in the stocks. He enacts a story for Mary about having dinner with Wordsworth, Keats, Haydon, and "old deaf Landseer," to whom he shouts part of their conversation. Charles talks of a "red blubbery fellow," possibly "old Ritchie," who, according to Charles, describes himself as a controller of stamps. Charles concludes his story by telling Mary that they are a pair that the world has never seen, she in a straight jacket for madness and he in the stocks for public drunkenness.

The light fades, allowing Charles and Mary to go off stage where she quickly gets out of her straight jacket and runs back onstage carrying a package of books of *Tales from Shakespeare*, the book she and her brother wrote together. They see that her name has been left off the title page. Charles is angry and wants to punch Godwin, but Mary urges him to let it go and take a copy to Hazlitt, stopping to have a drink with Coleridge.

Lamb asks Coleridge to stop wailing and Mary comes in asking if a crowd has died in the parlor. Coleridge says that Wordsworth has broken with him and wishes he had married a woman like Mary. She suggests he write to Wordsworth and to his wife. Coleridge complains about the man from Porlock who knocked on the door as Coleridge was writing down his masterpiece about Kubla Khan. When Mary says he must face his demons like everyone else, Coleridge leaves. Lights fade and come up on Mary and the upstage group.

Mary says she is haunted by the fear that she will be ill again. Mother wants the cat and asks Mary if she also murdered Aunt Hetty. Aunt Hetty says she is right there, and Mary tells Mother that she had a nightmare that Mother had come back from the dead to ask her questions, like an oral examination at a university. Mother then fires a series of questions that Mary answers, after which Mother tells Father that she had carnal relations with Old Salt every Friday for seventeen years. Charles, from the darkness, asks Mary whom she is speaking to, and the light changes so that the others are in the shadows. But the voices upstage keep talking to Mary, and she tells Charles that she has to go back to the madhouse. She says they will walk along the street on Christmas Day and pretend that they are sane. The ghost people watch them go and Mother, after wishing them Merry Christmas, calls for the cat and the lights fade out.

The Passion of Merlin and Vivien in the Forest of Broceliande is a short one-act for a man and a woman. Merlin is not "incredibly ancient" but he is considerably older than Vivien. We hear the sound of birds and thunder and see leaf shadows as the lights come up on a moss-covered tree stump. Merlin sits on the stump and takes a drink from a small flask that Vivien offers. He says he has taught her everything he knows. She replies that he has made her laugh a thousand times and never took advantage of her. She says she wants to give him something and Merlin notices that his hands feel like claws and his heels seem rooted to the ground. She says the potion is beginning to work and he is turning into a tree. Merlin feels betrayed, but she says that he taught her that trees were holy things and that she needs to be by herself. Merlin's arms begin twisting upwards, "palms up, finger spread like twigs." She kisses him and puts the locket he gave her for protection on his upturned claw-like hand. She leaves and we hear the birds and the rain in the darkness after Merlin says how proud of her he is.

Another play in the Pendragon cycle, *Pianos* is set inside a barn in Armitage, Ohio, in 1908. Myrtle Casey and her husband Willy, both 98, are talking about the barn full of pianos that Willy has collected over the years. Myrtle is tired of having cows in the house because there is no room for them in the barn. She tells Willy they are the laughingstock of Pendragon County, that no one can play broken pianos, and that it's dangerous to have pianos stacked forty feet high. Willy says the pianos can be fixed and reminds

Myrtle that she nagged him to get a piano. She says it is dangerous for eleven-year-old Jimmy to be climbing stacks of pianos. She calls to Jimmy and we hear a sound like something running across on a keyboard. Willy doesn't hear the sound but Myrtle thinks Jimmy is up on top of the pianos. We hear another piano sound and Willy calls to Jimmy to come down. He tells Myrtle that God is in the pianos, music is God's revelation, and the pianos are like a mountain one climbs to get to one's salvation. He goes off left to save Jimmy.

Myrtle warns him but we hear piano noises as, offstage, Willy climbs up, saying that he has had a vision and the ultimate revelation will come when he has climbed the mountain of pianos. He shouts his readiness to receive the meaning of existence. Myrtle looks up in horror, covers her face and screams as we hear a horrible cacophony of falling pianos. Lights black out and we hear Willy's voice in the darkness telling Myrtle that he heard God's voice. When he begins to describe what the Lord said we hear "an even louder cacophony of many, many falling pianos as Willy screams." Then silence and the sound of chickens clucking.

Plum Pudding (3m, 2w) takes place in France in the 19th century and requires a table with some chairs and an empty arch doorway up center. Lights come up on Emile and Julie in her apartment. A large covered pan is on the table and Julie tells Emile that it is indeed plum pudding that he smells. Emile says that he has a mystical feeling about plum pudding and wishes his friend, Monsieur Fortgibu, were present. Entering through the arch from an earlier time comes Fortgibu as the lights dim a bit on Julie, and Emile recalls a time when he was a boy in 1805 and was invited to dinner at Fortgibu's home. Fortgibu says that he has just returned from England where he ate "the most wonderful dish," one that he believes has never before been served in France. This "almost supernaturally delicious" dish is called Plum Pudding. Fortgibu tells Emile what he knows of the origin and history of plum pudding before wandering off into the stage right darkness looking for his big spoon.

Julie tells Emile that Fortgibu sounds a bit off his rocker, but Emile says that she has to hear what happened ten years later, when he passed by an out-of-the-way restaurant and smelled something "mysteriously evocative," plum pudding. Emile says he walked into the restaurant and was told by the waiter, who has come through the arch, that the last plum pudding has been ordered by another gentleman. The gentleman turns out to be Fortgibu, who comes through the arch, gray at the temples, but still vigorous. Julie says that it was just a coincidence, but Emile says that he shared the plum pudding again with Fortgibu, who thinks that their chance meeting after ten years means something, and that life is very much like plum pudding. He complains of feeling dizzy and again goes off into the shadows.

Emile tells Julie that it has been 27 years since his first encounter with Fortgibu and 17 since the second, and both involved plum pudding. Julie says she doesn't know anyone named Fortgibu and suggests that Emile has made up the story. A maid enters to announce the arrival of Monsieur Fortgibu, and a very old and confused Fortgibu appears in the archway, asking for Roxanne, who apparently lived before her death in the apartment above Julie's. Emile tells Fortgibu that he has met him three times in his life and all three times plum pudding was present. Fortgibu thinks that it might mean something, but it's more likely the illusion of coherence. He says that plum pudding is part of "a jumble of random fluctuations in an ocean of meaningless cosmic gibberish," part of a "rich hotch-potch of abstruse symbology." At Julie's invitation, he sits to join them for the plum pudding.

In *Praying Mantis*, Stephen and Laura are sitting on a back porch swing on a late summer night (sound of crickets) in 1994. Laura says she likes listening to crickets and watching the fireflies, feeling safe but thinking that something is waiting out there. She asks Stephen if he thinks she is unstable because her father and mother were unstable and abandoned her. He says nobody gets over anything. She says he is talking like he's trying out rough drafts of his novel. She asks if the novel is about her mother and if there is a praying mantis in it. He says he married her mother because he loved her and Laura's father had left them destitute. She wonders why he stayed when her mother left. Stephen tells her that her mother once told him that she would cut the hands off anyone who hurt her child. She says that she has seen him trying to be good to her and she can't help suspecting his motives. He says he will never hurt her but she says he will hurt her because he loves her. She says she is cold and is going inside. She asks if he is coming inside. He says no, but she doesn't move as the light fades and goes out.

The setting for *The Red Ettin* (2m, 2w) is "somewhere or other," represented by a unit set with a bed, table, chairs, and a hat rack. "The actors move. The set doesn't. Engrave these words onto your eyeballs." We hear ravens as light comes up on Jack and Widow. Widow tells Jack that his two dead brothers were also named Jack and that he had a sister who was eaten by a big red thing. Jack starts again to tell the story of a Widow who lived on a small bit of ground which she rented from a farmer. She interrupts, asking which Jack he is talking about, and then continues to tell about asking Jack to bring her a bucket of water, but the bucket had a hole in it and so she could only make him a small cake to take with him on his adventure. She says that if he gives her half the cake she will bless him; if he takes the whole cake she will curse him. He took the whole cake and she hasn't seen him since. Jack says his brother gave him a knife to keep until he came back. If the knife became rusty, then something terrible had happened to the brother. Each morning Jack would unwrap the knife from the red engineer's kerchief (his father's, according to Widow, who was cut into three pieces by a locomotive when he was lying on the tracks thinking of her beautiful, naked body). One morning the knife was brown with rust and Jack knew it was time to find his brother.

Jack continues his narration of the story as we hear sounds of sheep, and Shepherd appears, saying the sheep belong to The Red Ettin, who, according to a song, stole the King of Scotland's pretty daughter and tied her up naked in his big brass bed. Shepherd says a young man who looked like Jack, hearing the story, decided to rescue the girl, but he's dead because The Red Ettin has three heads and eats young fellows like Jack with fried potatoes and ketchup. Shepherd gives Jack directions to The Red Ettin's castle, hands him a pig's eyeball to give to the old woman in the castle, and leaves.

Jack narrates how he followed Shepherd's directions, coming to a field full of two-headed bulls, noting that, "You'll need to use your imagination for that. We have a limited budget here. We only had enough for the sound effects." We hear the sound of enraged two-headed bulls charging, the sound of a door slamming, and see firelight come up on Old Woman (played by the actor who did Widow). After he gives her the eyeball, she tells him the King of Scotland's daughter is tied up in the tower but that it's a trap and he must remember three things—a ball bat, roller skates, and meat tenderizer. When Jack says she looks remarkably like his mother, she says she's not getting cast as the Princess any more and must leave to put the eyeball in a pickle jar, explaining that "the greater part of dramaturgy is just figuring out how to get people in and out of doors." She says if he needs to save money on the corkscrew staircase he can just turn out the lights. In the blackout we hear the daughter moaning.

Jack turns up a lamp and we see her tied on the bed, a blanket barely covering her. Jack says he has come to save her and cuts the ropes with his knife. She wants him to give her his clothes, telling him he can wear the blanket. She wants him to get pizza for her before The Red Ettin kills him as he has killed all the Jacks before him. She says if he does kill the three-headed bull he can do whatever he wants with her. He says he wants a girl who loves him for himself. She says the story always wins and he is just another character. But she offers him a baseball bat as he leaves for the barn and then finds roller skates under her bed as light fades on her and comes up on The Red Ettin, a large older man (played by the actor who did Shepherd) drinking at a table.

He tells Jack that his three-headed bull costume is on the hat rack and says that Jack would eat those who came to kill him because we play the role we're cast in. "Lines make the man." He offers Jack a drink and Jack sits at the table with him. Red tells Jack that his name is Albert and that he killed The Red Ettin and took over the business. He says he is Jack's father and tells Jack he feels dizzy because of the muscle relaxer he put in the wine that acts as a meat tenderizer. When Jack falls to the floor Red takes an ax and gets ready to cut off Jack's head. With a war cry, King of Scotland's Daughter zooms in on roller skates and hits Red three times in the head with the baseball bat. She kisses Jack as Widow walks in holding a pair of galoshes and introduces King of Scotland's Daughter as Ethel, his sister. After Widow leaves, King of Scotland's Daughter asks Jack if he wants to start in on the sexual intercourse. When he says they can't because she's his sister, she replies that she is royalty and "we do that sort of thing all the time." She suggest that they cut Albert up in three pieces so he will fit on the grill and tells Jack that he could take over, inheriting the family business, becoming The Red Ettin. The Jacks will come to save her; he'll kill them; they'll barbecue them. She says that with the barbecue sauce and the wine and the meat tenderizer they could pull in pretty good money, perhaps start franchising fast food barbecue places. She says that sometimes you're offered a role you can't say no to, and, when Jack hesitates, she says she will let him tie her up.

Rainy Night at Lindy's is a long one-act for seven men and two women set in "a mythological delicatessen in New York City." There is a counter with a phone "and perhaps an old-fashioned cash register" and table and chairs surrounded by darkness, creating the feeling of "a busy and somewhat iconic film noir city on a rainy night" in November, 1928. In the darkness we hear the sound of rain and wind and a tapping telegraph key as Walter Winchell, seated at a table with a round microphone, speaks to "Mr. and Mrs. America and all the ships at sea," announcing that Arnold Rothstein, a notorious gambler reputed to be the mastermind behind the fixing of the 1919 World Series, is in a hospital fighting for his life.

The phone rings and is answered by Abe, the cashier. Leo and Clara, the owners of the deli, speak of Rothstein, a regular customer that Clara doesn't like, comparing him to a spider. Clara tells Abe and Leo that they are to take no more phone messages for him. Leo asks Clara to be quiet before she gets them in trouble, and Moe, "a big, beefy gangster," asks if the lobster on his plate is male or female, since he only eats female lobsters. Leo assures him the lobster is female. Rothstein enters and asks if there are any messages for him. He asks where Damon Runyon is, and the phone rings. Clara tells Abe to answer it; he does, listens, and says it is a wrong number. Rothstein tells Abe that he is expecting an important call, but as Leo escorts Rothstein to a table, Clara tells Abe, "No messages."

Ring Lardner enters, exchanges pleasantries with Abe, and lets Rothstein know that he detests him for fixing the World Series. Rothstein says it was nine years ago and that Ring's problem is that he wants to believe in things and gets angry when things don't turn out the way he hopes. Leo tries to get Ring to a table away from Rothstein and Moe. Rothstein says that he hears a scratching sound, like rats, but that it can't be rats because he hears the sound in other places. Runyon comes in, exchanges insults with Ring, and is told by Rothstein that he (Rothstein) lost three hundred and twenty-two thousand dollars in a crooked poker game. The phone rings; Abe answers, announces a wrong number, and hangs up. Rothstein says that Abe has a tell that lets him know when Abe is lying. Abe says he is not supposed to take any more messages for Rothstein, but when Rothstein asks him what the message was, Abe says that Humpty said for Rothstein to meet him at the Park Central Hotel, Room 349, in half an hour.

Inez, a chorus girl, enters and tells Rothstein that she has been waiting backstage for him for forty-five minutes. He says he has a meeting but that he'll be right back. She says that he's never going to divorce his wife and marry her. Rothstein replies that divorces are expensive and he has to pay Humpty three hundred and twenty-two thousand dollars. The phone rings and Abe says he is pretending not to tell Rothstein that there isn't another call for him. Rothstein takes the phone and then says that he has to be going to his appointment. Runyon advises him to pay the money, but Rothstein says it is a matter of principle. Ring accuses him of giving Jack Dempsey bad olive oil before the Tunney fight and asks if Rothstein got a thrill out of ruining baseball. Inez wants Rothstein to discuss his wife before he leaves for his appointment, and Rothstein says his wife is divorcing him because he doesn't sleep with her. Rothstein offers Moe his gun, but Moe thinks he should keep it. Runyon thinks Rothstein should take Moe with him. Rothstein insists that Moe take the gun and go to their office and pick up some money in case "the conversation" doesn't go well.

Rothstein leaves and Inez wants Moe to follow him, but Moe says he has to do what he's told and that he is "actually a relatively civilized individual." Inez says that she will give Moe "anything" if he goes to the hotel and makes sure Rothstein is all right. Ring tells Moe that his lobster plate has balls on it. Leo says the lobster does not have balls and then accuses Abe of buying male lobsters. Clara says that lobsters don't have balls, pops one in her mouth, and says that it is tapioca. Inez wants Moe to get to the hotel but he leaves to get money from Eugene. She berates the writers, blames Ring for distracting

Moe, and runs out. Ring says he knows everything is a game but that he wants the game to be fair, not fixed. Runyon tells him he's in the wrong country.

The phone rings; Abe answers: wrong number. Lights come down on the deli area and up on Winchell banging on his telegraph key and announcing that Rothstein, found shot in the stomach at the Park Central Hotel, died of his injuries. He was last seen at Lindy's Delicatessen, "home of giant corned beef sandwiches, delicious apple pancakes, and the greatest cheesecake in the world."

Rasputin is a long one-act play for two characters—a girl, Anastasia, and Rasputin, "a tall, gaunt man with piercing eyes, long black hair and a black beard." The unit set "surrounded by darkness" has a bed, a table, and some wooden chairs. Anastasia begins with a "once upon a time" story of a girl who is lost in a forest in the winter. A leaf tells her to go to the Czar, who looks very much like her father, and who orders the world to come alive. The girl wakes up and realizes she has been dreaming and is nearly covered with snow in the dark forest.

From the darkness the voice of Rasputin tells her that she must tell him her name, date of birth, place of residence, and names of family members. Anastasia keeps saying that she does not know, that she cannot remember. He tells her to close her eyes and asks her what she sees. She remembers riding through the woods on a wagon in the night with snow falling. She says she has sisters and a brother and that she comes from a palace where she was a Grand Duchess.

Rasputin lights a lamp so that she can see him. He asks her if she is from Ekaterinburg, a name she refuses to say, but he tells her that if she will not speak her name she is reducing those who created her to nothing. She finally says her name and then the names of her sisters—Tatiana, Marie, and Olga, and her brother Aleksy. Rasputin says she remembers someone else, but Anastasia says she doesn't want to remember him because he smells like death and is a horrible person. Rasputin says she lived in a brothel and her father was a pig-fancying moron. She says her father was Emperor of Russia. Rasputin asks her what she is doing in this shithole. He pours some vodka into a tin cup, drinks some, and offers the cup to her. She takes it and throws the vodka in his face. He wonders whether it would be kinder of him to help her remember or help her to forget. He says he can have intercourse with her whenever he wants but he prefers the challenge of seducing her. He says if she will take just one drink of vodka he will tell her where her parents and siblings are. But when she takes the drink he says she must tell him where her family is or else kiss him. She finally says, "Ekaterinburg," and he asks her if she remembers sitting in his lap as he told her stories. He repeats the "once upon a time" story which Anastasia said at the beginning of the play, with the variation that the leaf tells the girl to go to God.

Rasputin says that her father was a very stupid man who sent thousands of soldiers out to be butchered, and he is now in Ekaterinburg with the rest of his family, dead, covered with dirt and being eaten by worms. Anastasia describes how they were taken to a cellar and shot. She was hit and stabbed until she lost consciousness; she thinks she must have died and is in hell. When Rasputin mentions the wagon, she remembers a man telling her that he found her still alive as he was burying the corpses and took pity on her. She wonders why she didn't die with the rest and Rasputin suggests that, perhaps, as she was dying in the cellar, she imagined the woods, and the wagon, and the cottage, and him; that perhaps this is a vision she has just before her death. She asks which version is true—is this a vision or did she really escape? He says she must choose the role she will play: a madwoman who thinks she is the Grand Duchess Anastasia, a conniving Polish whore imper-sonating Anastasia, the Grand Duchess herself miraculously saved but driven mad by what happened, or the girl dying in the basement. When she says she is cold he puts his coat over her shoulders, and she tells again the story of the girl lost in the dark forest with the variation that the leaf sends her to Death. She pauses, then says that her name means resurrection. Rasputin kisses her tenderly on the lips and as the light fades and goes out we hear the sound of the wind.

Ravished, a longer three-character (2m, 1w) one-act, takes place in the present "or not far from there" on a simple unit set: DR a small wooden table with a vase full of red roses, R a bed, DL a wooden table with chairs, DC a glow like the embers of a fire, and UCL some sense of a garden. Lights come up on Lucrece, sitting on the bed, with Tarquin drinking at the table and Coll standing RC looking at Lucrece who is looking at Tarquin. Lucrece speaks in phrases of a man making love to her, and Coll asks what happened to her. She asks if the friend he sent to her, John Tarquin, has talked about her. Coll denies sending Tarquin to their home, but Tarquin speaks to Lucrece, saying that he promised Coll that he would come to see her. He says Coll spoke of her, of missing her.

Lucrece wonders why Coll never wrote to her, and Tarquin says that personal communications are forbidden by the private company they work for that does things for the government. He asks Lucrece the color of her eyes and as they look at each other Coll says he doesn't understand what Tarquin was doing with her. He says there was an explosion and that he was uncon-scious for a while and that there are memories he can't retrieve, but he does not understand why he would have made Tarquin swear to come and see her. He says that whatever Tarquin told her was a lie.

Lucrece then turns to Tarquin and asks him to tell her exactly what Coll said about her. Tarquin says that Coll showed him a photograph of her standing in a hallway by some roses and that he and Coll would sit by the embers of a fire at night, waiting, and Coll would talk about her. Coll has moved downstage and sits by the fire, telling Tarquin about Lucrece, and Tarquin tells her that Coll was terrified that he would forget her and described her over and over so he would not forget. Coll describes how he made love to Lucrece, and Tarquin tells her that they were in a dangerous and unnatural situation and that Coll needed to talk.

She asks Tarquin why he came to see her and then asks Coll the same question. Coll denies sending Tarquin but admits he might have said things he doesn't remember. Tarquin asks Coll what he thinks Lucrece does when Coll is not there and says he envies Coll's certainty about her. Lucrece asks Tarquin if he liked Coll, and Tarquin says that Coll had some weaknesses, that people who talk too much and who don't pay attention and who want things they can't have are weak. He tells her she wants him to touch her because she spends her nights alone but that it's all a game, violence and lechery, and nothing satisfies.

Coll tells Lucrece that he dreamed she was naked in bed with Tarquin and woke up wanting to kill somebody. He repeats that he never sent Tarquin to her. Lucrece tells Tarquin that she doesn't believe anything he has told her, that he is some random maniac. Tarquin shows her a photograph of herself, and Coll tells Tarquin that she is sometimes too trusting, leaving doors and windows unlocked and walking around naked with the blinds up. Coll tries to talk with her but feels she is waiting for some lover who will be more exciting. Lucrece tells Tarquin that something is wrong with him and asks if the place where he has been has changed him. She asks if he thinks he has some kind of power over her and says that men love war because it gives them the power of life and death over women.

Coll then asks Lucrece what has happened to her, and she tells him that he has come home to somebody else. "This is the other side of the looking glass," she says. "You've cast yourself in this role, so pay attention. Learn your lines. All the dead people in the audience are watching." Coll thinks Tarquin did something to her, but she says that nothing happened, that Tarquin stayed in the guest room. When Coll asks Tarquin why he went to see Lucrece, Tarquin replies that Coll asked him to go. He says that he and Lucrece talked in the garden until it began to rain.

Time perspective switches back to Lucrece asking Tarquin about the lack of rain in the place where he has been, and he says he is a kind of messenger. Tarquin tells Coll that Lucrece may not be sane, and Coll then tells her that he has seen Tarquin. She says Coll is stupid for believing Tarquin when he said nothing happened when he visited her. Coll asks if Tarquin raped her. She asks Coll if "a man like that" would just stop in to say hello and wonders if Coll is excited by the idea of Tarquin forcing her. Coll takes a gun from his bag and turns to Tarquin, telling him he's going to kill him. Tarquin says he should go back to Lucrece and ask her what happened, and whatever she says will be the truth. Coll begs Lucrece to tell him the truth and she repeats that nothing happened. Coll leaves and we hear a loud gunshot, then birdsong. Tarquin asks Lucrece if she is all right. She wonders if he wants to come home with her after the funeral so she can kill him. "Well," he says, "you can try."

In *Relativity*, an elderly Albert Einstein and a middle-aged Kurt Godel sit on a bench in Princeton, New Jersey, in the autumn of 1954 as Kurt wonders why, in the movie, there are seven dwarfs and why he can't remember all their names. Kurt is convinced that mathematicians are trying to poison him and that the Wicked Queen has given Snow White a radioactive apple that makes the castle glow. He says there may be an infinite number of parallel variations of the fairy tale. Albert wants to go to one where they are not having this conversation. Kurt says there are time loops in Albert's equations that make it theoretically possible to visit the past. Kurt thinks it odd that Albert sat down on their walk, and Albert tells him he should find someone else to talk to because he can't live forever. Kurt says that since time is an illusion, there is no death. He says he has always been looked at as if he were some sort of insect. Albert, who has fallen asleep, wakes up and tells Kurt that he needs to make new friends so he will not be utterly alone. Kurt says that he happens to like the illusion of Albert's company. Albert says he has been trying to work out a grand unified theory but has failed. He says that he cannot start over because he will be dead in two months. Kurt says Albert is his friend and he loves him. That, he says, is not an illusion. Albert says the name of the last dwarf is Happy. Kurt says he doesn't think so, and Albert suggests they walk, but the light fades on them before they get up.

Three men and three women seated on wooden chairs provide the cast and setting for *Rwanda*. Each actor has a spotlight that comes up before the actor speaks. The male characters are Captain (middle-aged), Accused, and Brother; the females are Accuser, Witness, and Mother. Captain asks Accuser if she sees "him," and Accused is identified as the killer of her children. Accused denies the accusation, saying that it is a mistake. Captain orders him taken away and killed, but the light comes up on Witness who says Accused didn't do it, but she doesn't know who did. Accuser says that Witness is Accused's whore. Witness then says that she saw her Brother killing the children. A light comes up on Brother and then on Mother. Brother denies killing anyone, and Mother says Witness hates him and has been in a mental hospital. Witness agrees that she was in the hospital after she saw what her brother did. Accuser then agrees with Witness that Brother killed her children. Captain says that both Accused and Brother will be shot. Lights go out on them as Mother pleads with Accuser and Witness to change their stories. We hear the sound of two gunshots. Captain says they have a hundred more accusations to deal with before sunset. If they run out of bullets, they can strangle them. Accuser says the Captain killed her children, that she can see his killer's eyes. Witness invites Accuser to come with her to the Mountains of the Moon where they will drink the warm blood of their children.

Potter, a man, sits in a large chair and Jasmine, a woman, is at a small desk as we hear the sound of rain falling in *So This Is the Elephants' Burial Ground*. Potter comments on the heat and suggests that Jasmine could take off her clothing since they are "way out here in the bush" with no one around. Potter asks her a series of questions and is not pleased with her noncommittal answers. Jasmine says she went to the store to get bread and was told by the baker that his oven was hot. When Potter asks her who the letter she isn't writing is for, she says it's for whoever opens the door. She tells Potter that she saw a man waiting in the garden again and Potter says that she'll probably find his bones picked clean by predators. Potter says he was a war hero, decorated for shooting his Captain. He says he was well liked everywhere and that he won a prize for singing. He tells Jasmine that she adores him and asks her to bring him a book. When she asks what color the book is he says he is color blind. He says he wrote a book about silkworms many years ago when he was recovering from malaria and in love with a beautiful girl who played the violin. He says the girl died by stepping in quicksand. Then he accuses Jasmine of being careless and leaving three pennies on the carpet by the bed. Jasmine says the pennies must have fallen from the torn pocket of her coat. Potter asks her if she tore the coat at the baker's when he was showing her his oven, and Jasmine says she is going out to the elephants' burial ground to sing and dance naked in the moonlight. Potter tells her she's not going anywhere, that the baker was found burned to death in his own oven. Jasmine says she thinks she will stay in, and the lights fade out as we hear the sound of rain.

Patty, a 19-year-old blonde, and Sharon, a 19-year-old brunette, are wearing swim suits as they sit on lawn chairs at night in 1968 in the back yard of an apartment near the Arizona State University campus in *Under the Pomegranate Trees*, a shorter one-act. They talk about playing near a long row of pomegranate trees near the athletic fields where a girl named Cindy liked to tease the boys by pulling up her skirt. Sharon reminds Patty that she swam naked with some boys and Patty says that she was pretending to be Marilyn (Monroe). They speak of a Mrs. Cain who, Sharon says, tried to run her over with her car because she was jealous of her relationship with Ben. Patty says that Ben loved her and not Sharon. Patty tells Sharon that one evening she touched Ben "there" as they were sitting under the pomegranate trees and that she knows he will never forget. Sharon begins to cry and we hear the sound of an ice cream truck playing "The Band Played On." Patty talks about the excitement of having power over someone and asks Sharon if she would like her to touch her so that she would always remember being under the pomegranate trees.

The Watchers is a longer one-act play set in a room on the upper floor of an old building in a city. There is a table littered with pizzas and meatball sandwiches. On the table is an old phone; there are two wooden chairs facing the audience. The two men, Johnny Murphy and Joe Antonelli, have binoculars, and as the action begins Antonelli, the taller of the two, is looking through his binoculars at the auditorium darkness while Murphy is finishing a piece of pizza. Murphy tells Antonelli he is lucky because women like him and says that the "guy" they are looking for will never show up. Antonelli says that he sees the girl. Looking at her with his binoculars, Murphy says she is a sweet girl and wonders if it is her place. The men talk about a girl named Mary, skunks, crows, David Hume and billiard balls, nicknames, and the possibility of someone watching them as they watch others.

The girl apparently disrobes to take a shower and Murphy is convinced that she knows she is being watched. Antonelli suggests that Murphy's idea of an infinite regress of people watching other people could be a circle, a universe that is finite but unbounded. Murphy wonders if what they are doing is all they have ever done, that what they think is their past is an illusion, that they are in a room in hell. Antonelli says that even if they are being watched, if they are not aware of it, it doesn't matter. Murphy wonders why they are watching, or what the people did, or the person they should report to, or when they last got paid. When he asks Antonelli what he wants, Antonelli replies that he wants Murphy to shut up.

Antonelli says that he wants to touch the girl they are watching, or at least be in the same room with her. He says that when Murphy went to the bathroom, he called her on the phone but hung up when she answered. He thinks though that the call had meaning for her. He says he remembered the girl's phone number, but he doesn't know how, and he thinks he used to know her. He thinks he might try to bump into her on the street and ask directions, but Murphy says he knows he can't do that because it would be fraternization which is against the rules. Murphy says that maybe he can't keep quiet because he wants Antonelli to kill him.

The telephone begins ringing, again and again, until Antonelli picks it up. No one is there. Looking through his binoculars, Antonelli says he thinks he sees a man in the shadows. Murphy thinks that he and Antonelli have been set up by unknown persons for unknown reasons. He says that he saw Antonelli crying as the man and the woman across the street were "doing the act of darkness." Antonelli denies it but Murphy believes the phone call was to make sure they were still in the room and that someone is coming for them. Antonelli loses his temper and tells Murphy he doesn't want to look any more, that he wants to be blind. There are five loud knocks on the door, a pause, five more, a pause as the men look at each other, then three very loud knocks and blackout.

What Shall I Do for Pretty Girls? is a long one-act play in 15 scenes for four characters—William Butler Yeats, Maud Gonne, Iseult (their daughter), and Georgie, Yeats' wife. A simple unit set represents different locations in France and London from 1917 to 1938. We hear the ocean and the sounds of many birds as the lights come up on Maud (late 40s) and Yeats (early 50s) in 1917 on the Normandy coast. The noise of her birds makes it difficult for them to hear what the other is saying until Yeats closes the door. Maud wonders if Yeats has come to ask her again to marry him, since her husband has recently died. She says she is worried about her daughter and thinks that Yeats should propose to her. Yeats says that Iseult asked him to visit, but Maud wants him to convince Iseult to come to Ireland with her to escape the war. Maud is terrified that her daughter will be killed before she has had a chance to live.

The lights fade and come up on Yeats and Iseult walking on the beach. She has overheard at least part of his conversation with her mother and asks if Yeats would like to kiss her and ask her to marry him. He does; she refuses. Yeats says he doesn't want to be alone anymore and wants children. The lights fade on them and come up on Iseult and Maud in the house as Maud asks her if she had a nice walk with Yeats. Maud tells her daughter that Yeats deserves a bit of happiness before he's too old to enjoy it. Iseult tells her mother that she is moving to London, and the scene shifts to a tea shop in

London as Iseult tells Yeats that she can't marry him. He says that he has found someone named Georgie Hyde-Lees that he may ask to marry him.

In darkness we hear the sounds of a violent thunderstorm as lights come up on Georgie and Yeats on their honeymoon. Yeats is upset because he feels he has betrayed Maud, Iseult, and her. Georgie sits at a desk with pencil and paper and says that the pencil is automatically writing, that she has no control over it. Fascinated, Yeats reads what has been written and puts other pieces of paper under her hand, an event he describes to Maud in the next scene, telling her that every night they receive "page after page of complex messages from a bewildering variety of entities in the spirit world." He says that when Georgie's hand cramps the spirit voices talk in her sleep, giving him precise and detailed instructions about how to give his wife pleasure in bed.

In the next scene, Georgie is lying in bed in a trance, speaking to Yeats in "a strange, unearthly, but somewhat dignified voice" about letting Iseult work out her own destiny. He follows the spirit voice's instructions to get his wife some tea and then rub her feet. When he leaves, Georgie sits up in bed and says, "Shit and onions!" Then, in the eighth scene, Iseult and Georgie are having lunch in the tea shop and Georgie tells her that the spirits are concerned about Yeats spending so much time tormenting himself about Iseult. Georgie offers to introduce Iseult to one or two eligible young men. Iseult says that Georgie's spirits are a "great load of bullocks" and calls her a charlatan. Georgie says that she and Yeats are moving to Ireland and that she is pregnant.

The scene changes to Maud's house in Ireland where Maud and Iseult have come in out of the rain, Maud having escaped from an English prison. Yeats tells Maud that she can't stay in her own house because Georgie is six months pregnant and is sick with pneumonia. He pleads with her to go, saying that he is terrified his wife will lose the baby. Maud stomps out into the rain and Iseult kisses Yeats, saying she wishes the child were hers. The scene ends as Georgie shouts at Yeats to close the door.

Yeats, now a father, is walking in a park in London with Iseult, cautioning her about her friendship with Ezra Pound. She says she has had sexual intercourse with Pound but that it should have been Yeats. She asks him to let her find her own happiness, or unhappiness. He says he reserves the right to worry. The lights fade on them and come up on Maud visiting Yeats and Georgie, complaining that Iseult has married a young man who gets drunk and beats her, is unfaithful to her, and abuses and humiliates her in public. Maud wants Yeats to convince Iseult to leave her husband. Georgie agrees and Yeats leaves. In the next scene Iseult tells him that she is pregnant and he insists that she leave with him.

Lights come up on Maud in prison, an effect created by the shadows of bars on the floor. We hear a cell door slamming shut as Yeats walks into the light and tells her that he is angry that the loveliest woman he ever knew "has turned herself into a bitter old crone for the sake of politics." She refuses to let him get her out of jail, but asks that he take Iseult (who lost her baby) and her son. Iseult appears, "looking haggard," and Maud orders her to go with Yeats. After the light fades on them we hear the sound of a ticking clock and Yeats tells Georgie that he has been getting Iseult out of prison. Georgie chides him for spending time with a "damned farting swami" and says that he never loved her. He says that they have their two children and she says that he has his "damned stupid metaphors for poetry."

The last scene takes place in a farmhouse (created by the sound of chickens) in the late 1930s. Iseult tells Yeats that he married exactly the right woman but that she would run off with him to France if he wanted. Maud comes on to ask Yeats if he is going to propose to her one last time. Iseult tells Yeats that "only the poets win." She and her mother sit on a bench on either side of Yeats, each taking one of his hands. Iseult wonders in they have gotten everything wrong, and Yeats says that they could have done nothing else, that, if one is lucky, one loves, and "that's all there is to be said about it."

As *William Roach at Valley Forge* begins we hear wind blowing in the darkness and the light comes up on two soldiers, William Roach and his friend Cobby, huddled before a fire as snow falls. William tells Cobby that he was sent to America to bring back a cousin, Mary Clark, who ran off rather than marry a man she had been promised to. Cobby says he has heard the story many times and doesn't want to hear it again. He complains about being cold and hungry and miserable and wonders why they are marching back and forth on snow and frozen mud until their feet bleed. William says they are fighting for freedom and that the war began over taxes. He tells Cobby to avoid being negative, drinks from a flask, and, after some discussion, passes the flask to Cobby. We learn that William married Mary Clark, and Cobby thinks she must be insane to think that the Duke of York is her uncle. The men talk about watching a performance of Addison's *Cato*, and William tells Cobby that they will win the war by outlasting the English and then everybody will be free. He says he doesn't understand why Mary agreed to marry him but tells Cobby that he can meet her when the revolution is over. He starts to give a cheer for the revolution, expecting Cobby to join him, but Cobby sits frozen, eyes open, as the snow falls on them and the lights go to black.

In *The Wind Among the Reeds*, two characters from the Pendragon cycle,
Molly Rainey, 63, and her husband Cletis, 67, are having breakfast in the
kitchen. It is summer and Cletis is talking to a parakeet in a bird cage,
explaining to Molly that he is trying to teach the bird to talk. He asks if there
is any meat loaf left and is told by Molly that what he ate was dog food, not
meat loaf. Molly is bored and is worried about their son, Billy, who lives in a
trailer, plays the tuba, and talks to his weiner dogs. Cletis defends Billy,
suggesting that he may be a misunderstood genius, but Molly says Billy is a
moron, that her life is a failure, and she wants a divorce. She starts taking
clothes out of the dresser to put in a suitcase, saying that she needs some
culture in her life and that Cletis has never taken her anywhere. Cletis reminds her that he took her to a vaudeville show at the Palace Theatre in
Canton, and he goes on to describe a French performer who did a whole
program of fart impressions, concluding by putting a tube up his ass, sticking
an ocarina on the end of the tube and playing the 1812 Overture. When Molly
says that she always wanted to be an opera singer, Cletis tells her that she
sounds like a moose with his balls caught in a wood chopper. Molly closes
the suitcase, leaves, then comes back, asking Cletis what he is going to do
without her since he can't see, drive, or cook. Cletis says he'll be fine and
wants to know what happened to set her off. She says that Lewis, her sister
Lizzy's husband, is going to die, and then she asks Cletis if he tried to kiss
her sister Jessie in the barn almost fifty years earlier. Cletis protests that they
were all teenagers back then and wonders why Molly didn't marry somebody
else. She says that Lizzy and Lewis really love each other and that she is
running away because she doesn't want to watch Cletis get old and die. Cletis
tells her that you can love something and stick with it until one of you dies or
you can run off and die alone. Molly starts unpacking her clothes and tells
Cletis that maybe she'll make meat loaf for lunch. Cletis starts talking to the
bird again and the lights fade and go out.

In *Wraith* (2m, 1w), set in a pub (a table and two chairs) in London in
1946, John Keir Cross and Stephen T. MacFarlane, both thin, pale, fair men
in their mid-thirties, talk about Cross' wife sleeping with both of them. Cross
says he has dedicated his latest book of stories to Mac, as a joke that no one
will get. He plagiarized the stories about ghosts, puppets, and wraiths from
Mac and Mac asks if he has seen his wraith, a Scotch doppelganger who
appears just before one dies. Cross says that his wife is with Montgomery,
and Mac says that she is lonely and that it must be difficult living with
someone like Cross. Cross says that a large rat once attacked his child after
he had tried to summon the Devil on his BBC radio program. Mac says the
only way to get rid of one's wraith is to die. Cross says he plans to drink

himself to death and wonders if anyone would notice if he strangled Mac. Mac says he will die when Cross dies. Mac leaves for the lavatory and Audrey, Cross' wife, enters, saying she has been nowhere for a long time but she is back and has read his book and liked parts of it very much. She says she is glad that he signed his own name rather than hiding behind the name MacFarlane. Cross says he can't leave until his friend returns, but Audrey tells him that the bartender says he has been sitting alone drinking and talking to himself. Cross and Audrey leave and Mac enters, says that he's been left to pay the tab, and finishes the drink Cross left for him.

Chapter Three

Monologues

MEN

In *Blitz*, part of the Pendragon cycle, Andrew McDuffy Rose, a 42-year-old actor, speaks to the audience from a table in a New York City bar in 1975. He tells us how, as a child during the Blitz in London, he and his brother and sister decided to tell their parents that they refused to be sent to a safer place in the country. He speaks of actors running impromptu line rehearsals of Shakespeare in air raid shelters as bombs were exploding, and he remembers one of the very best performances they ever gave to an audience of three. Nothing since, he says, has ever seemed so real to him as that time and place. He thinks that somehow the stage performances touched a strange, deep, archetypal truth. He tells us his brother Duncan is a competent, intelligent actor but doesn't have the fire that audiences are drawn to. When, at night in a strange city, he hears sirens, he remembers how they told their parents that they felt it was their duty to remain and play their parts, and how their parents allowed them to stay. He wants to feel again that moment when his father was so proud of him.

In darkness we hear the sound of a foghorn and Doctor Sinistrati appears out of the fog in *Doctor Sinistrati on Zombie Island*, welcoming us to the island and telling us that he is evil and has locked us in his cabinet of horrors. He says it does not matter that Aquanetta cannot act because she is "unspeakably beautiful." He says that we are dreaming the dream he has put in our heads and that the sound of the movie is poor because the nitrates are disintegrating the film He says that in his scenes with Aquanetta she looks only at his left ear perhaps because she is afraid his eyes will turn her into a zombie or perhaps because she fears he will see that she has no idea what the hell she is doing. But she is a nice girl, the kind you want to bring home to Mother in a cardboard box. He tells us that the zombies are having a picnic but that he would not want to be a zombie sitting in a darkened movie theatre "watching crap like this." He tells us his punishment for coming to America is to be surrounded by zombies in Hollywood, the zombie capital of the universe. Although he has worked with all the greats and near-greats, he is very lonely and has been unable to escape from the island. His theory is that no one is paying to watch "these unspeakable monstrosities," that the theatre is empty and the film keeps repeating endlessly. He thinks he hears a fog horn and cups his hand to his ear. After a moment, we hear the fog horn. He says the excursion boat is here and that the devourer will be arriving soon. Again he says he hears the fog horn and cups his hand to his ear. Again we hear the fog horn, and he begins his welcome with the opening words of the monologue as the light on him fades and goes out.

The Captain in *Event Horizon*, a middle-aged man in a pilot's uniform, addresses the audience as if they were passengers on a vehicle traveling in space, telling them that soon they will be arriving at the Event Horizon, the end of the observable universe, from which nothing can return. Although all hopes and choices end, he says, they may draw some comfort knowing that somewhere in the Event Horizon there is everything that ever existed. He says they are probably asking themselves why they didn't have more sexual intercourse when they had the chance, but, he says, it would have been over before they knew what was happening, like everything else in their lives. He does, however, thank the Flight Attendant, Sally, for a "magical layover" in Toledo. He tells the passengers that they have always been completely at the mercy of circumstances far beyond their control or comprehension, that they have always lived on the edge of an abyss, in darkness, where every day is Judgement Day. He hopes they have had a pleasant journey and as he is wishing them luck and thanking them, his voice stops and the lights black out.

In *The Little People*, O'Mulligan, an old Irishman, sits in a wooden chair illuminated by firelight on a dark stage. He speaks of the Little People, whom he loves and has seen many times. He leaves dark chocolates, creamed corn, and applesauce out for them at night. He says the Little People are mischievous and change the tv channel when he falls asleep and once they painted his tallywhacker green with a little smiley face on top. He says the Little People are good, with tender emotions. Around Christmas every year "we" put out mouse traps with dark chocolate and, if the trap doesn't kill them, their necks are snapped and then they are fried in butter. The women and little babies, he says, are delicious, their little heads crunching like walnuts. He loves the Little People, but he prefers enchiladas.

Ben, in *Mulberry Street*, speaks to the audience about a story told by his grandfather shortly before he died about coming as an immigrant to Mulberry Street in New York and encountering a little girl afraid to go into the tenement because, she says, there is something in the dark of the hallway, two floors up, that whispers at her. Little more than a boy himself, the grandfather agrees to precede the little girl up the stairs. The light in the second floor hallway had burned out, and the grandfather heard something like a whisper as he stood in the dark, listening, trying to see, and suddenly felt that he had been in this situation before, back in Italy. He remembered that the boys of his village, Savignano, would go down from their village and up the other side of the gorge to Greci, a village that was mostly Albanian. When they were younger, they fought with the Greci boys, but as they got older they would sneak over to meet the Albanian girls. They would meet them in an abandoned house halfway up the Greci side of the hill, a dangerous adventure because they might be caught. One night the grandfather had walked to the abandoned house and heard a whimpering sound, strange and unsettling. He had a choice: he could go into the house or he could turn around and go home. He recalled a story his mother had told him about David being told by the Lord to wait until he heard the wind stirring the tops of the mulberry trees where his enemies were hidden, and then to kill all he found. Perhaps the sound the grandfather heard was a ghost, or a girl, or an animal, or a trap. He hesitated for some time and then turned and went home, but he wondered if he'd done the right thing. Going back in the daylight, he found the house empty except for a small pile of bones, perhaps from a small animal. Now, in the hallway, he faces an uncannily similar moment of truth and this time he moves purposefully into the darkness.

The setting for *Nick Lucifer at Club Hell* is Nick's "somewhat less than respectable but rather alluring and very atmospheric establishment, Club Hell." The time could be the present or any decade from the 1920s to the 1950s. Nick is a middle-aged gangster who speaks to us from his table, nursing a drink. He describes being on top of the highest building in the city with the Old Man's kid, urging him to jump. Nick says he did it and survived with just a limp. But the truth, he says, was that the Old Man pushed him and he bounced off an awning, breaking his leg. But that started the legend that he can't be killed.

He calls the Old Man a psychopath, a destroyer who demands absolute obedience. He talks about the Old Man knocking up a virgin and getting some poor stooge to marry her, and when his son grows up he lets the kid get murdered. He talks, too, of Abe who is ordered by the Old Man to kill his own son. But the Old Man called off the hit. Nick says he slept with Lil, the Old Man's wife, but so did everyone else. He also slept with the wife of the other son after he saw her lying naked in the garden. He gave her an apple, not knowing that she and her husband would be thrown out of the garden.

Nick thinks the Old Man is a homicidal maniac who helped him set up his club so he would have someone to blame if anything goes wrong. Nick says he heard from Johnny, the kid from Patmos, that something big is coming down the pike. He says the Old Man is sick and may be dying. When he dies, Nick plans to take over, franchising Club Hell. But sometimes, Nick says, he thinks the Old Man isn't real, that Nick just made him up because he was too scared to be alone. But, he says, the floor show with naked girls will start in a couple of minutes. He offers a toast to his imaginary silent partner, wishing him a long and happy death, but planning to bring a gun when he dances on his grave, just in case. "You can't trust a son of a bitch like that."

In the darkness on stage we hear crickets and the sounds of woods at night, and then the lights for *Panther* come up on John Rose, a very old man, sitting on a fallen tree. The year is 1988 and John says that there is something waiting for him in the woods. He says that Jessie, his sister, long dead, told him to watch out for panthers. He reminisces about the members of his family who have passed, saying he would have died himself if he had not promised Jessie that, if she could not live to be a hundred, he would. He talks about seeing twenty-one wild turkeys, "like giant cockroach demons," race across his back yard. He tells us his dreams of uncovering a hole in the side of a hill that is a portal to some terrible place, and of being in a dark theatre and seeing a girl in black speaking to herself in a strange gibberish as she moves past him to her lover sitting alone in the front row. He feels warm breath near him in the darkness of the woods. He has endured his hundred years. He calls out "Jessie?" twice and the lights go to black.

The lone actor in *The Tale of Mr. McGregor* speaks from his walled garden which, he says, would be a paradise if it were not for the damned rabbits who eat all his vegetables, talk to the mice and crows, and wear clothes. The rabbits, "the damned Satanic rabbits," stare at him and are becoming more aggressive, attacking the cat and carving their names on the tool shed. The rabbits hang about the rubbish heap, smoking and drinking with the squirrels. He tells us that one day he found six baby bunnies and put them in a burlap bag, but when he showed them to his wife she said there were no bunnies but just a bunch of rotten fruit. His wife tells him that he is very sick and he says he sees bunnies laughing at him. He tells us that he lies in bed at night unable to sleep, seeing the red rabbit eyes staring at him, waiting to attack and drag him kicking and screaming to their holes where they will dismember him with little rabbit knives and bake him in a pie. "Help me. Somebody help me. Help me." The lights go out.

WOMEN

In *Beavers on Uranus* Portia speaks to her date (in the audience) about the evening being a complete waste of time. She says all guys are only interested in her boobs. She relates to the guy who's been strangling people with sock puppets. She says finding happiness in love is as likely as finding intelligent, lap-dancing beavers on Uranus. She tells him he would say just about anything to get her underpants off and wonders what he finds attractive about her. But she is pretty sure the answer would be more bullshit. She eats peanut butter and cheese before going to sleep so that she will be able to remember her nightmares, but now she can't sleep at all. She says falling in love is like stepping into a big shit hole because love makes us blind and stupid and we don't even see the person we think we're in love with because we just project onto them something that reminds us of somebody else that we think we used to love. Imagination kills, and love kills. But, she says, she is too tired and lonely and in despair to make him leave. She says this is his lucky night and that she will show him her sock puppet collection.

Rose, a young woman who sits on her bed wrapped in a sheet, tells us in *Bogle* of her experiences with a creature who has always been there, a shape changer who, in her dream, raped her in a bog and, in another dream, licked cream from her breasts. When she woke up she found it was the cat. She tells us not to laugh, that she is not trying to be funny, and asks why she has milk in her breasts. She says the creature is always out there, watching her, waiting to play tricks. It is a "horrible thing, impossibly old," but sometimes it appears as a young man who wants to touch her, and sometimes at night it sobs like a child begging to be let in. She warns us to keep windows closed at night because we can't let anything in, ever, because every intimacy is a violation. She repeats, "Don't touch me," and then says, "Listen," before the light fades out.

A young woman sitting wrapped in a sheet, barefoot, identified in the script as Rose, speaks the monologue *Croatoan*, a word carved into a tree or post of an abandoned fort on Roanoke Island. Rose says that she is incoherent and talks of being defiled, of seduction, of intercourse being another form of murder, of desire being pointless, of every act of love being a betrayal. She speaks of looking at old books in a shop on the wharf and going for a walk in the garden with a man she met there who may make love to her or beat her to death with his walking stick. She says a girl carved the word into a tree and then all the settlers disappeared into the woods and nobody knows what happened or what it means. She says it is time for us to go and the light fades and goes out.

Devoured is a short monologue spoken by Betty, 19, who lives in Pendragon County in east Ohio. The year is 1938 and Betty makes a little girl doll as she speaks a "once upon a time" story about an old Swedish woman who lived in the woods and made dolls and had many dogs. One day the old woman fell and broke her hip and the dogs devoured her and became wild. Later, a girl walked into the woods with her little sister and thought she saw an old man motioning to them to go deeper into the woods. The old man resembled a photograph she had of her grandfather, the man who had wanted to buy the old woman's property to build a hunting lodge but who had been struck by lightning and became delusional. She had been told that her grandfather, Judge Rooney, had died in 1889, but she thought he might still be alive and was beckoning her to go deeper into the woods. The girl got very lost and realized that her little sister had disappeared. The woods became foggy as the girl called out for her sister and tried to find her way out of the woods. When she sat down in the thick gloom to rest, she thought she heard something moving in the bushes near her and reached out her hand to find a little pile of bones. In the morning her father found her lying in a field near her house, but they never found her sister. The girl makes dolls now, Becky tells us, and can only make out shadows in a world that looks to her like a wilderness of thick, dense fog. She and the doll look out into the darkness. The doll has no eyes. Light fades and goes out.

Maura, a woman of 50 in *Drones*, speaks on a bare stage about drones coming every day and about the signs "Drones Save Lives" that are everywhere. She says no one knows where the drones are going to hit or who will be killed. But she thinks that if they kill you, you must have been guilty, and that a certain amount of quantum uncertainty is built into the system that may now be completely automated. She says that most of this place is a wasteland and someday there won't be any people left, just piles of rubble and skeletons, and flying about it all will be the drones, "like giant pterodactyls," dropping bombs on the ruins, "saving lives."

Entanglement, a monologue for a "very attractive woman in her thirties," is set in a bar. The woman, identified in the script as Laura, speaks to a man, "you," whom she later calls Albert, who has bought her a drink. She talks to him about ambiguity and making choices and tells of a novelist she knew who liked to think he was always right and wanted her to be wrong. He wanted to be right more than he wanted to have sex with her. She thinks "you" would say pretty much anything to get her clothes off, although he may also be wary of getting into some sort of entanglement he can't get out of. She wonders if people deserve contempt because they ask different kinds of questions. She says that if anyone had suggested in 1900 that what happens to one particle will affect another particle on the other side of the universe, they would have been ridiculed and destroyed. She says she doesn't mind him looking at her breasts and thinks that anything is ambiguous until someone pays attention to it. She says loneliness is the answer to every equation and that women who go into bars with mirrors are taking a chance, but so is the man who may go home with her. She asks Albert what he wants and says he must decide "right now."

Face in the Window is spoken by a woman identified in the script as Shelley. In dim light we can see three chairs and a window. Shelley tells us about a woman who takes the train to work in the city, passing through abandoned, devastated buildings where people once lived. Sometimes, she says, the tracks pass close to buildings where people live. One morning she sees a face of a young woman who raises a hand and presses her palm against the glass, as if asking for help. She doesn't see the woman on the ride home that night, but the next morning, in the same window, she sees what she had seen the previous morning. She thinks it must be a trick of the light, that the same girl would not be at the same window at exactly the same time in that exact posture. The next morning she sees the girl again and is unable to concentrate at work, staring at the wall while her phone rings. Her boss asks her if she's sick, and an old woman on the train home asks her if she's ill. She dreams of searching for the girl and the next morning calls in sick to work. She can't stop thinking of the girl and takes a cab to that part of the city where the building is. The cab driver is not happy about driving in that part of town and refuses to wait for her when she gets out. She goes into the building, thinks she hears music, and climbs the stairs. When she gets to what she thinks is the right floor, she goes to the side of the building facing the tracks and walks to the end of the hall. The number has been torn off the opened door, but she sees the window and the three chairs. Through the window she can see the tracks and hears the clatter of the train approaching. She looks out the window and, in the passing train, sees a girl looking back at her. She raises her hand and rests her palm against the glass. Lights out.

In *The Ghost Fragments*, Naomi thinks there are ghosts in her house, a place from which all passion must be removed. She says that someone is moving her furniture during the night. She misses a "him," a lover in whose office she would change out of her dance clothes into a dress. "Today," she says, he arrived in New Haven. She says that when she comes back to the house at night there is a light on in the closet, a light she never turns on. She wakes in the middle of the night, hearing voices, and discovers that the tv is on although she turned it off before she went to bed. She thinks ghosts are the residue of unsatisfied desires and, thinking her house haunted, researches old newspapers in the library and discovers that a family was murdered in the house, the father coming home to discover the butchery but finding his youngest daughter hiding in the upstairs closet. She thinks of "him" typing in a small room used by generations of graduate students. She says that the ghost house follows her wherever she goes. She says that, when he was leaving her to go to New Haven, he kissed her and she couldn't let him go. They made love and, in the morning, she smashed his head again and again with a heavy old clock on the bedstand. She never opens the closet and when the telephone rings she never answers it because she knows who it is.

A young actress speaks to and of Alfred Hitchcock in *Hitchcock Blonde*, calling him a "fat pig," "gutter cockney," "compulsive liar," and "compulsive thief," accusing him of spying on her, undressing her when she is uncon-scious, training birds to peck out her eyes, making her into a caricature of his desire, "the tortured eros of (his) Freudian freak show." She says he wants her to love him, but she hates him and he makes all love seem sick. She wonders why she is trapped with his "fat, ugly face forever leering" at her, his camera raping her. She calls out for someone to help her, to get her "out of this damned motel," so she can take "this fucking key" and "gouge out" his eyes.

As *Lighthouse* begins we hear in darkness the sound of seagulls and a bell from a bouy. Aggie, a woman in her thirties, speaks from a wooden chair as a light passes across her like the revolving beacon of a lighthouse, creating regularly space intervals of light and darkness. She says that people told her she would go mad, trapped in a lighthouse, but she thought that with her blue-eyed husband and three small children she would be content. She says she was very happy at first but then she began to see things, something slithering across the floor. She tells her husband that there are snakes in the lighthouse, but he doesn't believe her, and the snakes are so fast that no one could see them. She had nightmares and couldn't sleep as she prowled the lighthouse with a flashlight at night. She decided that the snakes were after her children and one night stepped on something that caused a horrible, stabbing pain in her heel. Her husband tells her she stepped on a walnut shell and was not bitten by a snake. She feels hate toward her husband and thinks that she has been inoculated with the wisdom of the serpent. When she fell asleep she dreamed that snakes were everywhere in the lighthouse. Realizing she had to save her children, she threw them from the windows. She then tells us, after a silence, that she was taken to a place where she couldn't hear the sea. They tell her the children are dead. When she asks if the snakes killed them she is told that there are no snakes in the lighthouse. But all she can see is a snake from her dream, a snake with cold blue eyes.

Loop is a monologue spoken by a young girl named Meredith standing by a lake in the autumn of 1954. She tells us that she does things that she cannot explain and, feeling guilty, keeps thinking about what she did over and over, like a movie loop from *The Creature from the Black Lagoon*. She says she tries to be a good person but then she does things she can't believe she's doing. She says sometimes she feels as if she is standing outside herself watching the incredibly stupid thing she's doing. But although the moment is gone, she keeps playing it over and over in her head. She says she hurts other people but she can't stop and can never explain. She thinks perhaps this is why her mother ran away, because she couldn't help it. She says she is like her mother and hates the movie about the creature from the black lagoon because at the drive-in she lost her virginity and got knocked up while that movie was playing. That was where she lost her soul and can't get it back. The baby is growing in her and she can't tell anybody because nobody understands and the loop of the creature coming out of the water keeps playing over and over and there's no place she can run to get away.

Jane, in *The Mountains of the Moon*, speaks a monologue naked under a white sheet on a white table. She says she is cold and can hear voices from other rooms but she has never had a dream like this. She remembers a party, someone looking in the window, and splintered panes of glass. She can't understand most of what the voices are saying but she remembers having a conversation with someone about humans' limited understanding of the universe. She says someone was following her, taking pictures of her; she can almost remember. She dreamed she woke up on the Mountains of the Moon, the source of the Nile, but also on the Moon. She remembers a G. M. Hopkins sonnet about the mind having mountains but she can't remember who she is. We hear the sound of a telephone ringing and then stopping. She thinks she may be pregnant. She says all dialogue is an illusion. She says she can see other people in the room, also naked under sheets and very cold. Her name, she says, is Jane Doe. She lies back on the table and pulls the sheet over her body. She tells "little baby" that God is coming to cut her open and bring her into the light. She pulls the sheet over her head and the light fades out

In *One Hundred Views of Mount Fuji*, a young woman, Mujina, speaks to the audience as if presenting a lecture, with slides, of pictures by Hokusai, who drew the mountain from every possible angle and said on his death bed that if he could live another five or ten years he might begin to understand something about drawing. The monologue continues as a series of imagistic sentences unconnected by narrative structure, with ambiguous pronoun referents, creating an intellectual-emotional complex involving death, violence, snow, reflections, burning, birds, animals, ghosts, demons, water, caves, trees, and sex, all perhaps associated with the various views of the mountain.

The Pine Barrens is spoken by a woman named Marla who tells us that as a teenager she saw a creature with wings, a horrible snout, and feet like hooves that flew in "this impossible clumsy, dorky way." She says she loves living in the Pine Barrens, in the presence of possible danger, and realizes that the creature she saw, the Jersey Devil, was her brother. When her Crazy Aunt Betty died, Marla tells us, she moved back to Betty's ramshackle house in the Pine Barrens and found the creature in her house one evening, making murmuring noises in the upstairs bathroom. She left some food on a tray outside the bathroom door and went to sleep. In the morning the food was gone, but she kept putting out food and discovered that the creature liked ham sandwiches and Ding Dongs and liked to sing or wail along with the radio. After months without seeing the creature, she noticed when she was outside that the upstairs bathroom window was open. The creature was getting out at night and coming back to spend the day with her. Needing company, Marla sang with the creature and told it all her troubles. She found out that the Delaware Indians used to live in the Pine Barrens and called it the place of the dragon, and she says there was a story about a woman named Leeds who in 1735 supposedly gave birth to something with "a forked tail, bat wings, hooves, and a horse's head." She says the Barrens have always been a place for the strange, oppressed, and odd because we are herd animals and kill what is different from us. She is afraid that if she opens the bathroom door to look the creature will go away and she'll never see it again. She says love isolates and eventually kills you and that she doesn't go anywhere or do anything except make ham sandwiches. She asks how her isolation is different from the life of anyone who's lucky enough to love something, because love is doomed and the only real love is love without hope for a person we have imagined. She says time is passing and she can't seem to move, but, she adds, everyone else is trapped, lost, doomed, strange. "We're all monsters," she says, but she thinks she is lucky because she has found somebody to love.

Professor Roeg, in *Pomerene Hall*, speaks from a circle of light as if rehearsing a guided tour, telling us the history of the Hall as we hear the sounds of all the activities the building has housed and that Roeg, a former student there, is describing: silverware and dishes clattering, girls laughing and splashing in water, running footsteps, water from a shower, a girl screaming, sneakers squeaking and basketballs bouncing, wind, pigeons, a creaking door, a girl sobbing, a shower room, girls whispering, a girl saying no, wind, again the girl saying no, and wind and pigeons. Roeg speaks of stories of supposedly haunted areas in the building and of her friend Cheryl whom she took on rides up a now abandoned shaft in a "small old-fashioned elevator." Roeg speaks of excess emotional energy permeating physical environments and of Cheryl leaving a trail of broken hearts in her wake, an epidemic of suicides. Cheryl "allowed herself to be violated by a monstrous troglodyte who sold drugs from the back of a Volkswagen bus" and who involved her in drugs and orgies. When Roeg warned Cheryl and told her she loved her, Cheryl looked at her with shock and pity and went to get her books in the changing room by the swimming pool. Roeg tried to restrain Cheryl and got "very, very angry," but does not remember what happened next. In the morning, she tells us, she went to Cheryl's apartment but it was empty and Roeg assumed she had gone to Mexico and that she would never see her again. And, she says, "I never have." But she has had dreams of Cheryl lying broken and dead at the bottom of the elevator shaft. She says she comes back to the blocked-up shaft at night, even after all the years have passed. She says she knows how to open the door at the top of the shaft. We then hear the sounds we have heard before but now jumbled together, ending with the slamming of a door. Blackout.

Olive, a waitress in *Psalms of Scattered Bones*, speaks to us about her boyfriend, Jacob, who, she says, was vain, a liar, carried a straight razor, didn't believe in God, and thought that life was Hell. She says that the sex was exciting although she laughed when he made love to her because it made her happy. She tells us of passing an old house on her way to work at the restaurant and noticing an old man looking out at her from a window at the top of the house. He was there, looking at her, every day when she walked to work and every night when she walked home, no matter how late. Sometimes she heard the sound of an old player piano, out of tune and skipping parts, and sometimes she smelled stew meat cooking. She says she teased Jacob about her having another admirer, and sometimes he would walk home with her and see the old man, whom he hated, looking down. Jacob became convinced that the old man had lots of money and decided to kill him. One cloudy, windy night, Jacob decided to kill the old man, but first he took Olive into the shadows of the ruined garden behind the house and made love to her and held her until she fell asleep. When she woke up, naked and very cold, she saw the old man looking down at her. She grabbed her clothes and ran home but Jacob wasn't there and she never saw him again. But she remembers two things about that morning: the smell of roasting flesh and, in the garden, the sight of hundreds and hundreds of bones.

In *The Rat-Catcher's Tale*, Nancy, an old woman in a circle of light on a dark stage, speaks to the audience as if they were children, telling them a bedtime story "with a very happy ending." She proceeds to narrate the story of the Pied Piper of Hamelin who rid the town of rats by playing his pipe and leading all the rats into the river. But the mayor refused to pay the piper's fee and at night the piper came back, played his pipe, and led all the children of the town into a mountain cave that was filled with rats. The people could hear the children screaming as the rats devoured them. When the people dug into the mountain they found "a great many little piles of bones." Nancy wonders if the children liked the "nice" story and tells them (us) that she is not really their Nanny but the Queen of the Rats who, with her subjects, is going to eat the members of the audience. The actor playing Nancy makes several choking noises and seems to pull the head of a squeaking rat from her mouth. The lights go to black but we hear the sound of squeaking in the dark. (Nigro adds a note to the effect that no live rat should ever be used in this production and suggests how the desired effect may be achieved.)

A long monologue, *Scarborough Fair*, is spoken by Cheryl, a woman in her early twenties, recalling a short-lived love affair with the man she is speaking to, telling him what he remembers. They each lived at the top of tower dormitories on a university campus and she describes the cooking and the music played in the basement of the dorms and the pitiful classroom situations with classes too large for their assigned rooms and the material presented through videotape. She describes how they met in Psych class and realized they both worked in the library. Her father, who taught at the university, had a study carrel on the top floor of the library. She says that she knew she was the girl inside his head the minute she met him. She says their souls are burning together, that she will be burning in his head the moment he dies. We learn that the man she is talking to is named Ben. Just when they are about to have sex in the library carrel, Cheryl tells Ben that if her boyfriend found out he would hurt Ben and she doesn't want him to be hurt. She tells Ben that she lives with this boyfriend, but she doesn't want Ben to leave her because it would make her insane again and probably kill her. She says that sometimes she has had sex with other men and women, when she was using drugs. She and Ben make love in the library eventually, and in Ben's red coach house where they would read *Finnegan's Wake* in the afternoons and fall asleep. She recalls their experiences together and her appreciation of Duns Scotus. When Ben is offered a scholarship to graduate school, he asked her if she wanted to go with him to Massachusetts. He says he won't go without her. During the troubles over the Vietnam War, when the soldiers came on campus, Ben took her to his father's house. She says that he will leave her and forget her, finding her in other women. She tells him that he

will go to Massachusetts and never see her again but she will own him
forever because he will always remember her.

In *Sycorax*, the woman speaks to her son, Caliban, about how being
pregnant with him saved her life in Algiers, where men fear a woman's mind
more than anything. Rather than kill her, they marooned her on the deserted
island where she gave birth to him. She says she cannot remember the spell
that imprisoned Ariel in a tree. She tells how when she was a girl Setebos
entered her as a blue stream of moonlight and taught her sorceries—how to
control the weather, control the flow of time, and fashion a robe of invisibil-
ity. By opening herself to the devil Setebos (devils are masks of God), she
gained power to do anything, but she tells her son that what the mind creates,
even magic, is nothing but a pile of cuttlefish bones. The ravens had overheard her boasting that she could control Setebos and reported this to him,
and he caused the men of Algiers to banish her. She thinks Setebos fears
silence, the silence that made all things, but she misses him and thinks
perhaps she was the last love of a dying god. She warns Caliban that people
are coming to the island who will hate him, not knowing who or what he is.
She says she has seen a man on a ship with a child in his arms who will try to
enslave Caliban with a book. She urges Caliban to steal the book and copulate with the man's daughter, peopling the island with Calibans. Seeing a red
flash in the sky she thinks Setebos has come to make love to her and she
leaves, telling her son not to look for her, for if he does all he will find will be
a pile of cuttlefish bones.

Another monologue for (an 18-year-old) Laura, *Telepathy*, is addressed to
an older man who is burning a book he has worked on for years. Laura says
she knows, a lot of the time, what the man is thinking. She says that just
before she goes to sleep she hears the voices of other people in her head. She
wonders why the man has been drinking so much lately and asks if he is
upset because she is leaving for college. She says she is grateful to him for
looking after her when her father left and her mother went crazy. She says
she learned from him that truth was a lie and that telepathy is not a rational
thing. She says she dreamed that she looked in the mirror and saw a praying
mantis looking back at her. She remembers another dream in which she is
wandering, covered in blood, through a house of mirrors, and sometimes she
dreams that Death comes to claim her and has her father's hands. She remembers that her father once put his hands around her mother's neck, strangling her after she had tormented him verbally for hours and then walked out

of their lives. She says the stepfather never touches her even though he wants to and suggests that her mother left because she knew of his desire. She says she is going to bed but will leave her door open in case he needs something in the middle of the night.

   Uncertainty, a third Laura monologue for an attractive woman in her late twenties, sitting at a wooden table in a circle of light, deals again with ambiguity and her inability to remember how she got blood on her hands. She says that there were a lot of people in the house and the next morning "he" was dead. She says she takes pills to help her sleep and admits to sleepwalking when she was a girl, dreaming she was sitting naked on the front lawn but feeling really cold and seeing the school bus go by with all the faces looking out the windows at her. She tells the person questioning her that she wants to go home and clean up that room. She says there were a lot of people and a lot of drinking, but it was friendly and she doesn't think anyone knew that the man was her stepfather who had showed up in the middle of the party during a thunderstorm. He says she hadn't seen him since she went off to college and she says that she would have had no reason to kill him, that once he had saved her from drowning with his strong hands. She says a big gray cat had gotten into the house and she remembers hearing owls and three women talking about our inability to know the position and velocity of a particle at the same time. She says her life is like that, sometimes she knows where she is but doesn't know where she's going, and sometimes she knows where she's going but doesn't know where she is. She asks if she dreamt that someone cut off his hands. She says she used to have a nightmare that she was looking into a mirror and a praying mantis was looking back at her. She says the man helped form her mind but that she had to leave and had lost touch. She says that the night before she left for college she came home late and found him burning his book. She knew he wanted to kiss her, but he didn't, and when she went to bed she left her door open but he didn't come in. She says she never called him or wrote to him and didn't pick up the phone when he called and put all his letters unopened in a box. She says that when he arrived on her doorstep in the rain, looking very sick, she took him up to the guest room and then went back to the party and continued drinking. In the morning, having awakened naked in her bed, she wrapped a sheet around her and went to the guest room and found blood everywhere. She thinks somebody must have come in during the night, that perhaps he was followed, that somebody was after him. She says she just wants to wake up or else go to sleep and not wake up at all and not dream. The worst thing, she says, is the uncertainty, never knowing for sure what's real, and maybe not wanting to know. She asks if she can go.

In *The Voice Folk*, Old Mother Heck speaks to us sitting before a fire in a cave where she lives in the woods outside Armitage. She warns us about the Voice Folk, who have been around long before the Indians and who are invisible to humans. But the mournful cry they make draws people to them until they are lost. One day, she says, she will go deep into the cave to see the Voice Folk and never come back.

In *Web* we see a screen with a constant flow of images, speeding up as the play progresses with more and more images of spiders and spiderwebs. In the darkness we hear a woman's voice, "friendly, reasonable, . . . not mechanical or robotic." The voice speaks in short sentences, telling the audience that "we" know everything about "you," including the date of your death and what you are thinking. The voice urges "you" to "stare into our magical glowing abyss" and never be alone again. Blackness.

Index

FULL-LENGTH PLAYS

SHORT(ER) PLAYS

Three Characters

Four Characters

More Than Four Characters

MONOLOGUES

Men

Women